Terms *of* Trade
glossary
of International Economics

TERMS *of* TRADE
glossary
of International Economics

Alan V. Deardorff
University of Michigan, USA

World Scientific

NEW JERSEY · LONDON · SINGAPORE · BEIJING · SHANGHAI · HONG KONG · TAIPEI · CHENNAI

Published by

World Scientific Publishing Co. Pte. Ltd.

5 Toh Tuck Link, Singapore 596224

USA office: 27 Warren Street, Suite 401-402, Hackensack, NJ 07601

UK office: 57 Shelton Street, Covent Garden, London WC2H 9HE

Library of Congress Cataloging-in-Publication Data
Deardoff, Alan V.
  Terms of trade : glossary of international economics / by Alan V. Deardorff.
    p. cm.
  Includes bibliographical references.
  ISBN-13 978-981-256-628-7   ISBN-13 978-981-256-603-4 (pbk)
  ISBN-10 981-256-628-7   ISBN-10 981-256-603-1 (pbk)
   1. International trade--Dictionaries. 2. International finance--Dictionaries. I. Title.

  HF1373.D43 2006
  330.03--dc22

2005044726

British Library Cataloguing-in-Publication Data
A catalogue record for this book is available from the British Library.

In-house Editor: Juliet Lee Ley Chin

Typeset by Stallion Press
Email: enquiries@stallionpress.com

Printed in Singapore

Contents

Introduction   vii

Acknowledgments   xi

Part I   Glossary of Terms in International
Economics   1
1. A–Z   3
2. 0–9 (Key to some numerical terms)   296

Part II   Picture Gallery   297
1. Edgeworth Production Box   299
2. Integrated World Economy Diagram   305
3. IS-LM-BP Diagram   308
4. Lerner Diagram   313
5. Offer Curve Diagram   322
6. Specific-Factors Model   331
7. Tariff in Partial Equilibrium   335
8. Trade and Transformation Curve Diagram   343

Part III   Lists of Terms in International
Economics by Subject   351
1. Arguments for Protection   353
2. International Commodity Agreements and Organizations   354
3. Effects   354
4. Empirical Findings   354
5. Fragmentation: Terms and Types   354

6. GATT Articles   355

7. Indexes   356

8. Memberships   357

9. Models   360

10. Non-tariff Barriers   360

11. Other Non-tariff Measures   361

12. Paradoxes   361

13. Preferential Trading Arrangements   361

14. Techniques of Analysis   362

15. Theoretical Propositions   362

16. Trade Disputes   363

17. Trade Rounds   363

18. United Nations Organizations   363

19. United States Government Units
    (dealing with international economic matters)   364

Part IV   Origins of Certain Key Terms in
          International Economics   365

Bibliography   371

Introduction

Have you ever wondered about the meaning of a word, a phrase, or an acronym in international economics? I often do. So I have looked them up, written their definitions, and listed these in a glossary that I have assembled over the last several years on my web site. With that I have frequently been able to refresh my own failing memory, since having written the definitions, I often forget them. I originally thought I was doing this for my students, both undergraduate and graduate, and I know that at least some of them have made use of it. So have others, all over the world, judging from the feedback that they have given me electronically. And so can you, if you need to.

This volume puts on paper what until now has been only on the web. I expect that some people will find it more useful, but others less useful, than the web version, which I will continue to maintain, although the information currently online — some from as early as 2000 — has been updated here to 2006. On the web you can click on terms that are defined elsewhere on the site, and of course you can't do that here. But such terms are indicated with page references to tell you that, and where, they are defined. Much as we are all attached to our computers these days, many of us still take comfort from using a book, and even I expect to keep this one beside me often, as I read both news and scholarship about international economics.

As I do, I am sure that I will find numerous additions that I will want to make to this, and I hope to continue adding to the online version when I find the time. The terms included here represent more than the beginning, but hardly the end, of an exhaustive effort to cover the field. With help from the many who have given me feedback, there is quite a bit here, including many terms that I would not have known about myself if others had not asked me about them.

The Glossary attempts, then, to cover all of the terms and concepts from international economics, including both international trade and international finance, at least at the introductory level. Because my own specialty is the economics of international trade, the coverage is inevitably much more thorough for that.

The **A–Z and 0–9 glossary** section includes definitions, cross references to definitions and, where appropriate, references to additional information elsewhere in the volume. The majority of the cross references are easy to follow (e.g., a cross reference to "capital" or "purchasing power parity" refers to the item of the same word or term, verbatim. In some cases, the references made are not verbatim — e.g., "biased", "price", and "mercantilist" (as they occur within the context of their usage) are cross-referenced to refer to the items "bias", "price definition" (and not "price control" or "price elastic") and "mercantilism" respectively.

Besides the glossary of terms, there is a **picture gallery** of some of the diagrams used to explain key concepts in international economics, including several that I have added for this print edition. Each basic diagram is accompanied by variations of it showing how it can be used, together with explanations and notes on its use. This section is followed by various **lists of terms** that occur frequently in international economics. Although most of these terms are defined in the glossary, this won't help you if you can't think of them. The lists put them into groups by subject to aid you in recalling them.

The volume ends with a **bibliography** of sources of the terms mentioned in the glossary. Prior to the bibliography is a short section on the **origins of terms** in international economics. This penultimate section of the Glossary records what I have been able to learn about the origins of some of the terms in international economics, especially in cases where a simple reference to a source in the bibliography is not sufficient. If I attribute a concept or a term (naming it) to a particular author, that means that I have personally checked the source and seen it used in the way that I describe. However, if I say or imply that this was the first use of a concept or term, then I obviously cannot always know that with certainty. If you know of prior uses that should be mentioned, I would be most grateful if you would let me know, preferably by e-mail to alandear@umich.edu.

Acknowledgments

As usual I have benefited from talking with a long list of people about this project, starting with my trade colleagues at Michigan: Bob Stern, Jim Levinsohn, Gordon Hanson, and Juan Carlos Hallak. Others who have answered questions or made suggestions include, alphabetically, Jagdish Bhagwati, Patrick Conway, Mike Finger, Keith Head, Doug Irwin, John Jackson, Paul Krugman, Jay Levin, Steve Magee, Rachel McCulloch, Mitsuaki Shindo and Charles van Marrewijk. By the time this volume goes to print, there will probably be more people to whom I should be giving credit. I also could never have done this without the help from my son, Ryan Deardorff, and my wife Pat.

I have taken full advantage of many other glossaries that are available. There are several on the web, including a surprising number dedicated to international trade. Many of these are apparently intended for those who actually do it, rather than for those of us who only study and teach about it.

In addition, I have consulted other sources including several textbooks, which are listed below. Some of these textbooks include their own glossaries of terms, which I have found especially useful both for identifying terms to define and for checking my own definitions.

- Bannock, Graham, R.E. Baxter and Evan Davis (1998). *Penguin Dictionary of Economics*, 6th edition. New York, NY: Penguin Books.
- Bhagwati, Jagdish, Arvind Panagariya and T.N. Srinivasan (1998). *Lectures on International Trade*, 2nd edition. Cambridge, MA: MIT Press.
- Black, John (1997). *A Dictionary of Economics*. New York, NY: Oxford University Press.

- Caves, Richard E., Jeffrey A. Frankel and Ronald W. Jones (1999). *World Trade and Payments: An Introduction*, 8th edition. Reading, MA: Addison Wesley Longman.
- Goode, Walter (1998). *Dictionary of Trade Policy Terms*, 2nd edition. Centre for International Economic Studies, University of Adelaide.
- Helpman, Elhanan and Paul R. Krugman (1985). *Market Structure and Foreign Trade: Increasing Returns, Imperfect Competition, and the International Economy*. Cambridge, MA: MIT Press.
- Hoekman, Bernard, Aaditya Mattoo and Philip English (eds.) (2002). *Development, Trade and the WTO: A Handbook*. Washington DC: World Bank.
- Husted, Steven and Michael Melvin (2001). *International Economics*, 5th edition. Boston, MA: Addison Wesley Longman.
- Jackson, John H. (1997). *The World Trading System*, 2nd edition. Cambridge, MA: MIT Press.
- Jackson, John H. and William J. Davey (1986). *Legal Problems of International Economic Relations*, 2nd edition. St. Paul, MN: West Publishing Co.
- Jones, Ronald W. and Peter B. Kenen (1985). *Handbook of International Economics*. Amsterdam: North Holland.
- Krugman, Paul R. and Maurice Obstfeld (2000). *International Economics: Theory and Policy*, 5th edition. Reading, MA: Addison Wesley Longman.
- Laird, Sam and Alexander Yeats (1990). "A Glossary of Nontariff Measures, Appendix 4". In *Quantitative Methods for Trade Barrier Analysis*. New York, NY: New York University Press.
- Mikic, Mia (1998). *International Trade*. New York: St. Martin's Press.
- Obstfeld, Maurice and Kenneth Rogoff (1996). *Foundations of International Macroeconomics*. Cambridge, MA: MIT Press.
- Pearce, David W. (1999). *The MIT Dictionary of Modern Economics*, 4th edition. Cambridge, MA: MIT Press.
- Wong, Kar-yiu (1995). *International Trade in Goods and Factor Mobility*. Cambridge, MA: MIT Press.

Part I
Glossary of Terms in International Economics

Absolute advantage
The ability to produce a good at lower cost, in terms of real resources, than another country. In a *Ricardian model* (page 237), cost is in terms of only labor. Absolute advantage is neither necessary nor sufficient for a country to export a good. See *comparative advantage* (page 42).

Absolute purchasing power parity
See *purchasing power parity* (page 223).

Absorption
Total demand for final goods and services *by* all residents (consumers, producers, and government) of a country (as opposed to total demand *for* that country's output). The term was introduced as part of the *absorption approach* (see below).

Absorption approach
A way of understanding the determinants of the balance of trade, noting that it is equal to income minus absorption. Due to *Alexander (1952)* (page 371).

Abundant
Available in large supply. Usually meaningful only in relative terms, compared to demand and/or to supply at another place or time. See *factor abundance* (page 101).

Abundant factor
The factor in a country's *endowment* (page 86) with which it is best endowed, relative to other factors, compared to other countries. May be defined by *quantity* (page 224) or by *price* (page 215).

Academic Consortium on International Trade
A group of academic economists and lawyers who are specialized in international trade policy and international economic law.

ACIT's purpose is to prepare and circulate policy statements and papers that deal with important, current issues of international trade policy.

Accession

The process of adding a country to an international agreement, such as the *GATT* (page 116), *WTO* (page 293), *EU* (page 89), or *NAFTA* (page 184).

Accession country

A country that is waiting to become a member of the *EU* (page 89).

Accommodating transaction

In the *balance of payments* (page 17), a transaction that is a result of actions taken officially to manage international payments; in contrast with *autonomous transaction* (page 16). Thus *official reserve transactions* (page 196) are accommodating, as may be *short-term capital flows* (page 246) that respond to expectations of *intervention* (page 150).

Accumulation

The acquisition of an increasing quantity of something. The accumulation of *factors* (page 101), especially *capital* (page 30), is a primary mechanism for economic growth.

ACIT

Academic Consortium on International Trade (page 3).

ACP countries

A group of African, Caribbean, and Pacific less developed countries that were included in the *Lomé Convention* (page 166) and now the *Cotonou agreement* (page 52). As of January 2006, the group included 78 countries.

Actionable subsidy

A *subsidy* (page 260) that is not prohibited by the *WTO* (page 293) but that member countries are permitted to levy *countervailing duties* (page 52) against.

Actual protection rate

Implicit tariff (page 133).

AD

Anti-dumping.

Ad valorem

Per unit of value (i.e., divided by the price).

Ad valorem equivalent

The ad valorem *tariff* (page 264) that would be equivalent, in terms of its effects on trade, price, or some other measure, to a *non-tariff barrier* (page 194).

Ad valorem tariff

Tariff (page 264) defined as a percentage of the value of an imported good.

ADB

1. *African Development Bank Group* (page 7).

2. *Asian Development Bank* (page 13).

Adjustable peg

An exchange rate that is *pegged* (page 207), but for which it is understood that the *par value* (page 204) will be changed occasionally. This system can be subject to extreme *speculative attack* (page 253) and *financial crisis* (page 106), since speculators may easily anticipate these changes.

Adjusted for inflation

Corrected for price changes to yield an equivalent in terms of goods and services. The adjustment divides nominal amounts for different years by price indices for those years — e.g. the *CPI* (page 54) or the *implicit price deflator* (page 133) — and multiplies by 100. This converts to **real** values, i.e. valued at the prices of the *base year* (page 20) for the price index.

Adjustment assistance

Government program to assist those workers and/or firms whose industry has declined, either due to competition from imports (*trade adjustment assistance* (page 272)) or from other causes. Such programs usually have two (conflicting) goals: to lessen hardship for those affected, and to help them change their behavior — what, how, or where they produce.

Adjustment mechanism

The theoretical process by which a market changes in disequilibrium, moving toward equilibrium if the process is stable. See *Walrasian* (page 290) and *Marshallian* (page 174) adjustment.

Administered price

A price for a good or service that is set and maintained by government, usually requiring accompanying *restrictions on trade* (page 235) if the administered price differs from the world price.

Administered protection

Protection (*tariff* (page 264)) or *NTB* (page 195)) resulting from the application of any one of several statutes that respond to specified market circumstances or events, usually as determined by an *administrative agency* (see below). Several such statutes are permitted under the *GATT* (page 116), including *anti-dumping duties* (page 10), *countervailing duties* (page 52), and *safeguards protection* (page 240).

Administrative agency

A unit of government charged with the administration of particular laws. In the United States, those most important for administering laws related to international trade are the *ITC* (page 153) and *ITA* (page 153).

Advance deposit requirement

A requirement that some proportion of the value of imports, or of import duties, be deposited prior to payment, without competitive interest being paid.

Advanced country

Developed country (page 67).

Advantage

Usually refers to a *cost advantage* (page 51), though it could refer to a strategic advantage (such as *first mover advantage* (page 107)) or to a superiority of technology or quality.

Adverse selection

The tendency for insurance to be purchased only by those who are most likely to need it, thus raising its cost and reducing its benefits.

Adverse terms of trade

A *terms of trade* (page 269) that is considered unfavorable relative to some benchmark or to past experience. *Developing countries* (page 67) specialized in *primary products* (page 217) are sometimes said to suffer from adverse or declining terms of trade.

AEC

African Economic Community (see below).

African Development Bank Group

A multinational *development bank* (page 67) for Africa.

African Economic Community

An organization of African countries that aims to promote economic, cultural and social development among the African economies. Among other things, it intends to promote the formation of *FTAs* (page 114) and *customs unions* (page 60) among regional groups within Africa that will eventually merge into an **African Common Market**.

African Growth and Opportunity Act

U.S. legislation enacted May 2000 providing tariff *preferences* (page 213) to African countries that qualify. As of January 2006, 37 countries had qualified.

AFTA

ASEAN Free Trade Area (page 12).

Agenda 21

A plan of action adopted at the *Rio Summit* (page 238) to promote sustainable development.

Agent

1. One who acts on behalf of someone else.

2. In *Principal-Agent theory* (page 218), the person whose job it is to act to the benefit of someone else (the *principal* (page 217)), but who may require some incentive to do so.

Agglomeration

The phenomenon of economic activity congregating in or close to a single location, rather than being spread out uniformly over space.

Agglomeration economy

Any benefit that accrues to economic agents as a result of having large numbers of other agents geographically close to them, thus tending to lead to *agglomeration* (see above). This is a basic feature of the *new economic geography* (page 190).

Aggregate demand

The total demand for a country's output, including demands for consumption, investment, government purchases, and net exports.

Aggregate measure of support

Variation of *aggregate measurement of support* (see below).

Aggregate measurement of support

The measurement of *subsidy* (page 260) to agriculture used by the *WTO* (page 293) as the basis for commitments to reduce the subsidization of agricultural products. It includes the value of price supports and direct subsidies to specific products, as well as payments that are not product specific.

Aggregate supply

The total supply of a country's output, usually assumed to be an increasing function of its price level in the short run but independent of the price level in the long run.

Aggregation

The combining of two or more kinds of an economic entity into a single category. Data on international trade necessarily aggregate goods and services into manageable groups. For macroeconomic purposes, all goods and services are usually aggregated into just one.

AGOA

African Growth and Opportunity Act (page 7).

Agreement on Agriculture

See *agriculture agreement* (page 9).

Agreement on Textiles and Clothing

The 10-year transitional program of the *WTO* (page 293) to phase out the quotas on textiles and apparel of the *MFA* (page 176).

Agricultural good

A *good* (page 120) that is produced by *agriculture* (see below). Contrasts with *manufactured good* (page 169).

Agriculture

Production that relies essentially on the growth and nurturing of plants and animals, especially for food, usually with land as an important input; farming. Contrasts with *manufacturing* (page 169).

Agriculture agreement

The agreement within the *WTO* (page 293) that commits member governments to improve *market access* (page 171) and reduce trade-distorting *subsidies* (page 260) in agriculture, starting with the process of *tariffication* (page 266).

Aid

Assistance provided by countries and by international institutions such as the *World Bank* (page 293) to *developing countries* (page 67) in the form of monetary grants, loans at low interest rates, *in kind* (page 137), or a combination of these.

Allocation

An assignment of economic resources to uses. Thus, in *general equilibrium* (page 117), an assignment of *factors* (page 101) to industries producing goods and services, together with the assignment of resulting final goods and services to consumers, within a country or throughout the world economy.

Allocative efficiency

Refers to whether or not an *allocation* (see above) is *efficient* (page 82). A change from an allocation that is not efficient, to one that is, may be termed an "increase in allocative efficiency.

Amber box

The category of *subsidies* (page 260) in the *WTO* (page 293) *agriculture agreement* (see above) the total value of which is to be reduced. It includes most domestic support measures that distort production and trade.

Amicus brief

A document filed in a legal proceeding by an interested party who is not directly part of the case. In the *WTO* (page 293) an issue has been whether to permit dispute settlement *panels* (page 203) to accept such submissions, especially from *NGOs* (page 191).

Amortization

The deduction of an expense in installments over a period of time, rather than all at once.

Amplitude

The extent of the up and down movements of a fluctuating economic variable; that is, the difference between the highest and lowest values of the variable. See *destabilizing speculation* (page 66).

AMS

Aggregate measure of support (page 8).

Analytical technique

See *technique of analysis* (page 268).

ANCERTA

Australia-New Zealand Closer Economic Relations Trade Agreement (page 15). Also **ANZCERTA** and just **CER**.

Andean community

An organization of five Andean countries — Bolivia, Colombia, Ecuador, Peru, and Venezuela — formed in 1997 out of the *Andean Pact* (see below). It provides for economic and social integration, including regional trade liberalization and a common external tariff, as well as harmonization of other policies.

Andean Pact

The *Cartagena agreement* (page 34) of 1969, which provided for economic cooperation among a group of five Andean countries; predecessor to the *Andean community* (see above).

Andean Trade Promotion and Drug Eradication Act

US legislation enacted in 2002 authorizing the U.S. president to provide *tariff preferences* (page 265) to countries in the Andean region in connection with the effort to curtail production of illegal drugs.

Anti-dumping duty

Tariff levied on *dumped* (page 76) imports. The threat of an anti-dumping duty can deter imports, even when it has not been used, and anti-dumping law is therefore a form of *non-tariff barrier* (page 194).

Anti-dumping suit

A complaint by a domestic producer that imports are being *dumped* (page 76), and the resulting investigation and, if dumping and injury are found, *anti-dumping duty* (see above).

Anti-trust policy
U.S. term for *competition policy* (page 44).

AOA
Agreement on Agriculture (page 8).

APC
Average propensity to consume (page 16).

APEC
Asia-Pacific Economic Cooperation (page 12).

Apparel
Clothing. The apparel sector is important for trade because, as a very *labor intensive* (page 156) sector, it is a likely source of *comparative advantage* (page 42) for *developing countries* (page 67). See *textiles and apparel* (page 270).

Apparent consumption
Production plus imports minus exports, sometimes also adjusted for changes in inventories. The intention here is not to distinguish different uses for a good within the country, but only to infer the total that is used there for any purpose.

Appellate body
The standing committee of the *WTO* (page 293) that reviews decisions of dispute settlement *panels* (page 203).

Applied tariff rate
The actual *tariff* (page 264) rate in effect at a country's border.

Appreciate
See *appreciation* (below).

Appreciation
A rise in the value of a country's currency on the *exchange market* (page 94), relative either to a particular other currency or to a weighted average of other currencies. The currency is said to **appreciate**. Opposite of *depreciation* (page 66).

Arbitrage
A combination of transactions designed to profit from an existing discrepancy among prices, exchange rates, and/or interest rates on different markets without risk of these changing. Simplest is simultaneous purchase and sale of the same thing

in different markets, but more complex forms include *triangular arbitrage* (page 280) and *covered interest arbitrage* (page 53).

Arc elasticity

See *elasticity* (page 83).

Argument for protection

A reason given (not necessarily a good one) for restricting imports by *tariffs* (page 264) and/or *NTBs* (page 195).

Armington assumption

The assumption that internationally traded products are *differentiated* (page 68) by *country of origin* (page 52). Due to *Armington (1969)* (page 371) in an international macroeconomic context, but now a standard assumption of international *CGE* (page 37) models, used to generate smaller and more realistic responses of trade to price changes than implied by *homogeneous products* (page 129).

Armington elasticity

The *elasticity of substitution* (page 84) between products of different countries.

Article XIX

The *Safeguards clause* (page 240) of the *GATT* (page 116).

Article XXIV

The article of the *GATT* (page 116) that permits countries to form *free trade areas* (page 113) and *customs unions* (page 60) as exceptions to the *MFN* (page 176) principle.

AS-AD

The model and/or diagram that determines the level of aggregate economic activity through the interaction of *aggregate supply* (page 8) and *aggregate demand* (page 8).

ASEAN

Association of Southeast Asian Nations (page 14).

ASEAN Free Trade Area

A *free trade area* (page 113) announced in 1992 among the ASEAN countries that is in the process of being implemented.

Asia-Pacific Economic Cooperation

An organization of countries in the Asia-Pacific region, launched in 1989 and devoted to promoting open trade and practical economic cooperation. As of January 2006, APEC had 21 member countries.

Asian crisis

A major *financial crisis* (page 106) that began in Thailand in July 1997 and quickly spread to other East Asian countries.

Asian Development Bank

A multilateral institution based in Manila, Philippines, that provides financing for development needs in countries of the Asia-Pacific region. As of January 2006, ADB had 43 developing member countries.

Asian Tigers

The *Four Tigers* (page 112).

Asset

An item of property, such as land, *capital* (page 30), money, a share in ownership, or a claim on others for future payment, such as a *bond* (page 24) or a bank deposit.

Asset approach

A theory of determination of the *exchange rate* (page 94) that focuses on its role as the price of an asset. With high *capital mobility* (page 33), equilibrium requires that expected *returns* (page 236) on comparable domestic and foreign assets be the same.

Asset bubble

See *bubble* (page 26).

Asset position

See *net foreign asset position* (page 189).

Assignment problem

How to use macroeconomic policies to achieve both *internal balance* (page 144) and *external balance* (page 100); specifically, with only *monetary* (page 179) and *fiscal* (page 107) policies available under *fixed exchange rates* (page 108), which instrument should be "assigned" to which goal? *Mundell (1962)* (page 379) showed that monetary policy should be assigned to external balance.

Assimilative capacity

The extent to which the environment can accommodate or tolerate pollutants.

Association agreement
Early predecessor to the *Europe agreements* (page 91) but excluding provision for political dialogue.

Association of Natural Rubber Producing Countries
An inter-governmental organization, formed by natural rubber producing countries to promote the overall interests of the commodity. See *international commodity agreement* (page 146).

Association of Southeast Asian Nations
An organization of countries in southeast Asia, the purpose of which is to promote economic, social, and cultural development as well as peace and stability in the region. Starting with five member countries in 1967, it had expanded to ten members as of January 2006.

Asymmetric information
The failure of two parties to a transaction to have the same relevant information. Examples are buyers who know less about product quality than sellers, and lenders who know less about likely *default* (page 63) than borrowers. Both are common in international markets.

Asymmetric shock
An *exogenous* (page 96) change in *macroeconomic* (page 168) conditions affecting differently the different parts of a country, or different countries of a region. Often mentioned as a source of difficulty for countries sharing a *common currency* (page 41), such as the *Euro zone* (page 90).

At par
At equality. Two currencies are said to be "at par" if they are trading one-for-one. The significance is more psychological then economic, but the long decline of the Canadian dollar "below par" with the U.S. dollar, and the more recent variation of the *euro* (page 90) between above and below par, also with the U.S. dollar, has been cause for concern.

At sight
See *payment at sight* (page 206).

ATC
Agreement on Textiles and Clothing (page 8).

ATPDEA

Andean Trade Promotion and Drug Eradication Act (page 10).

Australia-New Zealand Closer Economic Relations Trade Agreement

A free trade agreement formed in 1983 between Australia and New Zealand. Said to be one of the most comprehensive bilateral free trade agreements in the world, it was also the first to include trade in services. Identified as ANCERTA, ANZCERTA, and CER.

Autarky

The situation of *not* engaging in international trade; self-sufficiency. (Not to be confused with "autarchy," which in at least some dictionaries is a political term rather than an economic one, and means absolute rule or power.)

Autarky price

Price in autarky; that is, the price of something within a country when it is not traded by that country. Relative autarky prices turn out to be the most theoretically robust (but empirically elusive) measures of *comparative advantage* (page 42).

Auto Pact

See *Canada-US Auto Pact* (page 29).

Automatic licensing

The *licensing* (page 163) of imports or exports for which licenses are assured, for gathering information, or as a holdover from when licenses were not automatic. Depending on how the licensing is administered, automatic licensing can add to the bureaucratic and/or time cost of trade.

Automatic stabilizer

An institutional feature of an economy that dampens its macroeconomic fluctuations, e.g., an income tax, which acts like a tax increase in a boom and a tax cut in a recession.

Autonomous

Refers to an economic variable, magnitude, or entity that is caused independently of other variables that it may in turn influence; *exogenous* (page 96).

Autonomous transaction
In the *balance of payments* (page 17), a transaction that is not itself a result of actions taken officially to manage international payments; in contrast with *accommodating transaction* (page 4).

Average cost
Total cost divided by output.

Average product
The average product of a *factor* (page 101) in a firm or industry is its output divided by the amount of the factor employed.

Average propensity
The fraction of total income spent on an activity, such as consumption or imports. See *propensity* (page 222).

Average propensity to consume
The fraction of total (or perhaps *disposable* (page 71)) income spent on consumption. Contrasts with *marginal propensity to consume* (page 170).

Average propensity to import
The fraction of total income spent on imports; thus the ratio of *imports* (page 136) to *GDP* (page 122). Contrasts with *marginal propensity to import* (page 170).

Average tariff
An average of a country's tariff rates. This can be calculated in several ways, none of which are ideal for representing how protective the country's tariffs are. Most common is the *trade-weighted average tariff* (page 278), which under-represents *prohibitive tariffs* (page 222), since they get zero weight.

Backward bending
Refers to a curve that reverses direction, usually if, after moving out away from an origin or axis, it then turns back toward it.

The term is used most frequently to describe supply curves for which the quantity supplied declines as price rises above some point, as may happen in a labor supply curve, the supply curve for *foreign exchange* (page 109), or an *offer curve* (page 196).

Backward integration

Acquisition by a firm of its suppliers.

Backward linkage

The use by one firm or industry of produced inputs from another firm or industry.

BAFFLING PIGS and DUKS

Acronyms for the 12 original *members* (page 90) and non-members of the *Euro zone* (page 90). BAFFLING PIGS = Belgium, Austria, Finland, France, Luxembourg, Ireland, Netherlands, Germany, Portugal, Italy, Greece, and Spain. DUKS = Denmark, United Kingdom, and Sweden.

Balance of indebtedness

See *net foreign asset position* (page 189).

Balance of merchandise trade

The value of a country's merchandise exports minus the value of its merchandise imports.

Balance of payments

1. A list, or accounting, of all of a country's international transactions for a given time period, usually one year. Payments into the country (receipts) are entered as positive numbers, called *credits* (page 54); payments out of the country (payments) are entered as negative numbers called *debits* (page 61).

2. A single number summarizing all of a country's international transactions: the *balance of payments surplus* (page 18).

Balance of payments adjustment mechanism

Any process, especially any automatic one, by which a country with a *payments imbalance* (page 206) moves toward *balance of payments equilibrium* (page 18). Under the *gold standard* (page 119), this was the *specie flow mechanism* (page 252).

Balance of payments argument for protection

A common reason for restricting imports, especially under *fixed exchange rates* (page 108), when a country is losing *international reserves* (page 149) due to a *trade deficit* (page 273). It can be said that this is a *second best argument* (page 243), since a *devaluation* (page 67) could solve the problem without distorting the economy and therefore at smaller economic cost.

Balance of payments deficit

A negative *balance of payments surplus* (see below).

Balance of payments equilibrium

Meaningful only under a *pegged exchange rate* (page 207), this referred to equality of *credits* (page 54) and *debits* (page 61) in the *balance of payments* (page 17) using a traditional definition of the *capital account* (page 30). A *surplus* (page 262) or *deficit* (page 63) implied changing *official reserves* (page 197), so that something might ultimately have to change.

Balance of payments surplus

A number summarizing the state of a country's international transactions, usually equal to the *balance on current account* (see below) plus the balance on *financial account* (page 106) but excluding *official reserve transactions* (page 196), or omitting also other volatile short-term financial account transactions. It indicates the stress on a regime of *pegged exchange rates* (page 207).

Balance of trade

The value of a country's exports minus the value of its imports. Unless specified as the *balance of merchandise trade* (page 17), it normally incorporates trade in services, including earnings (interest, dividends, etc.) on financial assets.

Balance on capital account

A country's receipts minus payments for *capital account* (page 30) transactions.

Balance on current account

A country's receipts minus payments for *current account* (page 58) transactions. Equals the *balance of trade* (see above) plus net inflows of *transfer payments* (page 279).

Balanced budget

1. A government *budget surplus* (page 27) that is zero, thus with net tax revenue equaling expenditure.

2. A balanced budget change in policy or behavior is one in which a component of the government budget, usually taxes, is adjusted as necessary to maintain a balanced budget.

Balanced growth

Growth (page 123) of an economy in which all aspects of it, especially *factors of production* (page 103), grow at the same rate.

Balanced trade

1. A *balance of trade* (page 18) equal to zero.

2. The assumption that the *balance of trade* (page 18) must be zero in equilibrium, as would be the case with a *floating exchange rate* (page 108) and no *capital flows* (page 32). This is a standard assumption in *real models* (page 229) of international trade, which exclude financial assets.

Balassa index

See *revealed comparative advantage* (page 236).

Balassa-Samuelson effect

The hypothesis that an increase in the *productivity* (page 221) of *tradables* (page 272) relative to *non-tradables* (page 194), if larger than in other countries, will cause an *appreciation* (page 11) of the *real exchange rate* (page 228). Due to *Balassa (1964)* (page 371) and *Samuelson (1964)* (page 381).

Baldwin envelope

The *consumption possibility frontier* (page 48) for a large country, constructed as the *envelope* (page 86) formed by moving the foreign *offer curve* (page 196) along the country's *transformation curve* (page 279). Due to *Baldwin (1948)* (page 371).

Banana war

A *trade dispute* (page 274) between the *EU* (page 89) and the U.S. over EU preferences for bananas from former colonies. On behalf of U.S.-owned companies exporting bananas from South America and the Caribbean, the U.S. complained to the *WTO* (page 293), which ruled in favor of the U.S.

Bancor

The international currency proposed by Keynes for use as the basis for the international monetary system that was being constructed at the end of World War II. Instead, the *Bretton Woods*

System (page 26) that emerged was based on the U.S. dollar. See also *new bancor* (page 190).

Bank for International Settlements
An international organization that acts as a bank for *central banks* (page 35), fostering cooperation among them and with other agencies.

Bank rate
The interest rate charged by a central bank to commercial banks for very short term loans; the *discount rate* (page 70).

Barcelona Process
The *Euro-Mediterranean Partnership* (page 90).

Barrier
1. Any impediment to the international movement of goods, services, capital, or other factors of production. Most commonly a *trade barrier* (page 273).
2. An *entry barrier* (page 86).

Barter
The exchange of goods for goods, without using money.

Barter economy
An economic model of international trade in which goods are exchanged for goods without the existence of money. Most theoretical trade models take this form in order to abstract from macroeconomic and monetary considerations.

Base money
Monetary base (page 179).

Base year
The year used as the basis for comparison by a price index such as the *CPI* (page 54). The index for any year is the average of prices for that year compared to the base year; e.g., 110 means that prices are 10% higher than in the base year. The base year is also the year whose prices are used to value something in *real* (page 228) terms or after *adjusting for inflation* (page 5).

Basic balance
One of the more frequently used measures of the *balance of payments surplus or deficit* (page 18) under *pegged exchange rates* (page 207), the basic balance was equal to the *current account*

balance (page 58) plus the balance of *long-term capital flows* (page 166).

Basic import price

See *minimum price system* (page 177).

Basic needs

See *living wage* (page 164).

Basket

See *currency basket* (page 57).

Bastable's test

One of two conditions needed for *infant industry protection* (page 140) to be welfare-improving, this requires that the protected industry be able to pay back an amount equal to the national losses during the period of protection. See also *Mill's test* (page 177).

BEA

Bureau of Economic Analysis (page 28).

Beef hormone case

A *trade dispute* (page 274) that began in 1989 when the *EC* (page 78) banned imports of beef from cows that had been injected with growth hormones, arguing that the health effects of these hormones were suspect. The U.S. eventually complained under the *WTO* (page 293) in 1996, arguing the absence of scientific evidence of any harm, and in 1997 the WTO *panel* (page 203) agreed with the U.S.

Beggar-thy-neighbor

For a country to use a policy for its own benefit that harms other countries. Examples are *optimal tariffs* (page 200) and, in a recession, tariffs and/or *devaluation* (page 67) to create employment.

Benefit-cost analysis

Same as *cost-benefit analysis* (page 51).

Benign neglect

Refers to doing nothing about a problem, in the hope that it will not be serious or will be solved by others. Said to be U.S. policy toward its *balance of payments* (page 17) *deficit* (page 63) in the late 1960s, based on other countries' need for dollar *reserves* (page 235).

Bergsonian social welfare function

A *social welfare function* (page 249) that takes as arguments only the levels of utility of the individuals in society. Due to *Bergson (1938)* (page 372) as interpreted by *Samuelson (1981)* (page 381). Also called a **Bergson-Samuelson social welfare function**.

Bertrand competition

The assumption, sometimes assumed to be made by firms in an *oligopoly* (page 197), that other firms hold their prices constant as they themselves change behavior. Contrasts with *Cournot competition* (page 53). Both are used in models of international oligopoly, but Cournot competition is used more often.

Bias

1. Bias of technology, either *change* (page 268) or *difference* (page 268), refers to a shift towards or away from use of a *factor* (page 101). The exact meaning depends on the definition of *neutral* (page 189) used to define absence of bias. *Factor bias* (page 101) matters for the effects of technological progress on trade and welfare.

2. Bias of a trade regime refers to whether the structure of *protection* (page 222) favors importables or exportables, based on comparing their *effective rates of protection* (page 82). If these are equal, the trade regime is said to be **neutral**.

3. Bias of growth refers to *economic growth* (page 79) through *factor accumulation* (page 101) and/or *technological progress* (page 268) and whether if favors one sector or another. Growth is said to be *export biased* (page 97) if the export sector expands faster than the rest of the economy, *import biased* (page 134) if the import-competing sector does so.

Biased growth

See *bias* (above).

Bicycle theory

With regard to the process of *multilateral* (page 182) *trade liberalization* (page 275), the theory that if it ceases to move forward (i.e., achieve further liberalization), then it will collapse (i.e., past liberalization will be reversed). The idea was suggested by *Bergsten (1975)* (page 372) and named by *Bhagwati (1988)* (page 372).

Bid/ask spread

The difference between the price that a buyer must pay on a market and the price that a seller will receive for the same thing. The difference covers the cost of, and provides profit for, the broker or other intermediary, such as a bank on the foreign exchange market.

Big Mac index

An index of *PPP exchange rates* (page 212) based solely on the prices of the Big Mac sandwich in McDonald's restaurants around the world, published each spring by the *Economist*.

Bilateral

Between two countries, in contrast to *plurilateral* (page 210) and *multilateral* (page 182).

Bilateral agreement

An agreement between two countries, as opposed to a *multilateral agreement* (page 182).

Bilateral exchange rate

The *exchange rate* (page 94) between two countries' currencies, defined as the number of units of either currency needed to purchase one unit of the other.

Bilateral quota

An import (or export) *quota* (page 226) applied to trade with a single trading partner, specifying the amount of a good that can be imported from (exported to) that single country only.

Bilateral trade

The trade between two countries; that is, the value or quantity of one country's exports to the other, or the sum of exports and imports between them.

Bilateral transfer

A *transfer payment* (page 279) from one country to another.

Bill of exchange

Any document demanding payment.

Bill of lading

The receipt given by a transportation company to an exporter when the former accepts goods for transport. It includes the contract specifying what transport service will be provided and the limits of liability.

Binding

See *tariff binding* (page 264).

BIS

Bank for International Settlements (page 20).

Black market

An illegal market, in which something is bought and sold outside of official government-sanctioned channels. Black markets tend to arise when a government tries to fix a price without itself providing all of the necessary supply or demand. Black markets in foreign exchange almost always exist when there are *exchange controls* (page 93).

Bloc

See *trading bloc* (page 278).

Blue box

A special category of *subsidies* (page 260) permitted under the *WTO* (page 293) *agriculture agreement* (page 9), it includes payments that are linked to production but with provisions to limit production through production quotas or requirements to set aside land from production.

Bond

A debt instrument, issued by a borrower and promising a specified stream of payments to the purchaser, usually regular interest payments plus a final repayment of principal. Bonds are exchanged on open markets including, in the absence of *capital controls* (page 32), internationally, providing a mechanism for international *capital mobility* (page 33).

Bonded warehouse

See *foreign trade zone* (page 111).

Boom-bust cycle

A pattern of performance over time in an economy or an industry that alternates between extremes of rapid growth and extremes of slow growth or decline, as opposed to sustained steady growth. For an economy, this indicates an extreme form of the *business cycle* (page 28).

BOP

Balance of payments (page 17).

Border price

The price of a good at a country's border.

Border tax adjustment

Rebate of indirect taxes (taxes on other than direct income, such as a sales tax or *VAT* (page 288)) on exported goods, and levying of them on imported goods. May distort trade when tax rates differ or when adjustment does not match the tax paid.

Borderless world

The concept that national borders no longer matter, perhaps for some specified purpose.

Borrowing

The amount that an entity, usually a country or its government, has borrowed. Thus often the (negative of) the *net foreign asset position* (page 189) or the *national debt* (page 185).

BOT

Balance of trade (page 18).

Bound rate

See *tariff binding* (page 264).

Box

Used with a color, a category of *subsidies* (page 260) based on status in *WTO* (page 293): *red* (page 231) = forbidden, *amber* (page 9) = go slow, *green* (page 121) = permitted, *blue* (page 24) = subsidies tied to production limits. Terminology seems only to be used in agriculture, where in fact there is no red box.

Boycott

To protest by refusing to purchase from someone, or otherwise do business with them. In international trade, a boycott most often takes the form of refusal to import a country's goods.

BP curve

In the *Mundell-Fleming model* (page 183), the curve representing *balance of payments equilibrium* (page 18). It is normally upward sloping because an increase in income increases imports while an

increase in the interest rate increases *capital inflows* (page 32).
The curve is used under *pegged exchange rates* (page 207) for
effects on the *balance of payments* (page 17) and under *floating
rates* (page 108) for effects on the exchange rate.

Brain drain

The *migration* (page 176) of skilled workers out of a country. First
applied to the migration of British-trained scientists, physicians,
and university teachers in the early 1960's, mostly to the United
States.

Bretton Woods

A town in New Hampshire at which a 1944 conference launched
the *IMF* (page 132) and the *World Bank* (page 293). These, along
with the *GATT* (page 116)/*WTO* (page 293) became known as
the **Bretton Woods Institutions**, and together they comprise
the **Bretton Woods System**.

Bribe

A payment made to person, often a government official such as
a *customs officer* (page 59), to induce favorable treatment.

Broker's fee

The fee for a transaction charged by an intermediary in a market,
such as a bank in a foreign-exchange transaction.

Brown field investment

FDI (page 105) that involves the purchase of an existing plant
or firm, rather then construction of a new plant. Contrasts with
green field investment (page 121).

Brussels tariff nomenclature

An international system of classification for goods that was once
widely used for specifying tariffs. It was changed, in name only,
to the *CCCN* (page 59) in 1976 and later superseded by the
harmonized system of tariff nomenclature (page 125).

BTN

Brussels tariff nomenclature (see above).

Bubble

A rise in the price of an *asset* (page 13) based not on the current or prospective income that it provides but solely on expectations by market participants that the price will rise in the future.

When those expectations cease, the bubble bursts and the price falls rapidly.

Bubble economy

Term for an economy in which the presence of one or more *bubbles* (page 26) in its asset markets is a dominant feature of its performance. Japan was said to be a bubble economy in the late 1980s.

Budget constraint

1. For an individual or household, the condition that income equals expenditure (in a *static model* (page 257)), or that income minus expenditure equals the value of increased asset holdings (in a *dynamic model* (page 78)).

2. For a country, the condition that the value of exports equals the value of imports or, if capital flows are permitted, that exports minus imports equals the net *capital outflow* (page 33). It is equivalent to income from production equaling expenditure on goods plus net acquisition of foreign assets.

3. The curve, usually a straight line, representing either of these conditions.

Budget deficit

The negative of the *budget surplus* (see below); thus the excess of expenditure over income.

Budget surplus

Refers in general to an excess of income over expenditure, but usually refers specifically to the government budget, where it is the excess of tax revenue over expenditure (including transfer and interest payments).

Buffer stock

A large quantity of a *commodity* (page 41) held in storage to be used to *stabilize* (page 255) the commodity's price. This is done by buying when the price is low and adding to the buffer stock, selling out of the buffer stock when the price is high, hoping to reduce the size of price fluctuations. See *international commodity agreement* (page 146).

Building block

See *stumbling block* (page 259).

Built-in agenda

Issues that were scheduled for continued negotiations within the *WTO* (page 293) in the *Uruguay Round* (page 286) agreement. In addition to reviewing the implementation of various agreements, these included negotiations for further liberalization in agriculture and services.

Built-in stabilizer

Automatic stabilizer (page 15).

Bureau of Economic Analysis

The government agency within the United States Department of Commerce that collects macroeconomic data, especially the *National Income and Product Accounts* (page 186), as well as data on *balance of payments* (page 17) and *international investment* (page 148).

Business cycle

The pattern followed by macroeconomic variables, such as *GDP* (page 122) and *unemployment* (page 283) that rise and fall irregularly over time, relative to *trend* (page 280). There is some tendency for cyclical movements of large countries to cause similar movements in other countries with whom they trade.

Business Cycle Dating Committee

See *National Bureau of Economic Research* (page 185).

Buy American Act

U.S. legislation requiring that government purchases give preference to domestic producers unless imports are at least a specified percentage cheaper. This is an example of a *government procurement* (page 120) *NTB* (page 195) that was partially given up under the *Tokyo Round* (page 271).

Byrd amendment

A US law enacted in 2000 requiring that revenues from *antidumping duties* (page 10) and *countervailing duties* (page 52) be given to the U.S. domestic producers who had filed the cases.

Cabotage

1. Navigation and trade by ship along a coast, especially between ports within a country. Restricted in the U.S. by the *Jones Act* (page 154) to domestic shipping companies.

2. Air transportation within a country. Often restricted to domestic carriers, in an example of barriers to *trade in services* (page 274).

CACM

Central American Common Market (page 35).

CAFTA

U.S.-Central American Free Trade Agreement (page 287).

Cairnes-Haberler model

A trade model in which all factors of production are assumed immobile between industries. See *specific factors model* (page 253).

Cairns group

A group of agricultural exporting countries, currently (2006) numbering 17, that was formed in 1986 to act as a counterweight especially to the *EU* (page 89) in international negotiations on agriculture. Named after the city in Australia where the group first met, in August 1986.

Canada-US Auto Pact

The "Canada-United States Automotive Products Agreement of 1965" which reduced trade barriers on specified trade between Canada and the United States in automobiles and original-equipment auto parts.

Canada-US Free Trade Agreement

A *free trade agreement* (page 113) between Canada and the United States signed in 1989 and superseded by the *NAFTA* (page 184) in 1994.

Cancún Ministerial

The 5th *ministerial meeting* (page 177) of the *WTO* (page 293) held in Cancún, Mexico, September 2003 as part of the *Doha Round* (page 73) of multilateral trade negotiations. The meeting failed to reach agreement on a framework text for the round because of disagreements between the US/EU and the *G-20* (page 115), mostly over agricultural subsidies.

Canonical model of currency crises

This term has been used to refer to the model that *Krugman (1979b)* (page 377) presented of a *currency crisis* (page 57) that results when domestic policy is pursued in a manner inconsistent with a *pegged exchange rate* (page 207).

CAP

Common Agricultural Policy (page 41).

Capacity building

The term used repeatedly in the *Doha Declaration* (page 73) referring to the assistance to be provided to developing countries in establishing and administering their trade policies, conducting analysis, and identifying their interests in trade negotiations.

Capital

1. The plant and equipment used in production.

2. One of the main *primary factors* (page 217), the availability of which contributes to the *productivity of labor* (page 221), *comparative advantage* (page 42), and the *pattern of international trade* (page 206).

3. A stock of financial assets.

Capital abundant

A country is capital abundant if its *endowment* (page 86) of capital is large compared to other countries. Relative capital abundance can be defined by either the *quantity definition* (page 224) or the *price definition* (page 215).

Capital account

1. (Current definition) Since sometime in the 1990s, "capital account" refers to a minor component of international transactions, involving unilateral transfers of ownership of property. The common definition, below, describes what is now called the *financial account* (page 106).

2. (Common definition) A country's international transactions arising from changes in holdings of real and financial capital assets (but not income on them, which is in the *current account* (page 58)). Includes *FDI* (page 105), plus changes in private and official holdings of stocks, bonds, loans, bank accounts, and currencies.

3. (Bretton-Woods definition) Same as common definition except excluding *official reserve transactions* (page 196). This definition was used under the *Bretton Woods System* (page 26) of *pegged exchange rates* (page 207), but is less meaningful under *floating exchange rates* (page 108).

Capital account balance
  Balance on capital account (page 18).

Capital account deficit
  Debits (page 61) minus *credits* (page 54) on *capital account* (page 30). See *deficit* (page 63).

Capital account surplus
  Credits (page 54) minus *debits* (page 61) on *capital account* (page 30). Same as *balance on capital account* (page 18). See *surplus* (page 262).

Capital adequacy ratio
  The ratio of a bank's capital to its risk-weighted credit exposure. International standards recommend a minimum for this ratio, intended to permit banks to absorb losses without becoming insolvent, in order to protect depositors.

Capital augmenting
  Said of a *technological change* (page 268) or *technological difference* (page 268) if one production function produces the same as if it were the other, but with a larger quantity of capital. Same as *factor augmenting* (page 101) with capital the augmented factor. Also called *Solow neutral* (page 250).

Capital consumption allowance
  The name used in the *National Income and Product Accounts* (page 186) for *depreciation* (page 66) of capital.

Capital control

Any policy intended to restrict the free movement of capital, especially *financial capital* (page 106), into or out of a country.

Capital depreciation

See *depreciation* (page 66).

Capital flight

Large financial *capital outflows* (page 33) from a country prompted by fear of *default* (page 63) or, especially, by fear of *devaluation* (page 67).

Capital flow

International *capital movement* (page 33).

Capital gain

The increase in value that the owner of an asset experiences when the price of the asset rises, including when the currency in which the asset is denominated *appreciates* (page 11). Contrasts with *capital loss* (page 33).

Capital good

A good, such as a machine, that, once in place, becomes part of the *capital stock* (page 34).

Capital inflow

A net flow of capital, real and/or financial, into a country, in the form of increased purchases of domestic assets by foreigners and/or reduced holdings of foreign assets by domestic residents. Recorded as positive, or a *credit* (page 54), in the *balance on capital account* (page 18).

Capital infusion

An increase in *financial capital* (page 106) provided from outside a bank, corporation, or other entity.

Capital intensity

A measure of the relative use of capital, compared to other *factors* (page 101) such as labor, in a production process. Often measured by the ratio of capital to labor, or by the share of capital in factor payments.

Capital intensive

Describing an industry or sector of the economy that relies relatively heavily on inputs of capital, usually relative to labor, compared to other industries or sectors. See *factor intensity* (page 102).

Capital loss

The decrease in value that the owner of an asset experiences when the price of the asset falls, including when the currency in which the asset is denominated *depreciates* (page 66). Contrasts with *capital gain* (page 32).

Capital market imperfection

Anything that interferes with the ability of economic agents to borrow and lend as much as they wish at a fixed rate of interest that truly reflects probability of repayment. A common source of imperfection is *asymmetric information* (page 14).

Capital mobility

The ability of capital to *move* (see below) internationally. The degree of capital mobility depends on government policies restricting or taxing capital *inflows* (page 32) and/or *outflows* (see below), plus the *risk* (page 238) that investors in one country associate with assets in another.

Capital movement

Capital inflow (page 32) and/or *outflow* (see below).

Capital outflow

A net flow of capital, real and/or financial, out of a country, in the form of reduced holdings of domestic assets by foreigners and/or increased holdings of foreign assets by domestic residents. Recorded as negative, or a *debit* (page 61), in the *balance on capital account* (page 18).

Capital saving

A *technological change* (page 268) or *technological difference* (page 268) that is *biased* (page 22) in favor of using less capital, compared to some definition of *neutrality* (page 189).

Capital scarce

A country is capital scarce if its *endowment* (page 86) of capital is small compared to other countries. Relative capital scarcity can be defined by either the *quantity definition* (page 224) or the *price definition* (page 215).

Capital stock
The total amount of *physical capital* (page 209) that has been accumulated, usually in a country.

Capital using
A *technological change* (page 268) or *technological difference* (page 268) that is *biased* (page 22) in favor of using more capital, compared to some definition of *neutrality* (page 189).

Capitalism
An economic system in which *capital* (page 30) is mostly owned by private individuals and corporations. Contrasts with *communism* (page 42).

Capitalist
1. An owner (or sometimes only a manager) of *capital* (page 30).
2. Associated or identified with *capitalism* (see above).

Caribbean Basin Initiative
A *preferential trading arrangement* (page 214) originally enacted in 1983 by the United States, providing duty-free access to a group of Caribbean countries for selected products. It was renewed and extended in 2000.

Caribbean community
The Caribbean Community and Common Market was formed among four Caribbean countries in 1973 and had 15 members as of 2006. Its purpose is the promotion of economic integration among the member countries and coordination of foreign policies.

CARICOM
Caribbean Community and Common Market (see above).

Carriage of Goods by Sea Act
U.S. legislation governing ocean transport of cargo.

Carrier
A firm that provides transportation of persons or goods.

Cartagena agreement
The 1969 agreement, also known as the *Andean Pact* (page 10), that led ultimately to the *Andean community* (page 10).

Cartel
A group of firms or countries that seeks to raise the price of a good by restricting its supply. The term is usually used

for international groups, especially involving *state-owned firms* (page 256) and/or governments.

Cascading tariffs

Same as *tariff escalation* (page 264).

CBI

Caribbean Basin Initiative (page 34).

CCCN

Customs Cooperation Council Nomenclature (page 59).

Cecchini report

A 1988 report by a group of experts, chaired by Paolo Cecchini, examining the benefits and costs of creating a *single market* (page 247) in Europe, in accordance with provisions of the *Treaty of Rome* (page 280).

CEEC

Central and Eastern European countries (see below).

CEFTA

Central European Free Trade Agreement (page 36).

Ceiling

See *price ceiling* (page 214).

Central American Common Market

A group of Central American countries — El Salvador, Guatemala, Honduras, and Nicaragua — that formed a *common market* (page 41) in 1960, with Costa Rica added in 1962. It largely disintegrated in the 1970s and 80s due to military conflicts, but reformed as the **Central American Free Trade Zone** (but without Costa Rica) starting in 1993.

Central and Eastern European countries

Refers, informally, usually to the former communist countries of Europe.

Central bank

The institution in a country (or a *currency area* (page 57)) that is normally (but see *currency board* (page 57)) responsible for managing the supply of the country's money and the value of its currency on the foreign *exchange market* (page 94).

Central bank intervention

See *exchange market intervention* (page 94).

Central European Free Trade Agreement
A *free trade agreement* (page 113) initiated 1993 among the Czech Republic, Hungary, Poland, Slovakia, and Slovenia, now also including Bulgaria and Romania. Its purpose was in part to reverse the bias against trade among these neighboring countries that had developed during the process of *transition* (page 279).

Central Intelligence Agency
Intelligence gathering (and espionage) agency of the United States government, publisher of the *World Fact Book* (page 293).

Central parity
Par value (page 204).

Central planning
The guidance of the economy by direct government control over a large portion of economic activity, as contrasted with allowing *markets* (page 171) to serve this purpose.

CER
Australia-New Zealand Closer Economic Relations Trade Agreement (page 15).

Certainty
Precise knowledge of an economic variable, as opposed to belief that it could take on multiple values. Contrasts with *uncertainty* (page 282). One aspect of *complete information* (page 44).

CES function
A function with constant *elasticity of substitution* (page 84). CES is popular for both production and utility functions. Used extensively in *new trade theory* (page 190) as the *Dixit-Stiglitz* (page 73) utility function for *differentiated products* (page 68) under *monopolistic competition* (page 180). With arguments $X = (X_1, \ldots, X_n)$, the function is $F(X) = A[\Sigma_i a_i X_i^\rho]^{1/\rho}$, where a_i, A are positive constants and $\sigma = 1/(1 - \rho)$ is the elasticity of substitution. *For more on the origin of this term, please see* page 367.

CET function
Constant elasticity of transformation function (page 47).

Ceteris paribus
Latin phrase meaning, approximately, "holding other things constant." Used as shorthand for indicating the effect of one

economic variable on another, holding constant all other variables that may affect the second variable. Contrasts with *mutatis mutandis* (page 183).

CGE

Computable general equilibrium (page 45).

Chain of comparative advantage

A ranking of goods or countries in order of *comparative advantage* (page 42). With two countries and many goods, goods can be ranked by comparative advantage (e.g., by relative *unit labor requirements* (page 284) in the *Ricardian model* (page 237)). A country's exports will then lie nearer one end of the chain than its imports. With two goods, many countries can be ordered similarly.

Change in consumer surplus

The change in *consumer surplus* (page 48) due to a change in market conditions, usually a price change. For a price change, it is measured by the area to the left of the demand curve between the two prices, indicating a gain if price falls and a loss if it rises.

Change in producer surplus

The change in *producer surplus* (page 219) due to a change in market conditions, usually a price change. For a price change, it is measured by the area to the left of the (upward sloping part of the) supply curve between the two prices, indicating a gain if price rises and a loss if it falls.

Chapter 11

1. In *NAFTA* (page 184), this portion deals with *foreign direct investment* (page 109). Most controversially, it includes a provision for a firm from one member country that has invested in another to bring action against a unit of government in that country if it has acted to reduce the value of its investment.

2. A portion of U.S. bankruptcy law under which a firm can file for protection while it reorganizes.

Chicken war

A *trade dispute* (page 274) between the U.S. and the *EEC* (page 81) that began in 1962 when the EEC extended the *variable levy* (page 288) of the *CAP* (page 30) to poultry, tripling German tariffs on U.S. chickens. A *GATT* (page 116) *panel* (page 203) quantified the damage and led to U.S. retaliatory tariffs on cognac, trucks, and other goods. The U.S. 25% tariff on trucks today is a remnant of the chicken war.

Child labor
Employment of children under a specified minimum age.

Chinese Economic Area
Unofficial name for the area comprising Hong Kong, Taiwan, and either China as a whole or just its *special economic zones* (page 251).

CIA
1. Cash in advance.

2. *Central Intelligence Agency* (page 36).

CIF
The price of a traded good including *transport cost* (page 280). It stands for "cost, insurance, and freight," but is used only as these initials (usually lower case: c.i.f.). It means that a price includes the various costs, such as transportation and insurance, needed to get a good from one country to another. Contrasts with *FOB* (page 108).

CIS
Commonwealth of Independent States (page 42).

CITES
Convention on International Trade in Endangered Species of Wild Fauna and Flora, an agreement among originally 80 governments effective in 1975 to prevent trade in wild animals and plants from threatening their survival. It works by requiring licensing of trade in covered species.

Civil society
The name used to encompass a wide and self-selected variety of interest groups, worldwide. It does *not* include for-profit businesses, government, and government organizations, whereas it *does* include most *NGOs* (page 191).

Civil society organization
Non-governmental organization (page 193).

Classical

Referring to the writings, models, and economic assumptions of the first century of economics, including Adam Smith, David Ricardo, and John Stuart Mill.

Clear

A market is said to clear if supply is equal to demand. Market **clearing** can be brought about by adjustment of the price (or the exchange rate, in the case of the *exchange market* (page 94)), or by some form of government (or *central bank* (page 35)) intervention in or regulation of the market.

Clearing system

An arrangement among financial institutions for carrying out the transactions among them, including canceling out offsetting *credits* (page 54) and *debits* (page 61) on the same account.

Closed economy

An economy that does not permit economic transactions with the outside world; a country in *autarky* (page 15).

Closer economic relations

See *Australia-New Zealand Closer Economic Relations Trade Agreement* (page 15).

CMEA

Council for Mutual Economic Assistance (page 52).

Coase theorem

The proposition that the allocation of property rights does not matter for economic efficiency, so long as they are well defined and a free market exists for the exchange of rights between those who have them and those who do not. Due to *Coase (1960)* (page 373).

Cobb-Douglas function

A popular functional form for production and utility functions. With arguments $X = (X_1, \ldots, X_n)$, the function is $F(X) = A\Pi_i X_i^{\alpha}$, where $\Sigma_i \alpha_i = 1$ and A are positive constants. This function has *elasticity of substitution* (page 84) between arguments equal one. As a production or utility function, it has competitive expenditure shares equal to α_i.

Codex alimentarius
This is the "food code," consisting of standards, codes of practice, guidelines, and recommendations for producing and processing food. It is administered by the Codex Alimentarius Commission.

Coefficient
1. A number or symbol multiplied by a variable.
2. In a *regression analysis* (page 232), the estimated numerical association between one variable and another, usually taken to represent the sign and size of the causal effect of one on the other.

COGSA
Carriage of Goods by Sea Act (page 34).

Collective action problem
The difficulty of getting a group to act when members benefit if others act, but incur a net cost if they act themselves.

Collusion
Cooperation among firms to raise price and otherwise increase their profits.

COMECON
Council for Mutual Economic Assistance (page 52).

COMESA
Common Market of Eastern and Southern Africa (page 41).

Command economy
An economy in which decisions about production and *allocation* (page 9) are made by government dictate, rather than by decentralized responses to market forces.

Commercial bank
An institution that accepts and manages *deposits* (page 66) from households, firms and governments and uses a portion of those deposits to earn interest by making loans and holding securities.

Commercial paper
Short-term, negotiable debt of a firm; thus a *bond* (page 24) of short maturity issued by a company.

Commercial policy
Government policies intended to influence international commerce, including international trade. Includes *tariffs*

(page 264) and *NTBs* (page 195), as well as policies regarding exports.

Commodity

Could refer to any good, but in a trade context a commodity is usually a *raw material* (page 227) or *primary product* (page 217) that enters into international trade, such as metals (tin, manganese) or basic agricultural products (coffee, cocoa).

Commodity agreement

See *international commodity agreement* (page 146).

Commodity pattern of trade

The *trade pattern* (page 276) of a country or the world, focusing on goods and services traded as opposed to the *factor content* (page 102) of that trade.

Commodity prices

Usually means the prices of *raw materials* (page 227) and *primary products* (page 217).

Common agricultural policy

The regulations of the *European Union* (page 357) that seek to merge their individual agricultural programs, primarily by stabilizing and elevating the prices of agricultural commodities. The principle tools of the CAP are *variable levies* (page 288) and *export subsidies* (page 99).

Common currency

A *currency* (page 56) that is shared by more than one country. Thus the currency of a *currency area* (page 57).

Common external tariff

The single tariff rate agreed to by all members of a *customs union* (page 60) on imports of a product from outside the union.

Common market

A group of countries that eliminate all barriers to movement of both goods and factors among themselves, and that also, on each product, agree to levy the same tariff on imports from outside the group. Equivalent to a *customs union* (page 60) plus free mobility of factors.

Common Market of Eastern and Southern Africa

A trade agreement involving 21 nations of Eastern and Southern Africa. It went into effect in 1994, replacing a preferential trade area that had begun in 1982, with the aim of forming a *free trade area* (page 113) by 2000 and achieving other trade liberalization and transport facilitation over a period of 16 years.

Common tangent

A straight line that is tangent to two or more curves. Used in the *Lerner diagram* (page 369).

Commonwealth of Independent States

An organization formed in 1991 of the nations that had been part of the USSR.

Communism

An economic system in which *capital* (page 30) is owned by the government. Contrasts with *capitalism* (page 34).

Community indifference curve

One of a family of indifference curves intended to represent the preferences, and sometimes the wellbeing, of a country as a whole. This is a handy tool for deriving quantities of trade in a two-good model, although its legitimacy depends on the existence of *community preferences* (page 42), which in turn requires very restrictive assumptions. See *Leontief (1933)* (page 378).

Community preferences

A set of consumer preferences, analogous to those of an individual as might be represented by a *utility function* (page 287), but representing the preferences of a group of consumers. The existence of well-behaved community preferences requires restrictive assumptions about individual preferences and/or incomes.

Comparative advantage

The ability to produce a good at lower cost, relative to other goods, compared to another country. In a *Ricardian model* (page 237), comparison is of *unit labor requirements* (page 284); more generally it is of relative *autarky prices* (page 15). With perfect competition and undistorted markets, countries tend to export goods in which they have comparative advantage. See also *absolute advantage* (page 3). *For more on the origins of this term, please see* page 367.

Comparative static

Refers to a comparison of two equilibria from a *static model* (page 257), usually differing by the effects of a single small change in an *exogenous variable* (page 96).

Compensated demand curve

A *demand curve* (page 65) constructed under the assumption that demander's income is not held constant, but rather is varied to hold level of utility at a constant level. The *change in consumer surplus* (page 37) calculated from particular compensated demand curves measures *compensating variation* (see below) and *equivalent variation* (page 88).

Compensating variation

An amount of money that just compensates a person, group, or whole economy, for the welfare effects of a change in the economy, thus providing a monetary measure of that change in *welfare* (page 291). Same as *willingness to pay* (page 292). Contrasts with *equivalent variation* (page 88).

Compensation

1. The *GATT* (page 116) principle that members who violate GATT rules must compensate other countries by lowering tariffs or making other concessions, or be subject to *retaliation* (page 236).

2. The actual or potential payment by the winners from a change in trade or other policy to the losers, intended to undo the harm to the latter. Actual compensation is rare, but the potential for compensation is used as the basis for most evaluations of the *gains from trade* (page 116).

Compensation principle

As a basis for welfare comparisons, the idea that if a policy change (such as a tariff reduction) could be *Pareto improving* (page 204) if it were accompanied by appropriate *lump-sum* (page 167) transfers from winners to losers, then it is viewed as beneficial even when those transfers do not occur.

Compensation trade

Countertrade (page 52), including especially payment for *foreign direct investment* (page 109) out of the proceeds from that investment.

Competition

The interactions between two or more sellers or buyers in a single market, each attempting to get or pay the most favorable price. Economists usually interpret and model these interactions as among individual economic agents — firms or consumers. Popular terminology extends also to competition among nations, especially competing exporters.

Competition policy

Policies intended to prevent *collusion* (page 40) among firms and to prevent individual firms from having excessive market power. Major forms include oversight of mergers and prevention of price fixing and market sharing. Called "**anti-trust policy**" in the U.S. One of the *Singapore issues* (page 246).

Competitive

Used alone, this usually means *perfectly competitive* (page 209). Contrasts with *imperfectly competitive* (page 133).

Competitive advantage

Competitiveness (see below). Contrasts with *comparative advantage* (page 42).

Competitiveness

Usually refers to characteristics that permit a firm to compete effectively with other firms due to low cost or superior technology, perhaps internationally. When applied to nations, instead of firms, the word has a *mercantilist* (page 175) connotation.

Complete information

The assumption that economic agents (buyers and sellers, consumers and firms) know everything that they need to know in order to make optimal decisions. Types of **incomplete information** are *uncertainty* (page 282) and *asymmetric information* (page 14).

Complete specialization

1. Non-production of some of the goods that a country consumes, as in definition 2 of *specialization* (page 252).

2. Production only of goods that are exported or non-traded, but none that compete with imports.

3. Production of only one good.

4. Being the only country in the world to produce a good.

Composite currency

A currency defined as a specified combination of two or more currencies, normally existing only as a unit of account rather than as a physical currency. Examples include the *SDR* (page 242) and the *ECU* (page 81).

Compound tariff

A *tariff* (page 264) that combines both a *specific* (page 253) and an *ad valorem* (page 5) component.

Compulsory licensing

A legal requirement for the owner of a *patent* (page 205) to let other firms produce its product, under specified terms. Countries sometimes require foreign patent holders to *license* (page 163) domestic firms so as to improve access to the patented product at lower cost. This is permitted by the *TRIPs agreement* (page 281) for certain purposes, such as protecting public health.

Computable general equilibrium

Refers to economic models of microeconomic behavior in multiple markets of one or more economies, solved computationally for equilibrium values or changes due to specified policies. The equations are anchored with data from the countries being modeled, while behavioral parameters are either assumed or adapted from estimates elsewhere.

Comvariance

An analogue to *covariance* (page 53) for three variables. For three variables x, y, and z with values x_i, y_i, z_i, $i = 1, \ldots, n$, the comvariance is $\text{com}(x,y,z) = \Sigma_{i=1\ldots n}(x_i - \text{m}(x))(y_i - \text{m}(y))(z_i - \text{m}(z))$, where $\text{m}(\cdot)$ is the *mean* (page 175) of the values in its argument. Due to *Deardorff (1982)* (page 374).

Concave

Said of a curve that bulges away from some reference point, usually the horizontal axis or the origin of a diagram. More formally, a curve is concave from below (or concave to something below it) if all straight lines connecting points on it lie on or below it. Contrasts with *convex* (page 50).

Concentration

See *industrial concentration* (page 139).

Concentration ratio

A common measure of *industry concentration* (page 139), defined as the percent of sales in the industry accounted for by the largest n firms. n is some small number such as 4 or 6, and the result is called the "n-firm concentration ratio."

Concertina tariff reduction

The reduction of a country's highest tariff to the level of the next highest, followed by the reduction of both to the level of the next highest after that, and so forth. Also called the **concertina rule**. This is known to raise welfare if all goods are net substitutes.

Concession

The term used in *GATT* (page 116) negotiations for a country's agreement to *bind* (page 24) a tariff or otherwise reduce import restrictions, usually in return for comparable "concessions" by other countries. Use of this term, with its connotation of loss, for what economic theory suggests is often a source of gain, is part of what has been called *GATT-Speak* (page 117).

Concessional financing

Loans made by a government at an *interest rate* (page 143) below the *market rate* (page 173) as an indirect method of providing a *subsidy* (page 260).

Conditionality

The requirements imposed by the *IMF* (page 132) and *World Bank* (page 293) on borrowing countries to qualify for a loan, typically including a long list of budgetary and policy changes comprising a *structural adjustment program* (page 259).

Cone of diversification

See *diversification cone* (page 72).

Conservative social welfare function

A *social welfare function* (page 249) that takes special account of the costs to individuals of losing relative to the *status quo* (page 257), and that therefore seeks to avoid large losses to significant groups within the population. Due to *Corden (1974)* (page 373).

Consignment

1. Something that is put into the care of another, as when a batch of traded goods is consigned to a shipper for transport to another location.

2. A method of marketing in which the seller entrusts a product to an agent, who then attempts to sell it on the seller's behalf, or "on consignment."

Constant dollars

Dollars of constant *purchasing power* (page 223). That is, corrected for inflation. More precisely includes reference to a *base year* (page 20) for comparison, e.g., "in constant 1992 dollars." Same as *constant prices* (see below).

Constant elasticity of substitution function

See *CES function* (page 36).

Constant elasticity of transformation function

A function representing an economy's *transformation curve* (page 279) along which the *elasticity of transformation* (page 84) is constant.

Constant prices

See *constant dollars* (above).

Constant returns to scale

A property of a production function such that scaling all inputs by any positive constant also scales output by the same constant. Such a function is also called *homogeneous of degree one* (page 128) or *linearly homogeneous* (page 164). CRTS is a critical assumption of the *HO model* (page 128) of international trade. Contrasts with *increasing returns* (page 138) and *decreasing returns* (page 63).

Consumer movement

One of four *modes of supply* (page 178) of *traded services* (page 274), this one entails the buyer moving (temporarily) to the foreign location of the seller, as in the case of tourism.

Consumer price index

A *price index* (page 215) for the goods purchased by consumers in an economy, usually based on only a small sample of what they consume. Commonly used to measure *inflation* (page 141). Contrasts with the *implicit price deflator* (page 133).

Consumer support estimate

Introduced by the *OECD* (page 196) to quantify agricultural policies, this measures transfers to or from consumers that are implicit in these policies. Since industrialized-country agricultural producers are routinely supported by raising prices, CSE estimates are usually negative. See also *PSE* (page 222).

Consumer surplus

The difference between the maximum that consumers would be willing to pay for a good and what they actually do pay. For each unit of the good, this is the vertical distance between the demand curve and price. For all units purchased at some price, it is the area below the demand curve and above the price. Normally useful only as the *change in consumer surplus* (page 37).

Consumption externality

An *externality* (page 100) arising from consumption.

Consumption possibility frontier

A graph of the maximum quantities of goods (usually two) that an economy can consume in a specified situation, such as *autarky* (page 15) and *free trade* (page 113). Used to illustrate the potential benefits from trade by showing that it can expand consumption possibilities.

Contagion

The phenomenon of a *financial crisis* (page 106) in one country spilling over to another, which then suffers many of the same problems.

Content protection

See *domestic content protection* (page 74).

Content requirement

See *domestic content requirement* (page 74).

Contingent protection

Administered protection (page 6).

Continuous time

The use of a continuous variable to represent time, as in an economic model.

Continuum model

A model in which some entities that are normally discrete and exist in finite numbers are modeled instead by a continuous variable. This can sometimes simplify the treatment of large numbers of entities. In trade theory, the most notable example is the *continuum-of-goods model* (see below).

Continuum-of-goods model

A class of trade models in which goods are indexed by a continuous variable, approximating the case of very large numbers of goods. The classic, *original* (please refer to page 367) examples are *Dornbusch, Fischer, and Samuelson (1977, 1980)* (page 374).

Contract curve

1. In an *Edgeworth box* (page 81) for consumption, the allocations of 2 goods to 2 consumers that are *Pareto efficient* (page 204). Starting with an allocation that may not be on the contract curve, it shows the ways that the consumers might contract to exchange the goods with each other.

2. In an *Edgeworth box* (page 81) for production, this name is sometimes also used for the *efficiency locus* (page 82).

Contracting party

A country that has signed the *GATT* (page 116). The term **Contracting Parties** with both words capitalized means all contracting parties acting jointly.

Contraction

Economic contraction (page 79).

Contractionary

Tending to cause aggregate output (*GDP* (page 122)) and/or the price level to fall. Term is typically applied to *monetary policy* (page 179) (a decrease in the money supply or an increase in interest rates) and to *fiscal policy* (page 107) (a decrease in government spending or a tax increase), but may also apply to other macroeconomic shocks. Contrasts with *expansionary* (page 97).

Convergence

The process of becoming quantitatively more alike. In an international context, it often refers to countries becoming more alike in terms of their *factor prices* (page 103) or in terms of their *per capita incomes* (page 207), perhaps as a result of trade or other forms of economic *integration* (page 142).

Convertible currency

A currency that can legally be exchanged for another or for gold. In times of crisis, governments sometimes restrict such exchange, giving rise to *black market* (page 24) exchange rates.

Convex

1. Said of a curve that bulges toward some reference point, usually the horizontal axis or the origin of a diagram. More formally, a curve is convex from below (or convex to something below it) if all straight lines connecting points on it lie on or above it. Contrasts with *concave* (page 45).

2. Said of a set that contains all straight line segments joining points within it.

Coordination

Cooperation in setting economic policy, especially across countries, so that policies of different governments reinforce each other rather than canceling each other out.

Copyright

The legal right to the proceeds from and control over the use of a created product, such a written work, audio, video, film, or software. This right generally extends over the life of the author plus fifty years. Copyright is one form of *intellectual property* (page 142) that is subject of the *TRIPS* (page 281) agreement.

Core inflation

The rate of *inflation* (page 141) excluding certain sectors whose prices are most *volatile* (page 289), specifically food and energy.

Core propositions

The core propositions of the *HO model* (page 128) are the *factor price equalization theorem* (page 103), the *Heckscher-Ohlin theorem* (page 126), the *Stolper-Samuelson theorem* (page 258), and the *Rybczynski theorem* (page 239), according to *Ethier (1974)* (page 374).

Corn laws

British regulations on the import and export of grain, mainly wheat, intended to control its price. The laws were repealed in 1846, signaling a shift toward *free trade* (page 113).

Corporate income tax

A tax on the profits of corporations. Differences in corporate tax rates across countries can be a cause of *foreign direct investment* (page 109) as well as *transfer pricing* (page 279).

Corporate tax

Corporate income tax (see above).

Correlation

A measure of the extent to which two economic or statistical variables move together, normalized so that its values range from -1 to $+1$. It is defined as the *covariance* (page 53) of the two variables divided by the square root of the product of their *variances* (page 288). The correlation is used in trade theory to express weak relationships among economic variables.

Correlation result

A theoretical property of models with arbitrary numbers of goods or other variables that takes the form of a correlation among variables rather than a strict prediction for each one. Thus represents a weaker average relationship among the variables. Used for *comparative advantage* (page 42) and other properties of trade models in *higher dimensions* (page 127).

Corruption

Dishonest or *partial* (page 205) behavior on the part of a government official or employee, such as a *customs* (page 59) or *procurement* (page 219) officer. Also actions by others intended to induce such behavior, such as bribery or blackmail.

Cost advantage

Possession of a lower cost of production or operation than a competing firm or country. In the case of countries, this could refer to an *absolute advantage* (page 3), although it is more likely a *comparative advantage* (page 42).

Cost-benefit analysis

The use of economic analysis to quantify the gains and losses from a *policy* (page 210) or program as well as their *distribution* (page 72) across different groups in a society.

Cost function
A function relating the minimized total cost in a firm or industry to output and *factor prices* (page 103).

Cost, insurance, freight
See *CIF* (page 38).

Cotonou agreement
A partnership agreement between the *EU* (page 89) and the *ACP countries* (page 4) signed in June 2000 in Cotonou, Benin, replacing the *Lomé Convention* (page 166). Its main objective is poverty reduction, "to be achieved through political dialogue, development aid and closer economic and trade cooperation."

Council for Mutual Economic Assistance
An international organization formed in 1956 among the Soviet Union and other communist countries to coordinate economic development and trade. It was disbanded in 1991. Also known as COMECON.

Countertrade
Trade in which part or all of payment is made in goods or services. See *barter* (page 20).

Countervailing duty
A tariff levied against imports that are subsidized by the exporting country's government, designed to offset (countervail) the effect of the *subsidy* (page 260).

Country of origin
The country in which a good was produced, or sometimes, in the case of a traded service, the home country of the service provider.

Country risk
The *risk* (page 238) associated with operating in, trading with, or especially holding the assets issued by, a particular country. In the case of assets, country risk helps to explain why borrowers in some country must pay higher *interest rates* (page 143) than borrowers from other countries, thus paying a country *risk premium* (page 238).

Country size
Any of many measures of the size of a country. For most economic comparisons, however, country size refers to *GDP* (page 117).

Coupon

The interest payment on a *bond* (page 24), so-named because bonds originally were pieces of paper with small sections, called coupons, that were cut off and exchanged for the interest payments.

Cournot competition

The assumption, often assumed to be made by firms in an *oligopoly* (page 197), that other firms hold their outputs constant as they themselves change behavior. Contrasts with *Bertrand competition* (page 22). Both are used in models of international oligopoly, but Cournot competition is used more often.

Cournot's law

That the sum of the balances of *payments* (page 17) or of *trade* (page 272) across all countries must be zero. Term seems to have been coined by, and perhaps only used by, *Mundell (1960, p. 102)* (page 379), who credited it to *Cournot (1897)* (page 373).

Court of International Trade

See *U.S. Court of International Trade* (page 286).

Covariance

A measure of the extent to which two economic or statistical variables move up and down together. For two variables x and y with values x_i, y_i, $i = 1, \ldots, n$, the covariance is $\text{cov}(x,y) = \Sigma_{i=1\ldots n}(x_i - \text{m}(x))(y_i - \text{m}(y))$, where $\text{m}(\cdot)$ is the *mean* (page 175) of the values in its argument.

Cover

To use the *forward market* (page 111) to protect against *exchange risk* (page 95). Typically, an importer with a future commitment to pay in foreign currency would buy it forward, and exporter with a future receipt would sell it forward, and a purchaser of a foreign bond would sell forward the expected proceeds at maturity. See *hedge* (page 127).

Covered interest arbitrage

A combination of transactions on two countries' securities and exchange markets designed to profit from failure of *covered interest parity* (page 54). A typical set of transactions would include selling bonds in one market, using the proceeds to buy *spot* (page 254) foreign currency and foreign bonds, and selling *forward* (page 111) the return at a future date. See also *one-way arbitrage* (page 198).

Covered interest parity

Equality of returns on otherwise comparable financial assets denominated in two currencies, assuming that the *forward market* (page 111) is used to *cover* (page 53) against *exchange risk* (page 95). As an approximation, covered interest parity requires that $i = i^* + p$ where i is the domestic interest rate, i^* is the foreign interest rate, and p is the *forward premium* (page 111).

Covered interest rate

The covered interest rate, in a currency other than your own, is the nominal interest rate plus the *forward premium* (page 111) on the currency; thus the percent you will earn holding the foreign asset while protecting against exchange-rate change by selling the foreign currency forward.

CPI

Consumer price index (page 47).

Crawling peg

An exchange rate that is *pegged* (page 207), but for which the *par value* (page 204) is changed frequently by small amounts and in a pre-announced fashion in response to signals from the *exchange market* (page 94).

Creation

See *trade creation* (page 273).

Credit

1. Recorded as positive (+) in the *balance of payments* (page 17), any transaction that gives rise to a payment *into* the country, such as an export, the sale of an asset (including *official reserves* (page 197)), or borrowing from abroad. Opposite of *debit* (page 61).

2. A loan. For example, a *trade credit* (page 273).

Credit crunch

A shortage of available loans. In well-functioning markets, this would simply mean a rise in *interest rates* (page 143), but in practice it often means that some borrowers cannot get loans at all, a situation of **credit rationing**.

Creditor nation

A country whose assets owned abroad are worth more than the assets within the country that are owned by foreigners. Contrasts with *debtor nation* (page 62).

Creeping inflation

This term seems to be used both for a rate of *inflation* (page 141) that is low but nonetheless high enough to cause problems, and for a rate of inflation that itself gradually moves higher over time.

Crony capitalism

Used to describe a *capitalist* (page 30) economy in which government or corporate officials and insiders provide lucrative opportunities for their friends and relatives. Term became popular during the *Asian crisis* (page 13) to describe some of the victim countries, but is now often used elsewhere as well.

Cross-border supply

The provision of an internationally *traded service* (page 274) across national borders without requiring physical movement of buyer or seller, as when the service can be provided by long-distance communication. One of four such *modes of supply* (page 178) of traded services.

Cross elasticity

1. An *elasticity* (page 83) that has been ignored by a student in a problem set.

2. The *elasticity* (page 83) of supply or demand for one good or service with respect to the price of another.

Cross hauling

The simultaneous shipment of the same product in opposite directions over the same route. The export of the same good by two countries to each other would be cross hauling, if it occurs at the same time.

Cross rate

1. The *exchange rate* (page 94) between two currencies as implied by their values with respect to a third currency.

2. Thus, since most currencies are commonly quoted in U.S. dollars, the exchange rate between any two currencies other than the dollar.

Cross subsidy

The use of profits from one activity to cover losses from another. Thus the use of high prices for some of a firm's products, for example, to permit it to price below cost for others. In international trade, this could be one explanation for *dumping* (page 76).

CRS

Constant returns to scale (page 47) = CRTS.

CRTS

Constant returns to scale (page 47).

Crude

Crude oil.

CSE

Consumer support estimate (page 48).

CSO

Civil society organization (page 38).

Cultural argument for protection

The view that imports undermine a country's culture and identity — for example by changing consumption patterns to ones more similar to those abroad, or by reducing demands for domestically produced art and music — and therefore that imports should be restricted.

Cumulation

In an *anti-dumping* (page 10) case against imports from more than one country, the summation of these imports for the purpose of determining *injury* (page 141). That is, the imports are deemed to have caused injury if all of them together could have done so, even if individually they would not.

Currency

1. The money used by a country; e.g., the national currency of Japan is the yen.

2. The physical embodiment of money, in the forms of paper bills or notes, and metal coins.

Currency area

A group of countries that share a common currency. *Originally* (page 368) defined by *Mundell (1961)* (page 379) as a group that have fixed exchange rates among their national currencies.

Currency basket

A group of two or more currencies that may be used as a *unit of account* (page 285), or to which another currency may be *pegged* (page 207).

Currency bloc

1. A group of countries that share a *common currency* (page 41); a *currency area* (see above).

2. A group of countries that peg their different national currencies to a single currency.

Currency board

An extreme form of *pegged exchange rate* (page 207) in which management of both the *exchange rate* (page 94) and the *money supply* (page 180) are taken away from the *central bank* (page 35) and given to an agency with instructions to back every unit of circulating domestic currency with a specified amount of foreign currency. Operates similarly to the *gold standard* (page 119).

Currency crisis

The crisis that occurs when participants in an *exchange market* (page 94) come to perceive that an attempt to maintain a *pegged exchange rate* (page 207) is about to fail, causing *speculation* (page 253) against the peg that hastens the failure and forces a *devaluation* (page 67).

Currency depreciation

See *depreciation* (page 66).

Currency factor

The portion of a *rate of return* (page 227) that is due to the currency in which the asset is denominated. The currency factor can be non-zero either because of *currency risk* (page 58) or because of expected *appreciation* (page 11) or *depreciation* (page 66).

Currency in circulation

The amount of a country's *currency* (page 56) that is in the hands of the public (households, firms, banks, etc), as opposed to sitting in the vaults of the *central bank* (page 35).

Currency intervention

Exchange market intervention (page 94).

Currency realignment

A change in the *par value* (page 204) of a *pegged exchange rate* (page 207).

Currency reserves

This usually means *international reserves* (page 149).

Currency risk

Uncertainty about the future value of a currency.

Currency speculation

To buy or sell a currency in anticipation of its *appreciation* (page 11) or *depreciation* (page 66) respectively, the intent being to make a profit or avoid a loss. See *speculation* (page 253).

Currency swap

See *swap* (page 262).

Currency union

A group of countries that agree to *peg* (page 207) their exchange rates and to coordinate their monetary policies so as to avoid the need for *currency realignments* (see above).

Current account

A country's international transactions arising from current flows, as opposed to changes in stocks which are part of the *capital account* (page 30). Includes trade in goods and services (including payments of interest and dividends on capital) plus inflows and outflows of *transfers* (page 279).

Current account balance

Balance on current account (page 18).

Current account deficit

Debits (page 61) minus *credits* (page 54) on *current account* (see above). See *deficit* (page 63).

Current account surplus

Credits (page 54) minus *debits* (page 61) on *current account* (page 58). Same as *balance on current account* (page 18). See *surplus* (page 262).

Current prices

Refers to prices in the present, rather than in some base year; e.g., "GDP at current prices" means *GDP* (page 122) as measured, in contrast to *real* (page 228) GDP, or "GDP at XXXX prices," where the latter is measured in the prices of year XXXX.

CUSFTA

Canada-US Free Trade Agreement (page 29).

CUSTA

Same as *Canada-US Free Trade Agreement* (page 29).

Customs area

A geographic area that is responsible for levying its own *customs duties* (see below) at its border.

Customs classification

1. The category defining the tariff to be applied to an imported good.

2. The act of determining this category, which may be subject to various rules and/or to the discretion of the *customs officer* (see below).

Customs Cooperation Council Nomenclature

An international system of classification of goods for specifying tariffs, called the *Brussels tariff nomenclature* (page 26) prior to 1976, and later superseded by the *harmonized system of tariff nomenclature* (page 130).

Customs duty

An import *tariff* (page 264).

Customs officer

The government official who monitors goods moving across a national border and levies *tariffs* (page 264).

Customs procedure

The practices used by *customs officers* (see above) to clear goods into a country and levy *tariffs* (page 264). Includes clearance procedures such as documentation and inspection, methods of determining a good's *classification* (page 59), and methods of assigning its *value* (see below) as the base for an *ad valorem* (page 5) tariff. Any of these can impede trade and constitute a *NTB* (page 195).

Customs Service
See *U.S. Customs Service* (page 286).

Customs station
An office through which imported goods must pass in order to be monitored and taxed by *customs officers* (page 59).

Customs union
A group of countries that adopt free trade (zero tariffs and no other restrictions on trade) on trade among themselves, and that also, on each product, agree to levy the same tariff on imports from outside the group. Equivalent to an *FTA* (page 114) plus a common external tariff.

Customs valuation
The method by which a *customs officer* (page 59) determines the value of an imported good for the purpose of levying an *ad valorem tariff* (page 5). When this method is biased against importing, it becomes an *NTB* (page 195).

CVD
Countervailing duty (page 52).

Cyclical unemployment
The portion of *unemployment* (page 283) that is due to the *business cycle* (page 28) and thus rises in *recessions* (page 229) but then disappears eventually after the recession ends.

De minimis
A legal term for an amount that is small enough to be ignored, too small to be taken seriously. Used to restrict legal provisions, including laws regarding international trade, to amounts of activity or trade that are not trivially small.

Deadweight loss

The net loss in economic welfare that is caused by a tariff or other source of *distortion* (page 72), defined as the total losses to those who lose, minus the total gains to those who gain. Usually identified in a supply-and-demand diagram in terms of *change in consumer* (page 37) and *producer surplus* (page 219) together with government revenue. The net of these appears as one or two *welfare triangles* (page 292).

Debase

To reduce the value of. Classically, a *currency* (page 56) is debased if its value in terms of gold or other precious metal is reduced.

Debenture

1. A debt that is not backed by collateral, but only by the credit and good faith of the borrower.

2. A certificate issued by *customs authorities* (page 59) entitling an exporter of imported goods to be paid back duties that have been paid when they were imported. Such a refund is called a *drawback* (page 75).

Debit

Recorded as negative (−) in the *balance of payments* (page 17), any transaction that gives rise to a payment *out of* the country, such as an import, the purchase of an asset (including *official reserves* (page 197)), or lending to foreigners. Opposite of *credit* (page 54).

Debt

The amount that is owed, as a result of previous borrowing. A country's debt may refer to the debt of its government or to that of the country as a whole.

Debt burden

The *debt* (see above) of a country, when large enough that *servicing* (page 244) it has become difficult.

Debt cancellation

The most extreme form of *debt relief* (page 62), in which a country's debts are completely forgiven, so that no repayment of interest or principal is required.

Debt crisis

A situation in which a country, usually a *developing country* (page 67), finds itself unable to service its debts.

Debt/equity swap

An exchange of debt for equity, in which a lender is given a share of ownership to replace a loan. Used as a method of resolving *debt crises* (see above).

Debt overhang

A situation in which the external debt of a country is larger than it will be able to repay. Often due to having borrowed in foreign currency and then had its own currency *depreciate* (page 66).

Debt relief

Any arrangement intended to reduce the burden of debt on a country, usually including forgiveness of part or all of what is owed to creditors who may include private banks and other entities, government, or *international financial institutions* (page 147).

Debt service

The payments made by a borrower on its debt, usually including both interest payments and partial repayment of principal.

Debt sustainability

The ability of a *debtor country* (see below) to *service* (page 244) its debt on a continuing basis and not go into *default* (page 63). After a *debt crisis* (see above), sustainability may be restored through debt *rescheduling* (page 234).

Debtor nation

A country whose assets owned abroad are worth less than the assets within the country that are owned by foreigners. Contrasts with *creditor nation* (page 55).

Decile

One of ten segments of a distribution that has been divided into tenths. For example, the second-from-the-bottom decile of an income distribution is those whose income exceeds the incomes of from 10% to 20% of the population.

Decouple

Refers to the provision of government support to an enterprise, usually a farm, in a manner that does not provide an incentive to increase production. Farm subsidies that are decoupled are included in the *green box* (page 121) and are therefore permitted by the *WTO* (page 293).

Decreasing cost

Average cost (page 16) that declines as output increases, due to *increasing returns to scale* (page 138).

Decreasing returns to scale

A property of a *production function* (page 220) such that changing all inputs by the same proportion changes output less than in proportion. Example: a function *homogeneous of degree less than one* (page 128). Also called simply **decreasing returns**. Not to be confused with *diminishing returns* (page 68), which refers to increasing some inputs while holding other inputs fixed. Contrasts with *increasing returns* (page 138) and *constant returns* (page 47).

Deep integration

Refers to economic *integration* (page 142) that goes well beyond removal of formal barriers to trade and includes various ways of reducing the international burden of differing national regulations, such as *mutual recognition* (page 184) and *harmonization* (page 124). Contrasts with *shallow integration* (page 245).

Default

Failure to repay a loan. International loans by governments and private agents lack mechanisms to deal with default, comparable to the legal mechanisms that exist within countries.

Deficiency payment

Payment to a producer of an amount equal to the difference between a guaranteed price and the market price, with the latter often determined on the world market. Thus a form of *subsidy* (page 260) to production.

Deficit

1. In the *balance of payments* (page 17), or in any category of international transactions within it, the deficit is the sum of debits minus the sum of credits, or the negative of the *surplus* (page 262).

2. In the government budget, the *deficit* is the excess of government expenditures over receipts from taxes.

Deficit financing

1. The method used by a government to finance its budget *deficit* (page 63), that is, to cover the difference between its tax receipts and its expenditures. The main choices are to issue bonds or to print money.

2. The assumption that a change in government spending or taxes will be financed by a change in the government budget deficit, rather than by an accommodating additional change in spending or taxes to keep the budget balanced. Example: a "deficit-financed increase in government purchases."

Deflation

A fall in the general level of prices. Unlikely unless the rate of *inflation* (page 141) is already low, it may then be due either to a surge in *productivity* (page 221) or, less favorably, to a *recession* (page 229).

Deflator

The ratio of a *nominal* (page 191) magnitude to its *real* (page 228) counterpart. Usually refers, as with the *GDP deflator* (page 117), when the real magnitude has been constructed from underlying data and not by simply deflating the nominal magnitude by a corresponding *price index* (page 215), in which case the deflator itself may be used as though it were a price index.

Deflection

See *trade deflection* (page 273).

Degressive

Declining with income or over time. A degressive income tax takes a smaller fraction of higher incomes. Degressivity in trade policy might be a *tariff* (page 264) the *ad valoren* (page 5) size of which is scheduled to decline over time, or a *quota* (page 226) that is scheduled to expand faster than demand for imports.

De-industrialization

A decline over time in the share of *manufacturing* (page 169) in an economy, usually accompanied by growth in the share of *services* (page 244). Typically accompanied by an increase in manufactured imports, it may raise concern that the country is losing valuable economic activity to others.

Delocalization

Another term for *fragmentation* (page 112). Used by *Leamer (1996)* (page 378).

Demand

1. The act of offering to buy a product.

2. The quantity offered to buy.

3. The quantities offered to buy at various prices; the *demand curve* (see below).

Demand curve

The graph of quantity demanded as a function of price, normally downward sloping, straight or curved, and drawn with quantity on the horizontal axis and price on the vertical axis. Demand curves for imports and for foreign exchange usually have the same qualitative properties as demand curves for goods, but for somewhat different reasons.

Demand deposit

A bank deposit that can be withdrawn "on demand." The term usually refers only to checking accounts, even though depositors in many other kinds of accounts may be able to write checks and thus regard their deposits as readily available.

Demand elasticity

Normally the *price elasticity* (page 215) of demand. References to other elasticities of demand, such as the *income elasticity* (page 137) are normally explicit. See *import demand elasticity* (page 134).

Demand function

The mathematical function explaining the quantity *demanded* (see above) in terms of its various determinants, including income and price; thus the algebraic representation of the *demand curve* (see above).

Demand price

The price at which a given quantity is demanded; thus the demand curve viewed from the perspective of price as a function of quantity.

Demand schedule

A list of prices and corresponding quantities demanded, or the graph of that information. Thus a *demand curve* (see above).

Demographic transition

The change that typically takes place, as a country *develops* (page 67), in the birth and death rates of its population, both of which tend eventually to fall as *per capita income* (page 207) rises.

Dependency theory

The theory that *less developed countries* (page 161) are poor because they allow themselves to be exploited by the *developed countries* (page 67) through international trade and investment.

Deposit

An amount of money placed with a bank for safekeeping, convenience, and/or to earn *interest* (page 143).

Depreciation

1. A fall in the value of a country's currency on the *exchange market* (page 94), relative either to a particular other currency or to a weighted average of other currencies. The currency is said to **depreciate**. Opposite of *appreciation* (page 11).

2. The decline in value or usefulness of a piece of *capital* (page 30) over time, and/or with use.

Deregulation

The lessening or complete removal of government regulations on an industry, especially concerning the price that firms are allowed to charge and leaving price to be determined by market forces.

Derived demand

Demand that arises or is defined indirectly from some other demand or underlying behavior; e.g., demand for foreign currency is derived from demand for foreign goods, bonds, etc., while demand for import of a homogeneous good is derived from domestic demand and supply.

Derogation

As used in the trade literature, this seems to mean a departure from the established rules, as when a country's policies are said to constitute a derogation from the GATT.

Destabilizing speculation

Speculation (page 253) that increases the movements of the price in the market where the speculation occurs. Movement may be defined by *amplitude* (page 10), *frequency* (page 114), or some other measure. See *stabilizing speculation* (page 255).

Destination principle

The principle in international taxation that *value added taxes* (page 287) be kept only by the country where the taxed product is being sold. Under the destination principle, value added taxes are collected on imports and rebated on exports. Contrasts with the *origin principle* (page 202).

Devaluation

1. *Depreciation* (page 66).

2. A fall in the value of a currency that has been *pegged* (page 207), either because of an announced reduction in the *par value* (page 204) of the currency with the peg continuing, or because the pegged rate is abandoned and the *floating rate* (page 108) declines.

3. A fall in the value of a currency in terms of gold or silver, meaningful only under some form of *gold standard* (page 119) or *silver standard* (page 246).

Develop

To experience a sustained and substantial increase in *per capita income* (page 207); thus to undergo *economic development* (page 79).

Developed country

A country whose per capita income is high by world standards.

Developing country

A country whose per capita income is low by world standards. Same as *less developed countries* (page 161). As usually used, it does not necessarily connote that the country's income is rising.

Development

Economic development (page 79).

Development bank

A multilateral institution that provides financing for development needs of a regional group of countries. Examples include the *African* (page 7), *Asian* (page 13), and *Inter-American development banks* (page 143).

Development finance

Provision of *credit* (page 54) to a *developing country* (page 67) to permit it to undertake *development projects* (see below) that it could not otherwise afford.

Development project

A project intended to increase a *developing country's* (page 67) ability to produce in the future. Such projects are most commonly additions to the country's *capital stock* (page 34), but they may involve improvements in *infrastructure* (page 141), educational facilities, discovery or development of *natural resources* (page 186), etc.

DFI

Direct foreign investment (page 69).

DFS model

One of the *continuum-of-goods* (page 49) models of *Dornbusch, Fischer, and Samuelson (1977, 1980)* (page 374).

Differential treatment

See *special and differential treatment* (page 251).

Differentiated product

1. A firm's product that is not identical to products of other firms in the same industry. Contrasts with *homogeneous product* (page 129).

2. Sometimes applied to products produced by a country, even though there are many firms within the country whose products are the same, if buyers distinguish products based on *country of origin* (page 52). This is called the *Armington assumption* (page 12).

Dillon Round

The fifth *round* (page 239) of multilateral trade negotiations that was held under *GATT* (page 116) auspices, commencing 1960 and completed 1961. It was the first to be given a name, after C. Douglas Dillon, U.S. Undersecretary of State under Eisenhower and Treasury Secretary under Kennedy.

Diminishing returns

The fall in the *marginal product* (page 169) of a *factor* (page 101) or factors that eventually occurs as input of that factor rises, holding the input of at least one other factor fixed, according to the *law of diminishing returns* (page 159).

Direct factor content

A measure of *factor content* (page 102) that includes only the factors used in the last stage of production, ignoring factors used in producing intermediate inputs. Contrasts with *direct-plus-indirect factor content* (see below).

Direct foreign investment

Foreign direct investment (page 109).

Direction of trade

Refers to the particular countries and kinds of countries toward which a country's exports are sent, and from which its imports are brought, in contrast to the commodity composition of its exports and imports. Thus the pattern of its *bilateral trade* (page 23).

Direct-plus-indirect factor content

A measure of *factor content* (page 102) that includes factors used in producing intermediate inputs, factors used in producing intermediate inputs *to* the intermediate inputs, and so forth. That is, it includes all primary factors that contributed however indirectly to production of the good. Contrasts with *direct factor content* (see above).

Directly unproductive profit-seeking activities

Activities that have no direct productive purpose (neither increasing consumer utility nor contributing to production of a good or service that would increase utility) and are motivated by the desire to make profit, typically from market distortions created by government policies. Examples are *rent seeking* (page 233) and revenue seeking. Term *coined* (page 368) by *Bhagwati (1982)* (page 372).

Director General

Title given to the persons who head certain international organizations, including the *WTO* (page 293).

Dirigiste

Centrally planned (page 36); that is, under the direction of a central authority, normally the government. Contrasts with decentralized, or a system in which economic decisions are determined by market forces in a *market economy* (page 172).

Dirty float
Same as *managed float* (page 168).

Disarticulation
The absence of linkage among sectors of an economy, so that growth in some does not spill over into improved productivity and wellbeing in others.

DISC
Domestic International Sales Corporation (page 74).

Discount
1. Any reduction in price or value, especially when below a stated or normal price.
2. To buy or sell *commercial paper* (page 40) at a price below face value to account for *interest* (page 143) to accrue before maturity.

Discount rate
1. The rate, per year, at which future values are diminished to make them comparable to values in the present. Can be either subjective (reflecting personal time preference) or objective (a market interest rate).
2. The interest rate that the *Fed* (page 105) charges commercial banks for very short-term loans of reserves. One of the tools of *monetary policy* (page 179).

Discrete time
The division of time into indivisible units. In economic models, these units represent periods, such as days, quarters, or years.

Discretionary licensing
See *licensing* (page 163).

Discriminatory tariff
A higher *tariff* (page 264) against one source of imports than against another. Except in special circumstances, such as *antidumping duties* (page 10), this is a violation of *MFN* (page 176) and is prohibited by the *WTO* (page 293) against other members.

Diseconomies of scale
Decreasing returns to scale (page 63).

Disequilibrium
1. Inequality of supply and demand.
2. An untenable state of an economic system, from which it may be expected to change.

Disintegration
Another term for *fragmentation* (page 112). Used by *Feenstra (1998)* (page 374).

Disinvest
1. To allow a *stock of capital* (page 34) to become smaller over time, either by selling parts of it or by allowing it to *depreciate* (page 66) without replacing it.
2. To reduce *inventories* (page 151), either absolutely or by more than any increase in plant and equipment.
3. To sell all or a portion of a *portfolio* (page 211) of *financial assets* (page 106).

Disparity
Inequality, usually *income disparity* (page 137).

Disposable income
Income minus taxes. More accurately, income minus direct taxes plus transfer payments; that is, the income available to be spent (including on imports) and saved.

Dispute settlement
In the *GATT* (page 116), the adjudication of disputes among parties. In the *WTO* (page 293) this is done by the *dispute settlement mechanism* (see below).

Dispute Settlement Body
The entity within the *WTO* (page 293) that formally deals with disputes between members. It consists of all WTO members meeting together to consider reports of *panels* (page 203) and the *appellate body* (page 11).

Dispute settlement mechanism
The procedure by which the *WTO* (page 293) settles disputes among members, primarily by means of a three-person *panel* (page 203) that hears the case and issues a report, subject to review by the *appellate body* (page 11).

Dissipate rent

To use up, in real resources, the full value of the economic *rents* (page 233) that are being sought by *rent seeking* (page 233).

Distortion

Any departure from the ideal of *perfect competition* (page 207) that therefore interferes with economic agents maximizing social welfare when they maximize their own. Includes taxes and subsidies, *tariffs* (page 264) and *NTBs* (page 195), *externalities* (page 100), *incomplete information* (page 138), and *imperfect competition* (page 133).

Distribution

1. The productive activity of getting produced goods from the factory into the hands of consumers.

2. The amounts of income or wealth in the hands of different portions of a population.

Diversification cone

For given prices in the *Heckscher-Ohlin model* (page 126), a set of *factor endowment* (page 102) combinations that are consistent with producing the same set of goods and having the same factor prices. Such a set has the form of a cone. Concept *first used* (page 368) by *McKenzie (1955)* (page 378).

Diversified portfolio

A *portfolio* (page 211) that includes a variety of assets whose prices are not likely all to change together. In international economics, this usually means holding assets denominated in different currencies.

Diversify

To produce more than one thing. In the *Heckscher-Ohlin model* (page 126) with two goods, it means to produce both of them. With more than two goods, it may mean to produce two, or it may mean to produce all of the goods that are possible.

Diversion

See *trade diversion* (page 274).

Dividend

The amount paid each quarter by a corporation to its stockholders for each share of stock.

Division of labor

Splitting a production process across multiple workers, each performing a different task repeatedly rather than having a single worker perform all tasks. *Adam Smith (1776)* (page 381) pointed out the increased *productivity* (page 221) that can result, as well as the potential for *gains from trade* (page 116) when division of labor takes place across countries.

Dixit-Stiglitz function

Really just a symmetric *CES function* (page 36), the innovation of *Dixit and Stiglitz (1977)* (page 374) was to allow the number of arguments to be variable. Used originally as a utility function, with *elasticity of substitution* (page 84) greater than one the function displays a *preference for variety* (page 213). Used as a component of a production function, the same property implies that costs fall with variety.

Dixit-Stiglitz utility

The *Dixit-Stiglitz function* (see above) used as a *utility function* (page 287).

Doha Declaration

The document agreed upon by the trade ministers of the member countries of the *WTO* (page 293) at the *Doha Ministerial* (see below) meeting. It initiates negotiations on a range of some 21 subjects. A distinctive feature is the emphasis placed on the interests of developing countries.

Doha Ministerial

The *WTO* (page 293) ministerial meeting held in Doha, Qatar, in November 2001, at which it was agreed to begin a new round of multilateral trade negotiations, the Doha Round.

Doha Round

The round of multilateral trade negotiations begun January 2002 as a result of agreement at the *Doha Ministerial* (see above). Also called the **Doha Development Round** or the Doha Development Agenda.

Dollar standard

An international financial system in which the U.S. dollar is used by most countries as the primary *reserve asset* (page 234), in contrast to the *gold standard* (page 119) in which gold played this role.

Dollarization

The official adoption by a country other than the United States of the U.S. dollar as its local currency.

Domestic

From or in one's own country. A domestic producer is one that produces inside the home country. A domestic price is the price inside the home country. Opposite of "foreign" or "world."

Domestic content protection

Use of trade policies such as *domestic content requirements* (see below) to increase the portion of a product's value that is provided by domestic factors of production, either in direct production or through produced inputs.

Domestic content requirement

A requirement that goods sold in a country contain a certain minimum of domestic *value added* (page 287).

Domestic credit

Credit extended by a country's central bank to domestic borrowers, including the government and commercial banks. In the United States, the largest component by far is the Fed's holdings of U.S. government bonds, but it also makes some short-term loans to banks to use as their reserves.

Domestic distortions argument for protection

See *second best argument* (page 242).

Domestic International Sales Corporation

A type of U.S. corporation, authorized in 1971, with income primarily from exports. Usually wholly owned U.S. subsidiaries, DISCs had special treatment in borrowing or taxation. A 1976 *GATT* (page 116) case found against the U.S., which reached a compromise settlement with the *EC* (page 78) in 1981. DISC was replaced in 1984 by *foreign sales corporations* (page 110).

Domestic law

The laws and legal system of a country, which may be constrained by international obligations such as *WTO* (page 293) membership. Sometimes a domestic law is inconsistent with such obligations and must be changed. This may be seen as a threat to the country's *sovereignty* (page 251).

Domestic market

The market within a country's own borders. *Dumping* (page 76), for example, may be defined by comparing the price charged for export with the price charged on the domestic market, i.e., to buyers within the exporting country.

Domestic resource cost

A measure, in terms of real resources, of the *opportunity cost* (page 200) of producing or saving *foreign exchange* (page 109). It is an *ex ante* (page 93) measure of *comparative advantage* (page 42), used to evaluate projects and policies. The term was introduced to the economics literature by *Bruno (1963, 1972)* (page 373).

Domestic support

A policy that assists domestic industry, including a *subsidy* (page 260) to production, payment not to produce, *price support* (page 216), and other means of increasing the income of producers.

Domestic trade

Commerce within a country; wholesale and retail trade.

Downstream dumping

The export of a good whose cost is reduced by access to a domestically produced intermediate input that is sold below cost. This is not (yet) eligible under any *anti-dumping* (page 10) statute for an anti-dumping duty.

Drawback

Rebate of import duties when the imported good is re-exported or used as input to the production of an exported good.

DRC

Domestic resource cost (see above).

DSM

Dispute settlement mechanism (page 71).

DUKS

See *baffling pigs* (page 17).

Dummy

In a *regression analysis* (page 232), a dummy (or **dummy variable**) is used to capture an explanatory variable that is either on (with a value of one) or off (zero). For example, in a *gravity equation* (page 121), the coefficient on a common-language dummy would measure the effect on trade flow between two countries of their sharing a common language.

Dumping

Export price that is "unfairly low," defined as either below the home market price (*normal value* (page 195)) (hence *price discrimination* (page 215)) or below cost. With the rare exception of successful *predatory dumping* (page 213), dumping is economically beneficial to the importing country as a whole (though harmful to competing producers) and often represents normal business practice.

Dumping margin

In a case of *dumping* (see above), the difference between the "*fair price* (page 104)" and the price charged for export. Used as the basis for setting *anti-dumping duties* (page 10).

Duopoly

An *oligopoly* (page 197) with two firms.

DUP activities

Directly unproductive profit-seeking activities (page 69).

Durable good

A good that can continue to be used over an extended period of time.

Dutch disease

The adverse effect on a country's other industries that occurs when one industry substantially expands its exports, causing a *real* (page 228) *appreciation* (page 11) of the country's currency. Named after the effects of natural gas discoveries in the Netherlands, and most commonly applied to effects of exports in *natural resource* (page 186) extractive industries on *manufacturing* (page 169).

Dutiable imports

Imports on which a positive duty, or tariff, is levied. (The term seems like it ought to include imports on which the duty is zero but which a government is somehow free, or able, to levy a positive duty. That does *not* seem to be the way the term is used, however.)

Duty

Tax. That is, an import duty is a tariff.

Duty drawback

See *drawback* (page 75).

Duty-free

Without *tariff* (page 264), usually applied to imports on which normally a tariff would be charged, but that for some reason are exempt. Travelers, for example, may be permitted to import a certain amount duty-free.

Dynamic comparative advantage

A changing pattern of *comparative advantage* (page 42) over time due to changes in *factor endowments* (page 102) or *technology* (page 268).

Dynamic economies of scale

A form of *increasing returns to scale* (page 138) in which *average cost* (page 16) declines over time as producers accumulate experience, so that *average product* (page 16) rises with total output of the firm or industry accumulated over time. See *learning by doing* (page 160), *infant industry protection* (page 140).

Dynamic effects

Refers to certain poorly understood effects of trade and *trade liberalization* (page 275), including both *multilateral* (page 182) and *preferential trade agreements* (page 213), that extend beyond the *static gains from trade* (page 256). Such dynamic effects are thought to make the *gains from trade* (page 116) substantially larger than in the *static model* (page 257).

Dynamic gains from trade

The hoped-for benefits from trade that accrue over time, in addition to the conventional *static gains from trade* (page 256) of trade theory. Sources of these gains are not well understood or documented, although there exists a variety of possible theoretical reasons for them and some empirical evidence that countries have benefited more than the static gains alone would suggest.

Dynamic model

Any model with an explicit time dimension. To be meaningfully dynamic, however, it should include variables and behavior that, at one time, depend on variables or behavior at another time. Models may be formulated in *discrete time* (page 70) or in *continuous time* (page 48). Contrasts with a *static model* (page 257).

Early harvest

A term, in *trade negotiations* (page 275), for agreeing to accept the results of a portion of the negotiations before the rest of the negotiations are completed.

Earnings

The total amount earned, usually by a worker as wages, or by a firm as profits.

Earth Summit

Rio Summit (page 238).

EBITDA

Earnings (see above) before *interest* (page 143), taxes, *depreciation* (page 66), and *amortization* (page 9) of a firm. Sometimes used as an optimistic indicator of potential profitability.

EC

European Communities (page 91).

ECB

European Central Bank (page 91).

Eco-dumping

Environmental dumping (page 86).

Econometrics

The application of statistical methods to the empirical estimation of economic relationships. Econometric analysis is used extensively in international economics to estimate the causes and effects of international trade, exchange rates, and international capital movements.

Economic and Monetary Union

The *currency area* (page 57) formed in 1999 as a result of the *Maastricht Treaty* (page 168). Members of the EMU share the common currency, the *euro* (page 90).

Economic contraction

The downward phase of the *business cycle* (page 28), in which *GDP* (page 122) is falling and *unemployment* (page 283) is rising over time.

Economic development

Sustained increase in the economic standard of living of a country's population, normally accomplished by increasing its stocks of *physical* (page 209) and *human capital* (page 130) and improving its *technology* (page 268).

Economic efficiency

The extent to which a given set of *resources* (page 235) is being allocated across uses or activities in a manner that maximizes whatever value they are intended to produce, such as output, market value, or utility. Contrasts with *engineering efficiency* (page 86), which focuses within a single activity on the output it produces per unit input.

Economic expansion

The upward phase of the *business cycle* (page 28), in which *GDP* (page 122) is rising and *unemployment* (page 283) may be falling over time.

Economic exposure

Same as *exchange rate exposure* (page 94).

Economic freedom

Freedom to engage in economic transactions, without government interference but with government support of the institutions necessary for that freedom, including *rule of law* (page 239), *sound money* (page 250), and *open markets* (page 199).

Economic geography

See *new economic geography* (page 190).

Economic growth

The increase over time in the capacity of an economy to produce goods and services and (ideally) to improve the wellbeing of its citizens.

Economic indicator
A variable that is measured and publicly reported and that is considered meaningful not only for itself but as a sign of how rapidly the larger economy is expanding or contracting.

Economic integration
See *integration* (page 142).

Economic interdependence
The extent to which economic performance (*GDP* (page 122), *inflation* (page 141), *unemployment* (page 283), etc.) in one country depends positively or negatively on performance in other countries.

Economic justice
1. Fairness and equity in economic affairs, presumably by having laws, governments, and institutions that treat people equally and avoid favoring particular individuals or groups.
2. As most often used, the term carries a connotation that economic justice can only be achieved by lessening the power and changing the practices of *international financial institutions* (page 147), *transnational corporations* (page 279), and rich-country governments.

Economic profit
Revenue from an activity minus the *opportunity cost* (page 200) of the resources used in that activity.

Economic rate of return
The net benefits to all members of society, as a percentage of cost, taking into account *externalities* (page 100) and other *market imperfections* (page 172).

Economic rent
See *rent* (page 233).

Economic sanction
The use of an economic policy as a *sanction* (page 240).

Economic union
A *common market* (page 41) with the added feature that additional policies — monetary, fiscal, welfare — are also *harmonized* (page 124) across the member countries.

Economic welfare
See *welfare* (page 291).

Economies of scale

Increasing returns to scale (page 138).

Economies of scope

The property that a firm's average cost falls as it produces a larger number of different products.

ECSC

European Coal and Steel Community (page 91).

ECU

European currency unit (page 91).

Edgeworth-Bowley box

A geometric device showing *allocations* (page 9) of 2 goods to 2 consumers in a rectangle with dimensions equal to the quantities of the goods. *Preferences* (page 213) enter as *indifference curves* (page 139) relative to opposite corners of the box, tangencies defining *efficient allocations* (page 82) and the *contract curve* (page 49). First drawn by *Pareto (1906)* (page 379), based *originally* (see page 368), though only partially, on a diagram of *Edgeworth (1881)* (page 374). This and the *Edgeworth production box* (see below) are often called just the **Edgeworth Box**, even though Edgeworth never drew either.

Edgeworth box

See *Edgeworth-Bowley box* (above) and *Edgeworth production box* (below). Refer to diagrams on pages 299–301.

Edgeworth production box

A variation of the consumption *Edgeworth box* (see above) that instead represents the *allocations* (page 9) of 2 factors to 2 industries for use in *production functions* (page 220). *Efficient allocations* (page 82) now appear as tangencies between *isoquants* (page 153), while the *contract curve* (page 49) becomes the *efficiency locus* (page 82).

EEA

European Economic Area (page 91).

EEC

European Economic Community (page 91).

Effect of trade

This term normally refers, often only implicitly, to the effect of a change in some policy or other *exogenous variable* (page 96) that will increase the quantity of trade. Since in trade models, trade itself is *endogenous* (page 85), the effects associated with a change in trade depend on what caused it.

Effective exchange rate

An index of a currency's value relative to a group (or *basket* (page 21)) of other currencies, where the currencies in the basket are given weights based on the amount of trade between the countries that use the currencies. Also called a *trade-weighted exchange rate* (page 278).

Effective protection

The concept that the protection provided to an industry depends on the tariffs and other trade barriers on both its inputs and its outputs, since a tariff on inputs raises cost. Measured by the *effective rate of protection* (see below).

Effective protective rate

Same as *effective rate of protection* (see below).

Effective rate of protection

A measure of the protection provided to an industry by the entire structure of *tariffs* (page 264), taking into account the effects of tariffs on inputs as well as on outputs. Letting b_{ij} be the share of input i in the value of output j, and t_i the tarrif on good i the ERP of industry j is $ERP_j = (t_j - \Sigma_i b_{ij} t_i)/(1 - \Sigma_i b_{ij})$. Due to *Corden (1966)* (page 373).

Effective tariff

Effective rate of protection (see above).

Efficiency

See *economic efficiency* (page 79).

Efficiency locus

The set of *efficient allocations* (see below) in an *Edgeworth production box* (page 81). It is usually a curve, similar to a *contract curve* (page 49), and in fact is sometimes called that.

Efficient allocation

An *allocation* (page 9) that it is impossible unambiguously to improve upon, in the sense of producing more of one good without producing less of another.

Efficient market

A market in which, at a minimum, current price changes are independent of past price changes, or, more strongly, price reflects all (publicly) available information. Some believe foreign *exchange markets* (page 94) to be efficient, which in turn implies that future exchange rates cannot profitably be predicted.

EFTA

European Free Trade Association (page 91).

Elastic

Having an elasticity greater than one. For a *price elasticity* (page 215) of *demand* (page 65), this means that expenditure rises as price falls. For an *income elasticity* (page 137) it means that expenditure share rises with income, a *superior good* (page 261). Contrasts with *inelastic* (page 140) and *unit elastic* (page 284). Elastic demand for either exports or imports is sufficient to satisfy the *Marshall-Lerner condition* (page 173).

Elastic offer curve

An *offer curve* (page 196) along which import demand is always *elastic* (see above). It is therefore not *backward bending* (page 16). Contrasts with *inelastic offer curve* (page 140).

Elasticities approach

1. The method of analyzing the determination of the *balance of trade* (page 18), especially due to a *devaluation* (page 67), that focuses on the *price elasticities* (page 215) of *exports* (page 97) and *imports* (page 136). According to this approach, the effect depends critically on the *Marshall-Lerner condition* (page 173).
2. The explanation of *exchange rates* (page 94) using supply and demand curves.

Elasticity

A measure of responsiveness of one economic variable to another — usually the responsiveness of quantity to *price* (page 215) along a supply or demand curve — comparing percentage changes ($\%\Delta$) or changes in logarithms (d ln). The **arc elasticity** of x with respect to y is $\varepsilon = \%\Delta x / \%\Delta y$. The **point elasticity** is $\varepsilon = \mathrm{d}\ln x / \mathrm{d}\ln y = (y/x)(\mathrm{d}x/\mathrm{d}y)$.

Elasticity of demand for exports

This is normally the *price elasticity* (page 215) of demand for exports of a country, either for a single industry or for the aggregate of all imports. Equals the *elasticity of demand for imports* (see below) of the entire rest of the world, and it therefore also enters the *Marshall-Lerner condition* (page 173).

Elasticity of demand for imports

This is normally the *price elasticity* (page 215) of demand for imports of a country, either for a single industry or for the aggregate of all imports. The latter plays a critical role in determining how the country's *balance of trade* (page 18) responds to the exchange rate. See *Marshall-Lerner condition* (page 173).

Elasticity of substitution

The elasticity of the ratio of two inputs to a production (or utility) function with respect to the ratio of their marginal products (or utilities). With *competitive* (page 44) demands, this is also the elasticity with respect to their price ratio. For example, with factors L, K and factor prices w, r, the elasticity of substitution of a production function $F(K, L)$ is $\sigma = (wL/rK)\mathrm{d}(K/L)/\mathrm{d}(w/r)$.

Elasticity of transformation

The *elasticity* (page 83) of an economy's output of one good with respect to its output of another (holding other outputs, if there are any, constant).

EMA

European Monetary Agreement (page 92).

Embargo

The prohibition of some category of trade. May apply to exports and/or imports, of particular products or of all trade, vis a vis the world or a particular country or countries.

Emerging economy

1. Originally this term was applied to countries that had recently ceased to be part of the Soviet Union and its satellites, and thus emerging from *centrally planned* (page 36) *communist* (page 42) economies. The term drew attention to their transition to becoming *market economies* (page 172).

2. Rather quickly, perhaps acknowledging the importance of central planning and the failure of markets in many other countries, the term has expanded to encompass also *developing countries* (page 67), not necessarily ever communist, as they expanded the role of markets.

Emerging market

1. Same as *emerging economy* (page 84).

2. The *securities* (page 243) market of an *emerging economy* (page 84).

Emigration

The *migration* (page 176) of people *out of* a country.

Empirical finding

Something that is observed from real-world observation or data, in contrast to something that is deduced from theory.

Employment argument for protection

The use of a *tariff* (page 264) or other trade restriction to promote employment, either in the economy at large or in a particular industry. This is a *second best argument* (page 242), since other policies — such as a *fiscal stimulus* (page 107) or a production *subsidy* (page 260) — could achieve the same effect at lower economic cost.

EMS

European Monetary System (page 92).

EMU

Economic and Monetary Union (page 79).

Enabling clause

The decision of the *GATT* (page 116) in 1979 to give developing countries *special and differential treatment* (page 251).

Endogenous growth

Economic growth (page 79) whose long-run rate depends on behavior and/or policy.

Endogenous protection

Protection (page 222) that is explained as the outcome of economic and/or political forces. See *political economy of protection* (page 210).

Endogenous variable

An economic variable that is determined within a model. It is therefore *not* subject to direct manipulation by the modeler, since that would override the model. In trade models, the quantity of trade itself is almost always endogenous. Contrasts with *exogenous variable* (page 96).

Endowment

The amount of something that a person or country simply has, rather than their having somehow to acquire it. In the *HO model* (page 128) of trade theory, endowments refer to *primary factors* (page 217) of production, ignoring the fact that some of them — especially *capital* (page 30) and *skill* (page 247) — are deliberately accumulated.

Engine of growth

Term sometimes used to describe the role that *exports* (page 97) may have played in economic development, both of some of the regions of recent settlement in the nineteenth century and of today's *NICs* (page 191).

Engineering efficiency

See *economic efficiency* (page 79).

Entrepôt trade

The import and then export of a good without further processing, usually passing through an **entrepôt** which is a storage facility from which goods are distributed. See *re-exports* (page 231).

Entrepreneur

A person who starts a business.

Entry barrier

A natural or artificial impediment to a firm beginning to operate in an industry. Entry barriers give a *first mover advantage* (page 107) to firms already in an industry, and these are often national firms in competition with potential foreign entrants.

Envelope

The outermost points traced out by a moving curve.

Environmental dumping

Export of a good from a country with weak or poorly enforced environmental regulations, reflecting the idea that the exporter's cost of production is below the true cost to society, providing an unfair advantage in international trade. Also called *eco-dumping* (page 78).

Environmental Kuznets curve

An inverse U-shaped relationship hypothesized between per capita income and environmental degradation. Named after the *Kuznets curve* (page 155) dealing with inequality. Idea due to *Grossman and Krueger (1993)* (page 375).

Environmental protection argument for a trade intervention

The view that trade should be restricted in order to help the environment. Examples include embargos on imports made from endangered species, limits on imports produced by methods harmful to the atmosphere, and restrictions on investment into locations with lax environmental standards. This is usually a *second-best argument* (page 243).

Environmental subsidy

A *subsidy* (page 260) intended for environmental purposes. A subsidy for adapting existing facilities to new environmental laws or regulations is *non-actionable* (page 192) under *WTO* (page 293) rules.

EPU

European Payments Union (page 92).

EPZ

Export processing zone (page 99).

Equation of exchange

$M \times V = P \times Q$, where M is the quantity of money in an economy, V is the *velocity of money* (page 288), P is the price level, and Q is the real output of the economy. The equation is true by definition because it implicitly defines velocity of money. It is central to the *quantity theory of money* (page 225).

Equilibrium

1. A state of balance between offsetting forces for change, so that no change occurs.

2. In *competitive* (page 44) markets, equality of supply and demand.

Equilibrium level

The value taken on by an economic variable in *equilibrium* (see above), as opposed either to some other value, or to its rate of change.

Equilibrium position
Same as *equilibrium level* (page 87), though perhaps of several variables at once, perhaps as displayed in a graph.

Equity
Share in the ownership of a corporation; more commonly called a *stock* (page 257), as in the stock market.

Equivalent quota
The *quota* (page 226) that sets the same level of imports that is entering a country under a *tariff* (page 264), or perhaps under some other *NTB* (page 195).

Equivalent tariff
Tariff equivalent (page 264).

Equivalent variation
The amount of money that, paid to a person, group, or whole economy, would make them as well off as a specified change in the economy. Provides a monetary measure of the *welfare* (page 291) effect of that change that is similar to, but not in general the same as, *compensating variation* (page 43).

ERM
Exchange rate mechanism (page 94).

ERP
Effective rate of protection (page 82).

ERR
Economic rate of return (page 80).

Escalation
1. Regarding the structure of tariffs, see *tariff escalation* (page 264).
2. In the context of a *trade war* (page 278), escalation refers to the increase in tariffs that occurs as countries *retaliate* (page 236) again and again.

Escape clause
1. The portion of a legal text that permits departure from its provisions in the event of specified adverse circumstances.
2. The U.S. statute (section 201, 1974 trade act) that permits imports to be restricted, for a limited time and on a non-discriminatory basis, if they have caused injury to U.S. firms or

workers. The escape clause accords with the *safeguards clause* (page 240) (Article XIX) of the *GATT* (page 116).

Ethical trade

As used by the *ethical trading initiative* (see below), this term refers primarily to trade that conforms with high levels of *labor standards* (page 156), including the avoidance of *child labor* (page 38), *forced labor* (page 109), *sweatshops* (page 263), adverse health and safety conditions, and violations of *labor rights* (page 156).

Ethical trading initiative

An alliance of *multinational companies* (page 183), *nongovernmental organizations* (page 193), and labor unions seeking to promote and identify *ethical trade* (see above).

ETI

Ethical trading initiative (see above).

EU

European Union (page 357).

EU enlargement

The process of taking more member countries into the *EU* (see above).

Euler's theorem

1. The property of a function $X = F(V)$ that is *homogeneous of degree N* (page 128) that $\Sigma_i V_i \partial F / \partial V_i = NX$.

2. The useful implication of this that, for a *production function* (page 220) $X = F(V)$ with *constant returns to scale* (page 47), the competitive payments to factors sum to the value of output: $\Sigma_i w_i V_i = pX$.

Euratom

The European Atomic Energy Community, created in 1956 along with the *EEC* (page 81).

Euribor

Stands for the Euro Interbank Offered Rate, a euro-denominated interest rate charged by large banks among themselves on euro-denominated loans. Analogous to *LIBOR* (page 163) for the euro.

Euro
  The common currency of a subset of the countries of the *EU* (page 89), adopted January 1, 1999, with paper notes and coins put into circulation January 1, 2002.

Euro-Mediterranean Partnership
  An declaration at a 1995 conference in Barcelona between the 15 members of the *European Union* (page 357) and its 12 Mediterranean partners to enter a new phase in their relationship, promoting peace and stability, free trade, and cultural understanding. Also called the **Barcelona Process**.

Euro zone
  The countries of the *EMU* (page 85). That is, the *group* (page 90) of European countries, members of the *EU* (page 89), that adopted the common currency, the *euro* (see above). See *BAFFLING PIGS* (page 17).

Eurobond
  A *bond* (page 24) that is issued outside of the jurisdiction of any single country, denominated in a *eurocurrency* (see below).

Eurocurrency
  See *eurodollar* (below).

Eurodad
  A European network of *NGOs* (page 191) working to reduce poverty and empower the poor in developing countries through improved economic and financial policies.

Eurodollar
  Originally referred to U.S. dollar-denominated deposits in commercial banks located in Europe. Over time, the term came to include deposits in a commercial bank in *any* country denominated in *any* currency other than that of the country. Now sometimes called **eurocurrencies**.

Europe 1992
  An initiative, begun with the *Single European Act* (page 247) in 1987 by the *European Union* (page 357), to fully integrate the markets of the member countries by the end of 1992. The process involved extensive harmonization of laws and regulations that would otherwise interfere with the cross-border movement of goods and services.

Europe agreement

An agreement between the *EU* (page 89) and each of ten Eastern European countries (starting with Hungary and Poland in 1994) creating *free trade areas* (page 113) and establishing additional forms of political and economic cooperation in preparation for these countries' eventual membership in the EU.

European Central Bank

The central bank of the Euro zone — the group of countries using the euro as their currency.

European Coal and Steel Community

An economic agreement in 1951 among six countries of Western Europe — Belgium, France, Germany, Italy, Luxembourg, and Netherlands — that preceded formation of the *EEC* (page 81) and ultimately the *EU* (page 89).

European Communities

The name adopted in 1967 by the *European Economic Community* (see below) when it merged with the *ECSC* (page 81) and *Euratom* (page 89). This name and the acronym EC was used until 1992 when it was replaced by *European Union* (page 357).

European currency unit

A *composite currency* (page 45) that is a basket of most of the currencies of countries in the *European Union* (page 357). Conceived in 1979, it has been used as a *unit of account* (page 285) of the *European Monetary System* (page 92).

European Economic Area

The group of countries comprised of the *EU* (page 89) together with *EFTA* (page 83). The two groups have agreed to deepen their *economic integration* (page 80).

European Economic Community

A customs union formed in 1958 by the *Treaty of Rome* (page 280) among six countries of Europe: Belgium, France, Germany, Italy, Luxembourg, and Netherlands; predecessor to the *EC* (page 78) in 1967 and the *EU* (page 89) in 1992.

European Free Trade Association

A free trade area made up of countries in Europe that did not join the European Economic Community. EFTA was established in 1960 among Austria, Denmark, Norway, Portugal, Sweden,

Switzerland, and the United Kingdom. As of 2006 it includes Iceland, Liechtenstein, Norway, and Switzerland.

European Monetary Agreement

An intergovernmental organization administered by the *OECD* (page 196) that facilitated settlement of balance of payments accounts among its member states from 1958 to 1972. It replaced the *EPU* (page 87), and its functions were taken over by the *IMF* (page 132) in 1972.

European Monetary System

A *currency union* (page 58) formed by some of the members of the *EEC* (page 81) in 1979 that continued, with changing membership, until replaced by the *EMU* (page 85) and the *euro* (page 90) in 1999.

European Payments Union

An international arrangement for settling payments among member countries in Europe during a period in which many of the countries' currencies were not *convertible* (page 50). The EPU functioned from 1950 to 1958, after which it was replaced by the *EMA* (page 84).

European Recovery Program

See *Marshall Plan* (page 174).

European Union

A group of European countries that have chosen to integrate many of their economic activities, including forming a customs union and harmonizing many of their rules and regulations. Preceded by *EEC* (page 81) and *EC* (page 78). As of May 1, 2004, the EU had 25 *member countries* (page 357).

Even case

In international trade models with multiple goods and *factors* (page 101), this is the special case of an equal number of goods and factors. It is convenient for analysis, because the matrix of factor input requirements is square and therefore potentially *invertible* (page 151).

Everything But Arms

The name given by the *EU* (page 89) to its decision in 2001 to eliminate *quotas* (page 226) and *tariffs* (page 264) on all products except arms from the world's 48 poorest countries.

Ex ante analysis

Analysis of the effects of a policy, such as trade liberalization or formation of a *PTA* (page 222), based only on information available before the policy is undertaken. Also *prospective analysis* (page 222).

Ex post analysis

Analysis of the effects of a policy, such as trade liberalization or formation of a *PTA* (page 222), based on information available after the policy has been implemented and its performance observed. Also *retrospective analysis* (page 236).

Ex post tariff

Implicit tariff (page 133).

Excess demand

Demand (page 65) minus *supply* (page 261). Thus a country's demand for imports of a *homogeneous good* (page 128) is its excess demand for that good.

Excess profit

Profit of a firm over and above what provides its owners with a normal (market equilibrium) return to capital.

Excess supply

Supply (page 261) minus *demand* (page 65). Thus a country's supply of exports of a *homogeneous good* (page 128) is its excess supply of that good.

Exchange

1. To engage in *trade* (page 272), either within a country or internationally.

2. *Foreign exchange* (page 109).

Exchange control

Rationing of foreign exchange (page 227), typically used when the *exchange rate* (page 94) is fixed and the central bank is unable or unwilling to enforce the rate by *exchange-market intervention* (page 94).

Exchange equalization fund

The unit within a government or central bank that manages a *pegged exchange rate* (page 207). It manages *reserves* (page 235) of foreign currencies, which it uses to buy and sell domestic currency as needed to keep the exchange rate within specified bounds.

Exchange market

1. The market on which national currencies are exchanged for one another.

2. The actual exchange market, which exists primarily among large international banks. Others who wish to exchange currencies do it through these banks.

3. The theoretical representation of the exchange market as either the interaction of supply and demand arising from exchange-market transactions or as an asset market equilibrium between currencies.

Exchange market intervention

Usually done by a country's *central bank* (page 35), this is the purchase and sale of the country's currency on the *exchange market* (see above) in order to influence or fully determine its price. These transactions, unless they are *sterilized* (page 257), change the *monetary base* (page 179) of the country and thus its *money supply* (page 180).

Exchange rate

The price at which one country's currency trades for another, typically on the *exchange market* (see above).

Exchange rate determination

The process by which a country's *exchange rate* (see above) comes to be what it is. With a *floating exchange rate* (page 108), this may be modeled in various ways, including the *elasticities approach* (page 83), the *monetary approach* (page 178), the *portfolio approach* (page 211), and the *asset approach* (page 13).

Exchange rate exposure

The extent to which the stock-market value of a firm varies with changes in exchange rates. Also called *economic exposure* (page 79).

Exchange rate mechanism

A system that was operated by some *central banks* (page 35) within the *European Union* (page 357), which intervened in *exchange markets* (see above) to limit the fluctuations of their currencies relative to one another, while letting all of them collectively *float* (page 108).

Exchange rate overshooting

The response of an *exchange rate* (page 94) to a shock by first moving beyond where it will ultimately settle. Thought to help explain exchange rate *volatility* (page 289), this was first modeled by *Dornbusch (1976)* (page 374).

Exchange rate protection

The manipulation of the exchange rate so as to increase the domestic prices of, and demand for, domestically produced goods. Since an *undervalued currency* (page 283) stimulates demand for all domestically produced tradable goods, this form of protection, unlike *tariff protection* (page 265), can only be provided to the tradable sector as a whole, not to individual industries.

Exchange rate regime

The rules under which a country's *exchange rate* (page 94) is determined, especially the way the monetary or other government authorities do or do not *intervene* (page 150) in the *exchange market* (page 94). Regimes include *floating exchange rate* (page 108), *pegged exchange rate* (page 207), *managed float* (page 168), *crawling peg* (page 54), *currency board* (page 57), and *exchange controls* (page 93).

Exchange rate risk

Exchange risk (see below).

Exchange rate stability

Lack of movement over time in the *exchange rate* (page 94) of a country.

Exchange rationing

See *exchange control* (page 93) or *ration foreign exchange* (page 227).

Exchange risk

Uncertainty (page 282) about the value of an asset, liability, or commitment due to uncertainty about the future value of an exchange rate. Unless they *cover* (page 53) themselves in the *forward market* (page 111), traders with commitments to pay or receive foreign currency in the future bear exchange risk. So do holders of assets and liabilities denominated in foreign currency.

Exchange stabilization fund

A government institution sometimes used to handle *exchange market intervention* (page 94), charged with the explicit function of smoothing exchange rate fluctuations.

Excise tax

A tax on consumption of a particular good.

Exercise

To execute the terms of a contract. See *option* (page 201).

Exhaustion

In *intellectual property* (page 142) regimes, the transaction at which rights terminate. Under **national exhaustion**, rights end with first sale in a country, preventing *parallel imports* (page 204). Under **international exhaustion**, rights end with first sale anywhere, permitting parallel imports.

Exogenous

Coming from outside, usually in the context of an economic model, in which it means only that it is not explained within the model.

Exogenous growth

Economic growth (page 79) that occurs without being the result of deliberate policy or behavior. The term arises because *neoclassical growth models* (page 188) converge to a *steady state* (page 257) in which *per capita income* (page 207) is constant over time. Growth, then, requires *exogenous* (see above) *technical progress* (page 267).

Exogenous variable

A variable that is taken as given by an economic model. It therefore *is* subject to direct manipulation by the modeler. In most models, policy variables such as *tariffs* (page 264) and *par values* (page 204) of *pegged exchange rates* (page 207) are exogenous. Contrasts with *endogenous variable* (page 85).

Expansion

Economic expansion (page 79).

Expansionary

Tending to cause aggregate output (*GDP* (page 122)) and/or the price level to rise. Term is typically applied to *monetary policy* (page 179) (an increase in the money supply or a decrease in interest rates) and to *fiscal policy* (page 107) (an increase in government spending or a tax cut), but may also apply to other macroeconomic shocks. Contrasts *contractionary* (page 49).

Expectation

The expectation of a variable is the same as its *expected value* (see below), and is also used with both meanings.

Expected value

1. The mathematical expected value of a *random variable* (page 227). Equals the sum (or integral) of the values that are possible for it, each multiplied by its probability.

2. What people think a variable is going to be. In general, the expectation in this second sense may be more important than the first for determining behavior on a market, such as the *exchange market* (page 94).

Experience good

A product whose value can be better known after having consumed it. Producers of experience goods may temporarily charge a price lower than marginal cost to induce buyers to try the product. Done with an export, this would be legally considered *dumping* (page 76).

Export

1. A good that moves outward across a country's border for commercial purposes.

2. A product, which might be a service, that is provided to foreigners by a domestic producer.

3. To cause a good or service to be an export under definitions 1 and/or 2.

Export bias

Any *bias* (page 22) in favor of exporting. Most often applied to growth that is based disproportionately on accumulation of the *factor* (page 101) used *intensively* (page 143) in the export industry and/or *technological progress* (page 268) favoring that industry.

Export cartel

A *cartel* (page 34) of exporting countries or firms.

Export credit

A loan to the buyer of an export, extended by the exporting firm when shipping the good prior to payment, or by a facility of the exporting country's government. In the latter case, by setting a low interest rate on such loans, a country can indirectly *subsidize* (page 260) exports.

Export credit insurance

A program to guarantee payment to exporting firms who extend *export credits* (see above).

Export facilitation

Anything intended to make it easier to export, but usually refers to government services or programs with this objective.

Export-import company

A firm whose business consists mainly of international trade: buying goods in one country and selling them in another, thus both exporting and importing. Same as *import-export company* (page 134).

Export led growth

Growth of an economy over time that is thought to be caused by expansion of the country's exports. See *export promotion* (page 99), *engine of growth* (page 86).

Export licensing

See *licensing* (page 163).

Export limitation

Any policy that restricts exports.

Export multiplier

The *multiplier* (page 183) for a change in exports; that is, the increase in *GDP* (page 122) caused by a one-unit increase in exports.

Export performance requirement

Export requirement (page 99).

Export pessimism

The view that efforts to expand exports by *developing countries* (page 67) will lead to a decline in their *terms of trade* (page 269) because of an inability (due to weak demand) or unwillingness (expressed via *protection* (page 222)) of *developed countries* (page 67) to absorb these exports.

Export platform
The use of a country or region as a place to produce for export to another country. Used especially when a *preferential trade arrangement* (page 214) provides easier access to the destination country.

Export platform FDI
Foreign direct investment (page 109) from a source country into a host country for the purpose of exporting to a third country.

Export price index
Price index (page 215) of the goods that a country *exports* (page 97).

Export processing zone
A designated area in a country in which firms can import *duty-free* (page 77) so long as the imports are used as inputs to production of exports.

Export promotion
A strategy for *economic development* (page 79) that stresses expanding exports, often through policies to assist them such as *export subsidies* (see below). The rationale is to exploit a country's *comparative advantage* (page 42), especially in the common circumstance where an *overvalued currency* (page 203) would otherwise create bias against exports. Contrasts with *import substitution* (page 136).

Export quota
A quantitative restriction on exports, often the means of implementing a *VER* (page 289).

Export requirement
A requirement by the government of the host country of *FDI* (page 105) that the investor export a certain amount or percentage of its output.

Export subsidy
1. A subsidy to exports; that is, a payment to exporters of a good per unit of the good exported.

2. Sometimes applied to any payments to producers that lead to an increase in exports.

Export tariff

A tax on exports, more commonly called an *export tax* (see below).

Export tax

A tax on exports.

External balance

1. *Balance of payments equilibrium* (page 18).

2. Any *target* (page 263) value for the *balance on current account* (page 18), *balance on capital account* (page 18), or *balance of payments* (page 17).

External debt

The amount that a country owes to foreigners, including the debts of both the country's government and its private sector.

External diseconomy

Negative externality (page 187).

External economies of scale

A form of *increasing returns to scale* (page 138) in which productivity and thus costs of individual firms depend on the output of their entire industry, rather than just their own. Unlike more conventional (internal) scale economies, these are consistent with *perfect competition* (page 207).

External economy

Positive externality (page 211).

External increasing returns to scale

External economies of scale (see above).

Externalities argument for protection

The (*second best* (page 242)) argument that an industry should be *protected* (page 222) because it generates *positive externalities* (page 211) for other industries or consumers.

Externality

An effect of one economic agent's actions on another, such that one agent's decisions make another better or worse off by changing their utility or cost. Beneficial effects are *positive externalities* (page 211); harmful ones are *negative externalities* (page 187).

Facilitating payment

As permitted under the U.S. *Foreign Corrupt Practices Act* (page 109), a facilitating payment is a payment for "routine governmental action," such as obtaining permits, processing papers, providing normal government services, etc. It is, in fact, a *bribe* (page 26), but a small one that does not induce any illegal or exceptional behavior.

Factor

1. *Primary factor* (page 217).

2. Sometimes refers to *any* input to production.

3. Anything that helps to cause something, as a "contributing factor."

Factor abundance

The *abundance* (page 3) or *scarcity* (page 241) of a *primary factor* (page 217) of production. Because, in the short run at least, the supplies of primary factors are more or less fixed, this can be taken as given for determining much about a country's trade and other economic variables. Fundamental to the *HO model* (page 128).

Factor accumulation

An increase in the quantity of a *factor* (see above), usually *capital* (page 30) or sometimes *human capital* (page 130).

Factor augmenting

Said of a *technological change* (page 268) or *technological difference* (page 268) if production functions differ by scaling of a factor input only: $F^2(V_1, V_2) = F^1(\lambda V_1, V_2)$, where $F^1(\cdot)$ and $F^2(\cdot)$ are the production functions being compared, V_1 is the factor being augmented, V_2 is a vector of all other factor inputs, and λ is a constant.

Factor bias

See *bias* (page 22).

Factor content

The amounts of *primary factors* (page 217) used in the production of a good or service, or a vector of quantities of goods and services, such as the **factor content of trade** of the **factor content of consumption**. Can be either *direct* (page 69) or *direct-plus-indirect* (page 69).

Factor content pattern of trade

The *trade pattern* (page 276) of a country or the world, focusing on *factor content* (see above) of the goods and services that are traded, as opposed to the *commodity pattern of trade* (page 41).

Factor cost

The cost of the *factors* (page 101) used in production. The term is used especially when the value of economic activity in a sector or an economy can be measured or valued either at "factor cost," adding up payments to factors, or at "**market value**," adding up revenues from goods sold.

Factor endowment

The quantity of a *primary factor* (page 217) present in a country. See *endowment* (page 86).

Factor intensity

The relative importance of one *factor* (page 101) versus others in production in an industry, usually compared across industries. Most commonly defined by ratios of factor quantities employed at common *factor prices* (page 103), but sometimes by *factor shares* (page 104) or by *marginal rates of substitution* (page 170) between factors.

Factor intensity reversal

A property of the *technologies* (page 268) for two industries such that their ordering of relative factor intensities is different at different factor prices. For example, one industry may be relatively capital intensive compared to the other at high relative wages and labor intensive at low relative wages. Some propositions of the *Heckscher-Ohlin model* (page 126) require the absence of FIRs.

Factor intensity uniformity

The absence of *factor intensity reversals* (see above).

Factor market

The market for a *factor* (page 101) of production, such as labor or capital, in which supply and demand interact to determine the equilibrium price of the factor.

Factor mobility

The degree to which a *factor* (page 101) of production, such as labor or capital, is able to move, either among industries or among countries, in response to differences in its *factor price* (see below), thus tending to eliminate such differences.

Factor movement

International factor movement (page 147).

Factor of production

Factor (page 101) (definition 1).

Factor price

The price paid for the services of a unit of a *primary factor* (page 217) of production per unit time. Includes the *wage* (page 290) or salary of labor and the *rental prices* (page 234) of land and capital. Does *not* normally refer to the price of acquiring ownership of the factor itself, which might be called the "purchase price."

Factor price equalization

The tendency for trade to cause *factor prices* (see above) in different countries to become identical. *Ohlin (1933)* (page 379) argued that trade would bring factor prices closer together. *Samuelson (1948, 1949)* (page 380) showed formally the circumstances under which they would actually become equal.

Factor price equalization theorem

One of the major theoretical results of the *Heckscher-Ohlin model* (page 126) with at least as many goods as factors, showing that *free* (page 113) and *frictionless trade* (page 114) will cause *FPE* (page 112) between two countries if they have identical, *linearly homogeneous* (page 164) technologies and their *factor endowments* (page 102) are sufficiently similar to be in the same *diversification cone* (page 72).

Factor price frontier

A curve in *factor space* (page 104) showing the minimum combinations of *factor prices* (see above) consistent with absence of profit in producing one or more goods, given their prices. Since, with *perfect competition* (page 207), profit implies disequilibrium, this shows a lower bound on equilibrium factor prices.

Factor-price space

A graph with *factor prices* (page 103) on the axes.

Factor proportions

1. The ratios of factors employed in different industries. See *factor intensities* (page 102).

2. The ratios of factors with which different countries are endowed. See *factor endowments* (page 102).

Factor proportions model

The *Heckscher-Ohlin model* (page 126) of trade.

Factor saving

Biased (page 22) in favor of using less of a particular factor.

Factor scarcity

See *factor abundance* (page 101).

Factor share

The fraction of payments to *value added* (page 287) in an industry that goes to a particular *primary factor* (page 217).

Factor space

A graph in which the axes measure quantities of *factors* (page 101).

Factor using

Biased (page 22) in favor of using more of a particular factor.

Fair price

In *anti-dumping* (page 4) cases, the price to which the export price is compared, which is either the price charged in the exporter's own domestic market or some measure of their cost, both adjusted to include any transportation cost and tariff needed to enter the importing country's market. See *dumping* (page 76).

Fairness argument for protection

The view that it is unfair to force domestic firms to compete with foreign firms that have an advantage, either in terms of low wages or due to foreign government policies. This misinterprets economic activity as a game, the purpose of which is to win, rather than as a means of using limited resources to satisfy human needs. See *level playing field* (page 162).

FAO

Food and Agriculture Organization of the United Nations (page 108).

FAS

Same as *FOB* (page 108) but without the cost of loading onto a ship. Stands for "free alongside ship."

Fast track

A procedure adopted by the U.S. Congress, at the request of the President, committing it to consider trade agreements without amendment. In return, the President must adhere to a specified timetable and other procedures. Introduced in the *Trade Act of 1974* (page 272). See *trade promotion authority* (page 276).

Favorable exchange rate

An *exchange rate* (page 94) different from the *market* (page 171) or *official* (page 196) rate, provided by the government on a transaction as an indirect way of providing a *subsidy* (page 260).

FDI

Foreign direct investment (page 109).

Fed

The Federal Reserve System (see below) of the United States.

Federal funds rate

The interest rate on very short-term loans from one commercial bank to another in the United States. This rate is used as a target for *monetary policy* (page 179) by the *Fed* (see above).

Federal Reserve System

The *central bank* (page 35) of the United States.

Fiat money

A money whose usefulness results, not from any intrinsic value or guarantee that it can be converted into gold or another currency, but only from a government's order (fiat) that it must be accepted as a means of payment.

Fifty Years Is Enough

50 Years Is Enough (page 296).

Final good

A good that requires no further processing or transformation to be ready for use by consumers, investors, or government. Contrasts with *intermediate good* (page 144).

Financial account

This is the term used in the *balance of payments* (page 17) statistics, since sometime in the 1990s, for what used to be called the "capital account." See *capital account* (page 30), the "common" definition 2.

Financial asset

An *asset* (page 13) whose value arises not from its physical embodiment (as would a building or a piece of land or capital equipment) but from a contractual relationship: stocks, bonds, bank deposits, currency, etc.

Financial capital

The value of *financial assets* (see above), as opposed to real assets such as buildings and capital equipment.

Financial crisis

A loss of confidence in a country's currency or other financial assets causing international investors to withdraw their funds from the country.

Financial instrument

A document, real or virtual, having legal force and embodying or conveying monetary value.

Financial intermediary

An institution that provides indirect means for funds from those who wish to save or lend to be channeled to those who wish to invest or borrow. Examples include banks and other depository institutions, mutual funds, and some government programs.

Financial market

A market for a *financial instrument* (see above), in which buyers and sellers find each other and create or exchange financial assets. Sometimes these are organized in a particular place and/or institution, but often they exist more broadly through communication among dispersed buyers and sellers, including banks, over long distances.

Financial market integration

Freedom of participants in the *financial markets* (see above) of two countries to transact on markets in both countries, thereby causing returns on comparable assets in the two countries to be equalized through *arbitrage* (page 11).

Financial stability

The avoidance of *financial crisis* (page 106).

FIR

Factor intensity reversal (page 102).

First best

See *second best* (page 242).

First degree homogeneous

Homogeneous of degree 1 (page 128).

First mover advantage

The advantage that a firm or country may derive from being the first to enter a market, or from being the first to use a new technology, advertising technique, etc.

First order condition

One of the mathematical necessary conditions for maximization, used routinely in solving economic models. Typically, it consists of setting equal to zero the derivative of the function being maximized (or its *Lagrangian* (page 157)) with respect to a variable that can be controlled.

First theorem of welfare economics

The proposition of *welfare economics* (page 292) that a *competitive* (page 44) *general equilibrium* (page 117) is *Pareto optimal* (page 204). A corollary is that *free trade* (page 113) is Pareto optimal among countries.

Fiscal deficit

A *deficit* (page 63) in the government budget of a country.

Fiscal policy

Any macroeconomic policy involving the levels of government purchases, transfers, or taxes, usually implicitly focused on domestic goods, residents, or firms. A **fiscal stimulus** is an increase in purchases or transfers or a cut in taxes.

Fisher effect

The theory that a change in the expected rate of *inflation* (page 141) will lead to an equal change in the *nominal interest rate* (page 192), thus keeping the *real interest rate* (page 229) unchanged. Due to *Fisher (1930)* (page 375).

Fixed cost

The cost that a firm bears if it produces at all and that is independent of its output. The presence of a fixed cost tends to imply *increasing returns to scale* (page 138). Contrasts with *variable cost* (page 288).

Fixed exchange rate

Usually synonymous with a *pegged exchange rate* (page 207). Although "fixed" seems to imply less likelihood of change, in practice countries seldom if ever achieve a truly fixed rate.

Flexible exchange rate

Same as *floating exchange rate* (see below).

Floating exchange rate

A regime in which a country's exchange rate is allowed to fluctuate freely and be determined without *intervention* (page 150) in the exchange market by the government or central bank.

Floor

See *price floor* (page 215).

FOB

The price of a traded good excluding *transport cost* (page 280). It stands for "free on board," but is used only as these initials (usually lower case: f.o.b.). It means the price after loading onto a ship but before shipping, thus *not* including transportation, insurance, and other costs needed to get a good from one country to another. Contrasts with *CIF* (page 38) and *FAS* (page 105).

FOC

First order condition (page 107).

FOGS negotiations

In the *Uruguay Round* (page 286), this portion of the negotiations dealt with the **Functioning of the GATT System** and resulted ultimately in the formation of the *WTO* (page 293) and its *dispute settlement mechanism* (page 71).

Food and Agriculture Organization of the United Nations

A *UN* (page 282) body whose purpose is to "defeat hunger" throughout the world mostly by sharing information and expertise.

Food security
   1. The reliable availability of a sufficient quantity and quality of nutritious food for a population.
   2. As used by some *NGOs* (page 191), the term also requires that localities or regions be *self sufficient* (page 244), in apparent ignorance of the impossibility of combining this with the first definition.

Footloose factor
   A *factor* (page 101) that can move easily across national borders, in contrast to one that, due to inclination or constraints, cannot. Footloose factors are sometimes thought to have an advantage in a *globalized* (page 119) economy.

Footloose industry
   An industry that is not tied to any particular location or country, and can relocate across national borders in response to changing economic conditions. Many *manufacturing* (page 169) industries seem to have this characteristic.

Forced labor
   The use of labor that is compelled to work, subject to physical punishment if it does not.

Foreign asset position
   The amount of assets that residents of a country own abroad. Also used to mean the *net foreign asset position* (page 189).

Foreign Corrupt Practices Act
   U.S. law, enacted 1977, that prohibits U.S. firms from bribing foreign officials to obtain or retain business. The law permits, however, *facilitating payments* (page 101).

Foreign debt
   The amount a country owes to foreigners. More precisely, the negative of the *net foreign asset position* (page 189).

Foreign direct investment
   Acquisition or construction of physical capital by a firm from one (**source**) country in another (**host**) country.

Foreign exchange
   Foreign currency; any currency other than a country's own.

Foreign exchange market
   The *exchange market* (page 94).

Foreign exchange rate
  The *exchange rate* (page 94).
Foreign exchange risk
  Exchange risk (page 95).
Foreign investment argument for protection
  The use of *protection* (page 222) to attract *FDI* (page 105) from abroad. It does work, since much FDI has been motivated by firms trying to get behind a *tariff wall* (page 266) to sell their products. In an otherwise *non-distorted economy* (page 193), however, the cost in terms of more expensive goods is higher than the benefit from additional capital.
Foreign portfolio investment
  Portfolio investment (page 211) across national borders and/or across currencies.
Foreign repercussion
  The feedback effect on a domestic economy when its macro-economic changes cause large enough changes abroad for those in turn to cause further changes at home. Most commonly, a rise in income stimulates imports, causing an expansion abroad that in turn raises demand for the home country's exports.
Foreign reserves
  International reserves (page 149).
Foreign reserves crisis
  The *financial crisis* (page 106) that results from (or causes) a central bank coming close to running out of *international reserves* (page 149).
Foreign Sales Corporation
  Refers to a provision of the U.S. tax code that grants income-tax rebates to American exporters if they form what may be a largely artificial foreign subsidiary called an FSC. This has been the subject of a *trade dispute* (page 274) with the *EU* (page 89), which complained to the *WTO* (page 293) that this constitutes an illegal *export subsidy* (page 99).
Foreign trade deficit
  Trade deficit (page 273).

Foreign trade zone

An area within a country where imported goods can be stored or processed without being subject to import duty. Also called a "free zone," "free port," or "bonded warehouse."

Formula approach

A procedure for organizing multilateral *trade negotiations* (page 275) using a formula for tariff reductions as a starting point.

Forward

On the *forward market* (see below).

Forward curve

In a *forward market* (see below), the pattern of *forward rates* (page 112), or *forward premia* (see below), over various time horizons.

Forward discount

Opposite of *forward premium* (see below).

Forward integration

Acquisition by a firm of a larger part of its distribution chain, moving it closer to selling directly to its ultimate customers.

Forward linkage

The provision by one firm or industry of produced inputs to another firm or industry.

Forward market

A market for exchange of currencies in the future. Participants in a forward market enter into a contract to exchange currencies, not today, but at a specified date in the future, typically 30, 60, or 90 days from now, and at a price (*forward exchange rate* (page 112)) that is agreed upon today.

Forward premium

The difference between a *forward exchange rate* (page 112) and the *spot exchange rate* (page 254), expressed as an annualized percentage return on buying foreign currency spot and selling it forward.

Forward price

In any *forward market* (see above), the price of the item being traded for delivery at a future date; in *exchange markets* (page 94), the *forward rate* (page 112).

Forward rate

Also called the **forward exchange rate**, this is the *exchange rate* (page 94) on a *forward market* (page 111) transaction.

Four-firm concentration ratio

See *concentration ratio* (page 46).

Four Tigers

The four Asian economies that were the first to show rapid economic development after the success of Japan: Hong Kong, South Korea, Singapore, and Taiwan.

FPE

Factor price equalization (page 103).

Fragmentation

The splitting of production processes into separate parts that can be done in different locations, including in different countries. One of many terms for the same phenomenon, this particular one (which I seem to favor) *originated* (page 369) with *Jones and Kierzkowski (1990)* (page 376).

Free capital markets

This is not a standard term, but it seems to be used, variously, to describe the absence of government regulation of international *capital flows* (page 32), the absence of government or central bank *intervention in exchange markets* (page 94), and the absence of interference with national financial and development policies by *international financial institutions* (page 147).

Free enterprise

A system in which economic agents are free to own property and engage in commercial transactions. See *laissez faire* (page 158), *economic freedom* (page 79).

Free entry

The assumption that new firms are permitted to enter an industry and can do so costlessly. Together with *free exit* (see below), it implies that profit must be *zero* (page 294) in equilibrium.

Free exit

The assumption that firms are permitted to leave an industry and can do so costlessly. See *free entry* (above).

Free list

A list of goods that a country has designated as able to be imported without being subject to tariff or import licensing.

Free on board

See *FOB* (page 108).

Free port

See *foreign trade zone* (page 111).

Free rider

Someone who enjoys the benefits of a *public good* (page 222) without bearing the cost. An example, in trade policy, is that trade liberalization benefits the majority of consumers without their lobbying for it. This may tip policy in the direction of protection, for which there are fewer free riders.

Free trade

A situation in which there are no artificial barriers to trade, such as *tariffs* (page 264) and *NTBs* (page 195). Usually used, often only implicitly, with *frictionless trade* (page 114), so that it implies that there are no barriers to trade of any kind. For a traded *homogeneous product* (page 129), it follows that *domestic* (page 74) and *world price* (page 293) must be equal.

Free trade area

A group of countries that adopt free trade (zero tariffs and no other policy restrictions) on trade among themselves, while not necessarily changing the barriers that each member country has on trade with the countries outside the group.

Free Trade Area of the Americas

A *preferential trading arrangement* (page 214) being negotiated among most of the countries (all but Cuba) of the western hemisphere.

Free trade association

Free trade area (see above).

Free trade zone

An *export processing zone* (page 99).

Free zone

See *foreign trade zone* (page 111).

Frequency

The speed of the up and down movements of a fluctuating economic variable; that is, the number of times per unit of time that the variable completes a cycle of up and down movement. See *destabilizing speculation* (page 66).

Frictionless trade

The absence of natural barriers to trade, such as transport costs.

Friedman rule

The rule for the optimal conduct of *monetary policy* (page 179) proposed by *Friedman (1969)* (page 375), that it should generate a rate of *deflation* (page 64) that makes the *nominal interest rate* (page 192) equal to zero.

FSC

Foreign Sales Corporation (page 110).

FTA

Free trade area (page 113).

FTAA

Free Trade Area of the Americas (page 113).

FTZ

Free trade zone (page 113).

Functional distribution of income

How the income of an economy is divided among the owners of different *factors of production* (page 103), into wages, rents, etc.

Futures market

A market for exchange (of currencies, in the case of the exchange market) in the future. That is, participants contract to exchange currencies, not today, but at a specified calendar date in the future, and at a price (exchange rate) that is agreed upon today.

G-7

A group of seven major industrialized countries whose heads of state have met annually since 1976 in summit meetings to discuss economic and political issues. The seven are United States, Canada, Japan, Britain, France, Germany, and Italy (plus the *EU* (page 89)).

G-8

The *G-7* (see above) plus Russia, which have met as a full economic and political summit since 1998.

G-10

A *group* of ten countries, members of the *IMF* (page 132), that together with Switzerland agreed to make resources available outside their *IMF quotas* (page 132). Since 1963 the governors of the G-10 central banks have met on the occasion of the bimonthly *BIS* (page 24) meetings.

G-20

1. An international forum of finance ministers and central bank governors from 19 countries and the *EU* (page 89), plus the *IMF* (page 132) and *World Bank* (page 293). Created in 1999 by the finance ministers of the G-7, it meets annually to discuss financial and economic concerns among industrialized economies and emerging markets.

2. A group of developing countries — established August 20, 2003 — that joined together in the *Cancún Ministerial* (page 30) of the *WTO's* (page 293) *Doha Round* (page 73) in order to negotiate collectively with the U.S. and E.U., especially seeking the elimination of developed-country agricultural subsidies. Membership in the group has fluctuated, but the name G-20 now seems to have stuck. The group has been led by Brazil, other important members including Argentina, China, India, and South Africa.

G-24

A group of developing countries established in 1971 with the aim of taking positions on monetary and development finance issues.

G-77

A coalition of developing countries within the *United Nations* (page 285), established in 1964 at the end of the first session of *UNCTAD* (page 283), intended to articulate and promote the collective economic interests of its members and enhance their negotiating capacity. Originally with 77 members, it now (in 2006) has 132.

Gains from trade

The net benefits that countries experience as a result of lowering import *tariffs* (page 264) and otherwise *liberalizing trade* (page 275).

Gains from trade theorem

The theoretical proposition that (in the absence of *distortions* (page 72)) there will be gains from trade for any economy that moves from *autarky* (page 15) to *free trade* (page 113), as well as for a *small open economy* (page 248) and for the world as a whole if tariffs are reduced appropriately. Due to *Samuelson (1939, 1962)* (page 380).

Game

A theoretical construct in *game theory* (see below) in which players select actions and the payoffs depend on the actions of all players.

Game theory

The modeling of strategic interactions among agents, used in economic models where the numbers of interacting agents (firms, governments, etc.) are small enough that each has a perceptible influence on the others.

Gastarbeiter

Guest worker (page 123).

GATS

General Agreement on Trade in Services (page 117).

GATT

General Agreement on Tariffs and Trade (page 117).

GATT articles
The individual sections of the GATT agreement, conventionally identified by their Roman numerals. Most were originally drafted in 1947, but are still included in the *WTO* (page 293).

GATT-Speak
Variation on *GATT-Think* (see below).

GATT-Think
A somewhat derogatory term for the language of *GATT* (page 116) negotiations, in which exports are good, imports are bad, and a reduction in a barrier to imports is a *concession* (page 46). Similar to *mercantilism* (page 175). Due to *Krugman (1991b)* (page 377).

GCC
Gulf Cooperation Council (page 123).

GDP
Gross domestic product (page 122).

GDP deflator
The *deflator* (page 64) for *GDP* (see above), thus the ratio of *nominal* (page 191) GDP to *real GDP* (page 229) (usually multiplied, as with a *price index* (page 215), by 100).

General Agreement on Tariffs and Trade
A multilateral treaty entered into in 1948 by the intended members of the *International Trade Organization* (page 150), the purpose of which was to implement many of the rules and negotiated tariff reductions that would be overseen by the ITO. With the failure of the ITO to be approved, the GATT became the principal institution regulating trade policy until it was subsumed within the *WTO* (page 293) in 1995.

General Agreement on Trade in Services
The agreement, negotiated in the *Uruguay Round* (page 286), that brings international trade in services into the *WTO* (page 293). It provides for countries to provide *national treatment* (page 186) to foreign service providers and for them to select and negotiate the service sectors to be covered under GATS.

General equilibrium
Equality of supply and demand in all markets of an economy simultaneously. The number of markets does not have to be large.

The simplest *Ricardian model* (page 237) has markets only for two goods and one factor, labor, but this is a general equilibrium model. Contrasts with *partial equilibrium* (page 205).

Generalized system of preferences

Tariff preferences for developing countries, by which developed countries let certain manufactured and semi-manufactured imports from developing countries enter at lower tariffs than the same products from developed countries.

Genetically modified organism

Plants or animals (or products thereof) whose genetic makeup has been determined or altered by genetic engineering. Trade in GMOs has been the source of disagreement and controversy between the US and the EU.

Geography

See *new economic geography* (page 190).

Giffen good

A good that is so *inferior* (page 140) and so heavily consumed at low incomes that the demand for it rises when its price rises. The reason is that the price increase lowers income sufficiently that the positive *income effect* (page 137) (because it is inferior) outweighs the negative *substitution effect* (page 260).

Gini coefficient

A measure of income inequality within a population, ranging from zero for complete equality, to one if one person has all the income. It is defined as the area between the *Lorenz curve* (page 166) and the diagonal, divided by the total area under the diagonal.

Global competitiveness

Competitiveness (page 44), applied internationally.

Global optimum

An *allocation* (page 9) that is better, by some criterion, than all others possible; *optimum optimorum* (page 201).

Global quota

An import *quota* (page 226) that specifies the permitted quantity of imports from all sources combined. This may be without regard to country of origin, and thus available on a first-come-first-served basis, or it may be allocated to specific suppliers.

Global trade analysis project
A project based at Purdue University, providing a data base and *CGE* (page 37) modeling tools for analysis of global trade.

Globalization
1. The increasing world-wide integration of markets for goods, services and capital that began to attract special attention in the late 1990s.
2. Also used to encompass a variety of other changes that were perceived to occur at about the same time, such as an increased role for large corporations (*MNCs* (page 178)) in the world economy and increased intervention into domestic policies and affairs by international institutions such as the *IMF* (page 132), *WTO* (page 293), and *World Bank* (page 293).
3. Among countries outside the United States, especially developing countries, the term sometimes refers to the domination of world economic affairs and commerce by the United States.

GMO
Genetically modified organism (page 118).

Gnomes of Zurich
Term used by the British Labor government to refer to Swiss bankers and financiers who engaged in currency *speculation* (page 253) that forced the *devaluation* (page 67) of the British pound in 1964.

GNP
Gross national product (page 122).

Gold exchange standard
A monetary system that sought to restore features of the gold standard in the 1920s and again in the *Bretton Woods System* (page 26), while economizing on gold. Instead of money being backed directly by gold, central banks issued liabilities against foreign currency assets (mostly U.S. dollars under Bretton Woods) that were in turn backed by gold.

Gold standard
A monetary system in which both the value of a unit of the currency and the quantity of it in circulation are specified in terms of gold. If two currencies are both on the gold standard, then the *exchange rate* (page 94) between them

is approximately determined by their two prices in terms of gold.

Good

A product that can be produced, bought, and sold, and that has a physical identity. Sometimes said, inaccurately, to be anything that "can be dropped on your foot" or, also inaccurately, to be "*visible* (page 289)." Contrasts with *service* (page 244). Trade in goods is much easier to measure than trade in services, and thus much more thoroughly documented and analyzed.

Government debt

The amount that a country's government has borrowed as a result of *budget deficits* (page 27), usually by issuing government *bonds* (page 24) or, in *developing countries* (page 67), from *international financial institutions* (page 147). Often called the *national debt* (page 185).

Government procurement

Purchase of goods and services by government and by state-owned enterprises. Transparency in government procurement is one of the *Singapore issues* (page 246).

Government procurement practice

The methods by which units of government and state-owned enterprises determine from whom to purchase goods and services. When these methods include a preference for domestic firms, they constitute an *NTB* (page 195). Subject of a *Tokyo Round code* (page 271) and later a *WTO* (page 293) *plurilateral agreement* (page 210).

Graduation

Termination of a country's eligibility for *GSP* (page 123) tariff preferences on the grounds that it has progressed sufficiently, in terms of per capita income or another measure, that it is no longer in need to *special and differential treatment* (page 251).

Grandfather clause

A provision in an agreement, including the *GATT* (page 116) but not the *WTO* (page 293), that allows signatories to keep certain of their previously existing laws that otherwise would violate the agreement.

Gravity equation

An estimated equation of the *gravity model* (see below).

Gravity model

A model of the flows of *bilateral* (page 23) trade based on analogy with the law of gravity in physics: $T_{ij} = AY_iY_j/D_{ij}$, where T_{ij} is exports from country i to country j, Y_i,Y_j are their national incomes, D_{ij} is the distance between them, and A is a constant. Other constants as exponents and other variables are often included. Due independently to *Tinbergen (1962)* (page 382) and *Pöyhönen (1963)* (page 380).

Gray area measure

A policy or practice whose conformity with existing rules in unclear, such as a *VER* (page 289) under the *GATT* (page 116) prior to the *WTO* (page 293).

Gray market

Refers to goods that are sold for a price lower than, or through a distributor different than, that intended by the manufacturer. Most commonly, goods that are intended by their manufacturer for one national market that are bought there, exported, and sold in another national market.

Green box

Category of *subsidies* (page 260) permitted under the *WTO* (page 293) *Agriculture Agreement* (page 9); includes those not directed at particular products; direct income support for farmers unrelated to production or prices; subsidies for environmental protection and regional development.

Green exchange rate

An exchange rate used within the *EU's* (page 89) *common agricultural policy* (page 41) to convert subsidy and support payments into local currencies, avoiding the variability of the rate set in the *exchange market* (page 94).

Green field investment

FDI (page 105) that involves construction of a new plant, rather then the purchase of an existing plant or firm. Contrasts with *brown field investment* (page 26).

Green room group

A group of GATT/*WTO* (page 293) member countries or their delegates — including the larger members and selected smaller and less developed ones — that have met together during negotiations (originally in a green room at WTO Geneva headquarters) to agree among themselves, before taking decisions to the full membership for the required consensus.

Gross domestic product

The total value of new goods and services produced in a given year within the borders of a country, regardless of by whom. It is "gross" in the sense that it does *not* deduct *depreciation* (page 66) of previously produced *capital* (page 30), in contrast to *NDP* (page 187).

Gross international reserves

International reserves (page 149), without any deduction for the fact that some of them may have been borrowed. Contrasts with *net international reserves* (page 189).

Gross national income

National income (page 185) plus *capital consumption allowance* (page 31).

Gross national product

The total value of new goods and services produced in a given year by a country's domestically owned factors of production, regardless of where. It is "gross" in the sense that, in contrast to *NNP* (page 191), it does *not* deduct *depreciation* (page 66) of previously produced *capital* (page 30).

Gross output

The total output of a firm, industry, or economy without deducting intermediate inputs. For a firm or industry, this is larger than its *value added* (page 287) which is net of its own intermediate inputs. For an economy, gross output is greater than *net output* (page 189), which deducts the amount of the good itself used as an intermediate input.

Gross substitutes

Two goods are gross substitutes if a rise in the price of one causes and increase in demand for the other.

Group of Seven (or Eight)
  G-7 (page 115) (or *G-8* (page 115)).
Group of Seventy-seven
  G-77 (page 116).
Group of Ten
  G-10 (page 115)
Group of Twenty
  G-20 (page 115)
Group of Twenty-four
  G-24 (page 116)
Growth
  See *economic growth* (page 79).
Growth accounting
  Decomposition of the sources of *economic growth* (page 79) into the contributions from increases in *capital* (page 30), labor, and other *factors* (page 101). What remains, called the *Solow residual* (page 250), is usually attributed to *technology* (page 268).
Grubel-Lloyd index
  The measure of the *intra-industry trade* (page 151) suggested by *Grubel and Lloyd (1975)* (page 375). For an industry i with exports X_i and imports M_i the index is $I = [(X_i + M_i) - |X_i - M_i|]100/(X_i + M_i)$. This is the fraction of total trade in the industry, $X_i + M_i$, that is accounted for by IIT (times 100).
GSP
  Generalized system of preferences (page 118).
GTAP
  Global trade analysis project (page 119).
Guest worker
  A foreign worker who is permitted to enter a country temporarily in order to take a job for which there is shortage of domestic labor.
Gulf Cooperation Council
  An agreement among six countries of the Persian Gulf region — Bahrain, Kuwait, Oman, Qatar, Saudi Arabia, and the United Arab Emirates — in 1981 with the aim of coordinating and integrating their economic policies.

Harberger-Laursen-Metzler effect

The conjecture or result that a *terms of trade* (page 269) deterioration will cause a decrease in savings due to the decrease in real income, and therefore that a *real* (page 228) *depreciation* (page 66) will cause an increase in real expenditure. Due to *Harberger (1950)* (page 375) and *Laursen and Metzler (1950)* (page 377).

Harberger triangle

The triangular area, or areas, in a supply and demand diagram that measures the net welfare loss, or *dead-weight loss* (page 61) due to a market *distortion* (page 72) or policy, such as a *tariff* (page 264).

Hard currency

A *currency* (page 56) that is widely accepted around the world, usually because it is the currency of a country with a large and stable market. Examples today include the U.S. dollar and the *euro* (page 90).

Hard peg

A *pegged exchange rate* (page 207) with a credible commitment never to change the *par value* (page 204), thus subordinating *monetary policy* (page 179) to the needs of the exchange market and denying access to *devaluation* (page 67) as a policy tool. In practice, the effects of a hard peg are achieved only through a *currency board* (page 57) or by adopting another country's currency, e.g. *dollarization* (page 74).

Harmful externality

Negative externality (page 187).

Harmonization

1. The changing of government regulations and practices, as a result of an international agreement, to make those of different countries the same or more compatible.

2. In the case of *tariffs* (page 264), this means making tariff rates more similar across industries and/or across countries.

Harmonized system

An international system for classifying goods in international trade and for specifying the tariffs on those goods. It was adopted at the beginning of 1989, replacing the previously used schedules in over 50 countries, including the *Brussels tariff nomenclature* (page 26).

Harrod neutral

A particular specification of *technological change* (page 268) or *technological difference* (page 268) that is *labor augmenting* (page 156).

Hat algebra

The *Jones (1965)* (page 376) technique for *comparative static* (page 43) analysis in trade models. By totally differentiating a model in the logarithms of its variables, a linear system is obtained relating small proportional changes (denoted by carats ($\hat{\ }$), or "hats") in terms of various elasticities and shares. (The published article used *, not $\hat{\ }$, because of typographical constraints.)

Havana charter

The charter for the never-implemented *International Trade Organization* (page 150). The draft was completed at a conference in Havana, Cuba, in 1948.

Headquarters services

The activities of a firm that typically occur at its main location and that contribute in a broad sense to its productivity at all of its locations and plants. These may include management, accounting, marketing, and *R&D* (page 226).

Heavily indebted poor countries

The name given to those poor countries with large debts, the target of initiatives to forgive that debt as a means of assisting *development* (page 67).

Heckscher-Ohlin core propositions

See *core propositions* (page 50).

Heckscher-Ohlin model

A model of international trade in which *comparative advantage* (page 42) derives from differences in relative *factor endowments* (page 102) across countries and differences in relative *factor intensities* (page 102) across industries. Sometimes refers only to the *textbook* (page 270) or *2x2x2* (page 281) model, but more generally includes models with any numbers of factors, goods, and countries. Model was originally formulated by *Heckscher (1919)* (page 375), fleshed out by *Ohlin (1933)* (page 379), and refined by *Samuelson (1948, 1949, 1953)* (page 380).

Heckscher-Ohlin-Samuelson model

Usually synonymous with the *Heckscher-Ohlin model* (see above), although sometimes the term is used to distinguish the more formalized, mathematical version that Samuelson used from the more general but less well-defined conceptual treatment of Heckscher and Ohlin.

Heckscher-Ohlin theorem

The proposition of the *Heckscher-Ohlin model* (see above) that countries will export the goods that use relatively *intensively* (page 143) their relatively *abundant* (page 3) *factors* (page 101).

Heckscher-Ohlin-Vanek model

The *Heckscher-Ohlin model* (see above) for the case of identical *techniques* (page 268) of production (due either to *FPE* (page 112) or *Leontief technologies* (page 161)), used to derive the strong prediction about the *factor content of trade* (page 102) known as the *Heckscher-Ohlin-Vanek theorem* (see below).

Heckscher-Ohlin-Vanek theorem

The prediction of the *Heckscher-Ohlin-Vanek model* (see above) that a country's net *factor content* (page 102) of trade equals its own factor endowment minus its world-expenditure share of the world factor endowment. That is, for country i, $F^i = V^i - s_i V^W$, where F^i is the factor content of its trade, V^i, V^W its and the world's factor endowments, and s_i its share of world expenditure. Due to *Vanek (1968)* (page 382).

Hedge

To offset risk. In the foreign exchange market, **hedgers** use the *forward market* (page 111) to *cover* (page 53) a transaction or *open position* (page 199) and thereby reduce *exchange risk* (page 95). The term applies most commonly to trade.

Hedonic pricing

The use of statistical techniques such as *regression analysis* (page 232) to determine, from the prices of goods with different measurable characteristics, the prices that are associated with those characteristics. The latter can then be used to construct what the comparable price of a good would be from its characteristics.

Helms-Burton Act

A United States law enacted in 1996 that penalized companies for doing business in Cuba. Since the law applied to non-U.S. companies as well as U.S. companies, other governments objected.

Herfindahl index

A standard measure of *industry concentration* (page 139), defined as the sum of the squares of the market shares (in percentages) of the firms in the industry.

Hicks neutral

Said of a *technological change* (page 268) or *technological difference* (page 268) if production functions differ by scaling of output only: $F^2(V) = \lambda F^1(V)$, where $F^1(\cdot)$ and $F^2(\cdot)$ are the production functions being compared, V is a vector of factor inputs, and $\lambda > 0$ is a constant.

High dimension

In trade theory, this refers to having more than two goods, factors, and/or countries, or to having arbitrary numbers of these. Contrasts with the *two-ness* (page 282) of the *2x2x2 model* (page 281).

High-powered money

Same as *monetary base* (page 179), in the sense of currency plus commercial bank reserves.

HIPC

Heavily indebted poor countries (page 125).

HO model

Heckscher-Ohlin model (page 126).

Home bias

A preference, by consumers or other demanders, for products produced in their own country compared to otherwise identical imports. This was proposed by *Trefler (1995)* (page 382) as a possible explanation for the *mystery of the missing trade* (page 184).

Homogeneous

1. Having the property that all constituent elements are the same, as a *homogeneous good* (see below).

2. Possessing a certain form of uniformity, as a *homogeneous function* (see below).

Homogeneous function

A function with the property that multiplying all arguments by a constant changes the value of the function by a monotonic function of that constant: $F(\lambda V) = g(\lambda)F(V)$, where $F(\cdot)$ is the homogeneous function, V is a vector of arguments, $\lambda > 0$ is any constant, and $g(\cdot)$ is some strictly increasing positive function. Special cases include *homogeneous of degree N* (see below) and *linearly homogeneous* (page 164).

Homogeneous good

A good all units of which are the same; a *homogeneous product* (page 129).

Homogeneous of degree 1

The same as *linearly homogeneous* (page 164) and, for a *production function* (page 220), *constant returns to scale* (page 47). See *homogeneous of degree N* (below).

Homogeneous of degree N

A *homogeneous function* (see above) where the monotonic function is the constant raised to the exponent N: $F(\lambda V) = \lambda^N F(V)$. For $N > 1$, see *increasing returns to scale* (page 138); for $N < 1$, see *decreasing returns to scale* (page 63).

Homogeneous of degree zero

The property of a function that, if you scale all arguments by the same proportion, the value of the function does not change. See *homogeneous of degree N* (page 128). In the *HO model* (page 128), *CRTS* (page 56) *production functions* (page 220) imply that *marginal products* (page 169) have this property, which is critical for *FPE* (page 112).

Homogeneous product

The product of an industry in which the outputs of different firms are indistinguishable. Contrasts with *differentiated product* (page 68).

Homohypallagic

Having a constant *elasticity of substitution* (page 84). One of the inventors of the *CES function* (page 36) tried to christen it this in *Minhas (1962)* (page 379), where he also explored its theoretical and empirical implications for the *Heckscher-Ohlin theorem* (page 126), but the name did not catch on.

Homothetic

A function of two or more arguments is homothetic if all ratios of its first partial derivatives depend only on the ratios of the arguments, not their levels. For competitive consumers or producers optimizing subject to homothetic utility or production functions, this means that ratios of goods demanded depend only on relative prices, not on income or scale.

Homothetic demand

Demand functions derived from *homothetic* (see above) preferences. The demand functions are not themselves literally homothetic.

Homothetic preferences

Together with *identical preferences* (page 132), this assumption is used for many propositions in trade theory, in order to assure that consumers with different incomes but facing the same prices will demand goods in the same proportions.

Homothetic tastes

Homothetic preferences (see above).

Horizontal discipline

The use of a rule, as in the regulations of trade policies under the *GATT* (page 116) or *GATS* (page 116), that applies across the board to all sectors of the economy.

Horizontal integration

Production of different varieties of the same product, or different products at the same level of processing, within a single firm. This may, but need not, take place in subsidiaries in different countries.

Horizontal intra-industry trade

Intra-industry trade (page 151) in which the exports and imports are at the same stage of processing. Likely due to *product differentiation* (page 220). Contrasts with *vertical IIT* (page 289).

Hormone dispute

See *beef hormone case* (page 21).

HOS model

Heckscher-Ohlin-Samuelson model (page 126).

Host country

The country into which a *foreign direct investment* (page 109) is made.

HOT

Heckscher-Ohlin theorem (page 126).

Hot money

Holdings of very *liquid* (page 164) assets, which may be sold or cashed on short notice and then removed from a country, often in response to expectations of *devaluation* (page 67) or other *financial crisis* (page 106).

HOV model

Heckscher-Ohlin-Vanek model (page 126).

HS

Harmonized system (page 125).

Hub and spoke integration

A pattern of economic *integration* (page 142) in which one country (the "hub") forms *preferential trading arrangements* (page 214) with two or more other countries (the "spokes") that do not form such arrangements with each other.

Human capital

1. The stock of knowledge and skill, embodied in an individual as a result of education, training, and experience, that makes him or her more productive.

2. The stock of knowledge and skill embodied in the population of an economy.

Hysteresis

1. The failure of an economic variable to return to its initial equilibrium after a temporary shock. For example, an industry or trade flow might disappear due to an exchange rate change, then not reappear after the change is reversed.

2. A time lag between a cause and an effect. (Though this seems to be the more standard dictionary definition, economists seem to prefer definition 1.)

IADB

Inter-American Development Bank (page 143).

IBRD

International Bank for Reconstruction and Development (page 145).

ICA

International commodity agreement (page 146).

Iceberg transport cost

A cost of transporting a good that uses up only some fraction of the good itself, rather than using any other resources. Based on the idea of floating an iceberg, which is costless except for the amount of the iceberg itself that melts. It is a very tractable way of modeling transport costs since it impacts no other market. Due to *Samuelson (1954)* (page 380).

ICOR

Incremental capital output ratio (page 138).

ICP

International comparison program (page 146).

ICSID

International Centre for Settlement of Investment Disputes (page 145).

IDA
International Development Association (page 146).

IDB
Inter-American Development Bank (page 143).

Identical preferences
The assumption that individuals — either within a country or in different countries — have the same preferences. To be useful, since individuals' and countries' incomes may differ, the assumption is often used together with *homothetic* (page 129) preferences.

IFC
International Finance Corporation (page 147).

IFI
International financial institution (page 147).

IIT
Intra-industry trade (page 151).

ILO
International Labor Organization (page 148).

Imbalance
1. Any departure from equality.
2. In the *balance of payments* (page 17), any *surplus* (page 262) or *deficit* (page 63).

IMF
International Monetary Fund (page 148).

IMF quota
The amount of money that each *IMF* (see above) member country is required to contribute to the institution, partly in their own currency and partly in U.S. dollars, gold, or other member-country currencies. A country's quota is based upon the country's *GDP* (page 122). Countries have voting power in the IMF in proportion to their IMF quotas.

Immigration
The *migration* (page 176) of people *into* a country.

Immiserizing growth
Economic growth that makes the country worse off. *Bhagwati (1958)* (page 372) *coined* (page 369) this term for growth that

expands exports and worsens the *terms of trade* (page 269) sufficiently that real income falls. *Johnson (1955)* (page 376) had shown that a market *distorted* (page 72) by a tariff could lose from growth and had also, independently, worked out conditions for Bhagwati's result.

Impairment

See *non-violation* (page 195).

Imperfect capital mobility

Any departure from *perfect capital mobility* (page 207), permitting interest rates or returns to capital to differ between countries.

Imperfect competition

Any departure from *perfect competition* (page 207). However, imperfect competition usually refers to one of the *market structures* (page 173) other than perfect competition.

Imperfectly competitive

Refers to an economic agent (firm or consumer), group of agents (industry), model, or analysis that is characterized by *imperfect competition* (see above). Contrasts with *perfectly competitive* (page 208).

Implicit price deflator

A broad measure of prices derived from separate estimates of real and nominal expenditures for *GDP* (page 122) or a subcategory of GDP. Without qualification the term refers to the GDP deflator and is thus an index of prices for everything that a country produces, unlike the *CPI* (page 54), which is restricted to consumption and includes prices of imports.

Implicit tariff

1. *Tariff revenue* (page 266) on a good or group of goods, divided by the corresponding value of imports. Often lower than the official or statutory tariff, due both to *PTAs* (page 222) and to failures in *customs collection* (page 60).

2. The difference between the price just inside a border and the price just outside it, especially in the case of a good protected by an import *quota* (page 226).

Import

1. A good that crosses into a country, across its border, for commercial purposes.

2. A product, which might be a service, that is provided to domestic residents by a foreign producer.

3. To cause a good or service to be an import under definitions 1 and/or 2.

Import authorization

The requirement that imports be authorized by a special agency before entering a country, similar to import *licensing* (page 163).

Import bias

1. Any *bias* (page 22) in favor of importing.

2. Applied to growth, it tends to mean a bias *against* importing, and against trading more generally. Thus growth that is based disproportionately on accumulation of the *factor* (page 101) used *intensively* (page 143) in the import-competing industry and/or *technological progress* (page 268) favoring that industry.

Import-competing

Refers to an industry that competes with imports. That is, in a two-good model with trade, one good is the export good and the other is the import-competing good.

Import demand elasticity

The *elasticity of demand for imports* (page 84) with respect to price.

Import duty

A *tariff* (page 264) on imports.

Import elasticity

Usually means the *import demand elasticity* (see above).

Import-export company

A firm whose business consists mainly of international trade: buying goods in one country and selling them in another, thus both exporting and importing. Same as *export-import company* (page 98).

Import license

The license to import under an import *quota* (page 226) or under *exchange controls* (page 93).

Import licensing

See *licensing* (page 163).

Import parity price

A price charged for a domestically produced good that is set equal to the domestic price of an equivalent imported good — thus the world price plus transport cost plus tariff.

Import penetration

A measure of the importance of imports in the domestic economy, either by sector or overall, usually defined as the value of imports divided by the value of *apparent consumption* (page 11).

Import price index

Price index (page 215) of the goods that a country *imports* (page 134).

Import promotion

Any policy that encourages imports. A policy of *export promotion* (page 99) generally has the side effect of stimulating imports as well. Today the term is more commonly used for policies used by developed countries intended to assist developing countries in exporting to them.

Import propensity

The *marginal propensity to import* (page 170) (or sometimes the *average propensity* (page 16), if they are different).

Import protection

See *protection* (page 222).

Import quota

See *quota* (page 226).

Import relief

Usually refers to some form of restraint of imports in a particular sector in order to assist domestic producers, and with the connotation that these producers have been suffering from competition with imports. If done formally under existing statutes, it is *administered protection* (page 6), but it may also be done informally using a *VER* (page 289).

Import substitute

A good produced on the domestic market that competes with imports, either as a *perfect substitute* (page 208) or as a *differentiated product* (page 68).

Import substituting industrialization

ISI — a strategy for economic development based on replacing imports with domestic production.

Import substitution

A strategy for *economic development* (page 79) that replaces imports with domestic production. It may be motivated by the *infant industry argument* (page 140), or simply by the desire to mimic the industrial structure of advanced countries. Contrasts with *export promotion* (page 99).

Import surcharge

A tax levied uniformly on most or all imports, in addition to already-existing tariffs.

Import surveillance

The monitoring of imports, usually by means of *automatic licensing* (page 15).

Import-weighted average tariff

See *trade weighted average tariff* (page 278).

Imports

The quantity or value of all that is *imported* (page 134) into a country.

Impossible trinity

The impossibility of combining all three of the following: *monetary independence* (page 179), *exchange rate stability* (page 95), and full *financial market integration* (page 106).

Impost

A tax or *tariff* (page 264). (This is not a commonly used word.)

Improve the terms of trade

To increase the *terms of trade* (page 269); that is, to increase the relative price of exports compared to imports. Because it represents an increase in what the country gets in return for what it gives up, this is associated with an improvement in the country's welfare, although whether that actually occurs depends on the reason prices change.

Improve the trade balance

This conventionally refers to an increase in exports relative to imports, which thus causes the *balance of trade* (page 18) to become larger if positive or smaller if negative. The terminology ignores that exports drain resources while imports satisfy domestic needs, and reflects instead the association of exports with either accumulation of wealth or jobs.

In kind

Referring to a payment made with goods instead of money.

Income

1. The amount of money (*nominal* (page 191) or *real* (page 228)) received by a person, household, or other economic unit per unit time in return for services provided or goods sold.

2. *National income* (page 185).

3. The return earned on an *asset* (page 13) per unit time.

Income disparity

Inequality of income, usually referring to differences in average *per capita* (page 207) incomes across countries.

Income distribution

A description of the fractions of a population that are at various levels of income. The larger are the differences in income, the "worse" the income distribution is usually said to be, the smaller the "better." International trade and *factor movements* (page 103) can alter countries' income distributions by changing prices of low- and high-paid *factors* (page 101).

Income effect

That portion of the effect of price on quantity demanded that reflects the change in real income due to the price change. Contrasts with *substitution effect* (page 260).

Income elastic

Having an *income elasticity* (see below) greater than one.

Income elasticity

Normally the income elasticity of demand; that is, the *elasticity* (page 83) of demand with respect to income.

Income inelastic

Having an *income elasticity* (see above) less than one.

Income redistribution argument for a tariff

The argument that tariffs should be used in order to redistribute income towards the poor. In a rich country, where unskilled labor is the scarce factor, this can make sense as explained in the *Stolper-Samuelson theorem* (page 258), but it is a *second-best argument* (page 243).

Incomplete information

See *complete information* (page 44).

Incomplete specialization

Production of goods that compete with imports.

INCOTERMS

International commercial terms; that is, the language of international commerce.

Increasing opportunity cost

The characteristic of an economy that the *opportunity cost* (page 200) of a good rises as it produces more of it, resulting in a *transformation curve* (page 279) that is *concave* (page 45) to the origin. In the *HO model* (page 126), this happens in spite of *CRTS* (page 56) if sectors have different *factor intensities* (page 102).

Increasing returns to scale

A property of a *production function* (page 220) such that changing all inputs by the same proportion changes output more than in proportion. Common forms include *homogeneous of degree greater than one* (page 128) and production with constant *marginal cost* (page 169) but positive *fixed cost* (page 108). Also called **economies of scale**, **scale economies**, and simply **increasing returns**. Contrasts with *decreasing returns* (page 63) and *constant returns* (page 47).

Incremental capital output ratio

The amount of additional *capital* (page 30) that a *developing country* (page 67) requires to increase its output by one unit; thus the reciprocal of the *marginal product* (page 169) of capital. Used as an (inverse) indicator of how efficiently a country is using the scarce capital it acquires.

Indebtedness

The amount that is owed; thus amount of an entity's (individual, firm, or government's) financial obligations to creditors.

Index

A quantitative measure, usually of something the measurement of which is not straightforward, such as an average of many diverse prices, or a concept such as economic development or human rights.

Index number

A numerical *index* (see above), usually indicating, by comparison with a base value of 100, the size of the index relative to a base year or other benchmark for comparison. Thus, for example, a *CPI* (page 54) of 115 in 2004 with a base year of 1999 means that prices have risen 15% from 1999 to 2004.

Index number problem

A question the answer to which depends on a choice of weights. E.g., the effect of trade on the *real wage* (page 229) of labor in the *specific factors model* (page 253) is an index number problem, depending on how much workers consume of (lower-priced) imported and (higher-priced) exported goods.

Index of openness

Openness index (page 200).

Indifference curve

A means of representing the preferences and wellbeing of consumers. Formally, it is a curve representing the combinations of arguments in a *utility function* (page 287) that yield a given level of utility.

Indirect exchange rate

The foreign-currency price of a unit of domestic currency. (This definition appears in several places, but it is a mystery to me why this is any less direct than its reciprocal.)

Industrial concentration

The extent to which a small number of firms dominates an industry, often measured by a *concentration ratio* (page 46) or by a *Herfindahl index* (page 127). Concentration is, in effect, the opposite of *competition* (page 44), although in an open economy imports complicate the relationship.

Industrial policy

Government policy to influence which industries expand and, perhaps implicitly, which contract, via *subsidies* (page 260), *tax breaks* (page 266), and other aids for favored industries. The purpose, aside from political favor, may be to foster *competitive advantage* (page 44) where there are beneficial *externalities* (page 100) and/or *scale economies* (page 241).

Industrialization

The establishment and subsequent growth of industrial production in a country, usually meaning heavy manufacturing.

Inelastic

Having an elasticity less than one. For a *price elasticity* (page 215) of *demand* (page 65), this means that expenditure falls as price falls. For an *income elasticity* (page 137) it means that expenditure share falls with rising income. Contrasts with *elastic* (page 83) and *unit elastic* (page 284).

Inelastic offer curve

An *offer curve* (page 196) with *inelastic* (see above) demand for imports. That inelasticity implies that exports decline as imports increase, and it therefore means that the offer curve is *backward bending* (page 16). Strictly speaking, the natural definition of an offer curve's elasticity would be negative in this case, not just less than one, but that definition is seldom used.

Inequality

Differences in *per capita* (page 207) income or household income across populations within a country or across countries.

Infant industry argument

The theoretical rationale for *infant industry protection* (see below).

Infant industry protection

Protection (page 222) of a newly established domestic industry that is less productive than foreign producers. If productivity will rise with experience enough to pass *Mill's* (page 177) and *Bastable's* (page 21) tests, there is a *second-best* (page 242) argument for protection. The term is very old, but a classic treatment may be found in *Baldwin (1969)* (page 371).

Inferior good

A good the demand for which falls as income rises. The *income elasticity* (page 137) of demand is therefore negative.

Inflation

Increase in the overall price level of an economy, usually as measured by the *CPI* (page 54) or by the *implicit price deflator* (page 133).

Inflation adjusted

Adjusted for inflation (page 5).

Inflation rate

The percentage increase in the price level per year. See *inflation* (above).

Infrastructure

The facilities that must be in place in order for a country or area to function as an economy and as a state, including the capital needed for transportation, communication, and provision of water and power, and the institutions needed for security, health, and education.

Injury

Harm to an industry's owners and/or workers. Import protection under the *safeguards* (page 240), *AD* (page 4), and *CVD* (page 60) provisions of the *GATT* (page 116) require a finding of *serious* (page 244) (for safeguards) or *material* (page 174) (for AD/CVD) injury (as determined by, in the U.S., the *ITC* (page 153)). Known as the **injury test**.

Innovation

The creation or introduction of something new, especially a new product or a new way of producing something.

Input-output

Refers to the structure of *intermediate transactions* (page 144) among industries, in which one industry's output is an input to another, or even to itself.

Input-output table

A table of all inputs and outputs of an economy's industries, including *intermediate transactions* (page 144), primary inputs, and sales to final users. As developed by Wassily Leontief, the table can be used to calculate *gross outputs* (page 122) and primary factor inputs needed to produce specified *net outputs* (page 189). *Leontief (1954)* (page 378) used this to find the *factor content* (page 102) of U.S. trade, generating the *Leontief paradox* (page 160).

Instability

The property of not being *stable* (page 255); thus, moving around over time, and/or uncertain in its movement over time.

Instrument

1. An economic variable that is controlled by policy makers and can be used to influence other variables, called *targets* (page 263). Examples are *monetary* (page 178) and *fiscal policies* (page 107) used to achieve *external* (page 100) and *internal balance* (page 144).

2. See *financial instrument* (page 106).

Integrated world economy

A hypothetical, theoretical benchmark in which both goods and *factors* (page 101) move costlessly between countries. The IWE is associated with a rectangular diagram depicting allocation of factors to countries, showing conditions for *FPE* (page 112). The name was coined by *Dixit and Norman (1980)* (page 374), but the concept and technique was introduced by *Travis (1964)* (page 382). Refer to diagrams on page 305.

Integration

Economic integration refers to reducing barriers among countries to transactions and to movements of goods, capital, and labor, including harmonization of laws, regulations, and standards. Common forms include *FTAs* (page 114), *customs unions* (page 60), and *common markets* (page 41). Sometimes classified as *shallow integration* (page 245) vs. *deep integration* (page 63).

Intellectual property

Products of the mind, such as inventions, works of art, music, writing, film, etc.

Intellectual property protection

Laws that establish and maintain ownership rights to intellectual property. The principal forms of *IP* (page 152) protection are patents, trademarks, and copyrights.

Intellectual property right

The right to control and derive the benefits from something one has invented, discovered, or created.

Intensive

Of production, using a relatively large amount of an input. See *factor intensity* (page 102).

Inter-American development bank

A *development bank* (page 67) for the countries of Latin America and the Caribbean.

Interbank rate

The rate of interest charged by a bank on a loan to another bank. See *LIBOR* (page 163).

Interdependence

See *economic interdependence* (page 80).

Interest

The amount paid by a borrower to a lender above the amount (the *principal* (page 217)) that has been borrowed.

Interest bearing account

An account in a bank or other financial institution that pays *interest* (see above) to the depositor.

Interest equalization tax

A tax levied between 1963 and 1974 by the United States of 15% on interest received from foreign borrowers, intended to discourage *capital outflows* (page 33).

Interest parity

Equality of returns on otherwise identical financial assets denominated in different currencies. May be *uncovered* (page 282), with returns including expected changes in exchange rates, or *covered* (page 53), with returns including the *forward premium* (page 111) or discount. Also called **interest rate parity**.

Interest rate

The rate of return on bonds, loans, or deposits. When one speaks of "the" interest rate, it is usually in a model where there is only one.

Interest rate parity

Interest parity (see above).

Inter-industry trade

Trade in which a country's exports and imports are in different industries. Typical of models of *comparative advantage* (page 42), such as the *Ricardian model* (page 237) and *Heckscher-Ohlin model* (page 126). Contrasts with *intra-industry trade* (page 151).

Intermediate good

Same as *intermediate input* (see below).

Intermediate input

An input to production that has itself been produced and that, unlike *capital* (page 30), is used up in production. As an input it is in contrast to a *primary input* (page 217) and as an output it is in contrast to a *final good* (page 105). A very large portion of international trade is in intermediate inputs.

Intermediate transaction

The sale of a product by one firm to another, presumably to be used as an *intermediate input* (see above).

Intermittent dumping

Dumping (page 76) that occurs for short periods of time, presumably to dispose of temporary surpluses of goods and not intended to eliminate competition. Same as *sporadic dumping* (page 254).

Intermodalism

The use of more than one form (mode) of transportation, as when a shipment travels by both sea and rail.

Internal balance

A *target* (page 263) level for domestic aggregate economic activity, such as a level of *GDP* (page 122) that minimizes unemployment without being inflationary. See the *assignment problem* (page 13). Contrasts with *external balance* (page 100).

Internal debt

The amount owed by a country to, in effect, itself. It includes, for example, the portion of the *government debt* (page 120) that is denominated in the country's own currency and held by domestic residents.

Internal economies of scale

Economies of scale (page 81) that are internal to a firm; that is, the firm's average costs fall as its own output rises. Likely to be inconsistent with *perfect competition* (page 207). Contrasts with *external economies of scale* (page 100).

Internal market

Term used for a target of European *integration* (page 142), which would remove all barriers between national markets so that they would become, in effect, a single European market.

Internalization

One of the three pillars of the *OLI paradigm* (page 197) for understanding *FDI* (page 105) and the formation of *multinational enterprises* (page 183), this refers to the advantage that a firm derives from keeping multiple activities within the same organization.

Internalize

To cause, usually by a tax or subsidy, an *external* (page 100) cost or benefit of someone's actions to be experienced by them directly, so that they will take it into account in their decisions.

International

Involving transactions or relations between nations. The term, according to *Suganami (1978)* (page 381), was coined by *Bentham (1789)* (page 372).

International adjustment process

1. Any mechanism for change in international markets.

2. The mechanism by which *payments imbalances* (page 206) diminish under *pegged exchange rates* (page 207) and *non-sterilization* (page 194). Similar to the *specie flow mechanism* (page 252), *exchange-market intervention* (page 94) causes *money supplies* (page 180) of *surplus* (page 262) countries to expand and vice versa, leading to price and interest rate changes that correct the *current* (page 58) and *capital account* (page 30) imbalances.

International Bank for Reconstruction and Development

The largest of the five institutions that comprise the *World Bank* (page 293) Group, IBRD provides loans and development assistance to middle-income countries and creditworthy poorer countries.

International Centre for Settlement of Investment Disputes

One of the five institutions that comprise the *World Bank* (page 293) Group, ICSID provides facilities for the settlement — by conciliation or arbitration — of investment disputes between foreign investors and their host countries.

International Cocoa Organization
An intergovernmental organization set up in 1973 to administer the International Cocoa Agreement, the most recent version of which was negotiated in 2001. See *international commodity agreement* (below).

International Coffee Organization
An intergovernmental organization set up in 1963 that administers the International Coffee Agreement. See *international commodity agreement* (below).

International commodity agreement
An agreement among producing and consuming countries to improve the functioning of the global market for a *commodity* (page 41). May be administrative, providing information, or economic, influencing world price, usually using a *buffer stock* (page 27) to *stabilize* (page 255) it. ICAs are overseen by *UNCTAD* (page 283).

International comparison program
A program currently coordinated by the *World Bank* (page 293) to gather extensive information about prices in many countries so as to ascertain the purchasing power of their currencies and thus permit international comparisons of *real incomes* (page 228).

International competitiveness
See *competitiveness* (page 44).

International Cotton Advisory Committee
An association of governments dealing with cotton. It grew out of an International Cotton Meeting in 1939. See *international commodity agreement* (above).

International Development Association
One of the five institutions that comprise the *World Bank* (page 293) Group, IDA provides interest free loans and other services to the poorest countries.

International economics
The study of economic interactions among countries — including *trade* (page 272), *investment* (page 151), financial transactions,

and movement of people — and the policies and institutions that influence them.

International exhaustion

See *exhaustion* (page 96).

International factor movement

The international movement of any *factor* (page 101) of production, including primarily labor and capital. Thus includes *migration* (page 176) and *foreign direct investment* (page 109). Also may include the movement of *financial capital* (page 106) in the form of international borrowing and lending.

International finance

The monetary side of international economics, in contrast to the *real* (page 228) side, or *real trade* (page 229). Often called also *international monetary economics* (page 148) or *international macroeconomics* (page 148), each term has a slightly different meaning, and none seems entirely right for the entire field. "International finance" is best for the study of international financial markets including exchange rates.

International Finance Corporation

One of the five institutions that comprise the *World Bank* (page 293) Group, IFC promotes growth in the developing world by financing private sector investments and providing technical assistance and advice to governments and businesses.

International financial institution

Usually refers to intergovernmental organizations dealing with financial issues, most often the *IMF* (page 132) and/or the *World Bank* (page 293).

International Fisher effect

The theory that exchange-rate changes will match, or be expected to match, international differences in nominal interest rates. It follows from the (domestic) *Fisher effect* (page 107) together with *purchasing power parity* (page 223).

International Grains Council

An intergovernmental organization, concerned with grains trade, that administers the Grains Trade Convention of 1995. See *international commodity agreement* (page 146).

International institution

An organization established by multiple national governments, usually to administer a program or pursue a purpose that the governments have agreed upon.

International investment

1. International *capital movement* (page 33)

2. *Foreign direct investment* (page 109).

International Jute Organization

The organization set up in 1984 to implement the International Agreement on Jute and Jute Products, 1982. See *international commodity agreement* (page 146).

International Labor Organization

A United Nations specialized agency that establishes and monitors compliance with international standards for human and labor rights.

International Lead and Zinc Study Group

The international organization formed in 1959 to share information about lead and zinc. See *international commodity agreement* (page 146).

International liquidity

Refers to the adequacy of a country's *international reserves* (page 149).

International macroeconomics

Same as *international finance* (page 147), but with more emphasis on the international determination of macroeconomic variables such as *national income* (page 185) and the *price level* (page 216).

International monetary economics

Same as *international finance* (page 147), but with more emphasis on the role of money and less on other financial assets.

International Monetary Fund

An organization formed originally to help countries to stabilize exchange rates, but today pursuing a broader agenda of financial stability and assistance. As of January 2006, it had 184 member countries.

International Olive Oil Council
The intergovernmental organization in charge of administering the International Olive Oil Agreement, which originated in 1956. See *international commodity agreement* (page 146).

International Organization for Migration
International organization assisting migrants and the management of migration.

International parity conditions
Refers collectively to *purchasing power parity* (page 223) and *interest parity* (page 143).

International political economy
A field of study within social science, especially political science, that addresses the interrelationships between *international economics* (page 146) and political forces and institutions.

International reserves
The assets denominated in foreign currency, plus gold, held by a central bank, sometimes for the purpose of *intervening* (page 150) in the *exchange market* (page 94) to influence or peg the *exchange rate* (page 94). Usually includes foreign currencies themselves (especially US dollars), other assets denominated in foreign currencies, gold, and a small amount of *SDRs* (page 242).

International Rubber Study Group
An intergovernmental organization, founded in 1944, that provides a forum for the discussion of matters affecting the supply and demand for both synthetic and natural rubber. See *international commodity agreement* (page 146).

International specialization
See *specialization* (page 252).

International Sugar Organization
An intergovernmental body that administers the International Sugar Agreement of 1992. See *international commodity agreement* (page 146).

International trade
See *trade* (page 272).

International Trade Administration

A part of the United States Department of Commerce, the ITA acts on behalf of U.S. businesses in global competition. In trade policy, its import administration has the duty of determining whether imports are dumped or subsidized.

International Trade Commission

An independent, quasi-judicial federal agency of the U.S. government that provides information and expertise to the legislative and executive branches of government and directs actions against unfair trade practices. In trade policy, its commissioners assess injury in cases filed under the *escape clause* (page 88), *antidumping* (page 4), and *countervailing duty* (page 52) statutes.

International Trade Organization

Conceived as a complement to the *Bretton Woods* (page 26) institutions — the *IMF* (page 132) and *World Bank* (page 293) — the ITO was to provide international discipline in the uses of trade policies. The *Havana charter* (page 125) for the ITO was not approved by the United States Congress, however, and the initiative died, replaced by the continuing and growing importance of the *GATT* (page 116).

International Tropical Timber Organization

An organization created in 1983 for consultation among producers and consumers of tropical timber. An objective was that all timber traded by members should originate from sustainably managed forests.

Internationalization

Another term for *fragmentation* (page 112). Used by *Grossman and Helpman (1999)* (page 375).

Intertemporal

Occurring across time, or across different periods of time.

Intertemporal trade

Trade across time, as when a country imports in one time period paying for the imports with exports in a different time period, earlier or later. An *imbalance* (page 132) in the *balance of trade* (page 18) is presumed to reflect intertemporal trade.

Intervention

See *exchange market intervention* (page 94).

Intervention currency

A currency that is commonly used by *central banks* (page 35) for *exchange market intervention* (page 94). See *reserve currency* (page 235).

Intra-industry trade

Trade in which a country exports and imports in the same industry, in contrast to *inter-industry trade* (page 143). Ubiquitous in the data, much IIT is due to *aggregation* (page 8). Can be *horizontal* (page 130) or *vertical* (page 289). *Grubel and Lloyd (1975)* (page 375) wrote the book on IIT.

Intramediate trade

Another term for *fragmentation* (page 112). Used by *Antweiler and Trefler (2002)* (page 371).

Intra-product specialization

Another term for *fragmentation* (page 112). Used by *Arndt (1997)* (page 371).

Inventories

Goods being kept on hand for future use in production or future sale.

Invertible

Said of a matrix if its inverse exists. That is, a matrix A is invertible if there exists another matrix B such that $BA = I$, where I is the identity matrix.

Investment

1. Addition to the stock of *capital* (page 30) of a firm or country.
2. Purchase of an *asset* (page 13), real or financial.
3. The use of resources today for the purpose of increasing productivity or income in the future.

Invisible

In referring to international trade, used as a synonym for "*service* (page 244)." "Invisibles trade" is trade in services. Contrasts with *visible* (page 289).

Invoice

The itemized bill for a transaction, stating the nature of the transaction and its cost. In international trade, the **invoice price** is often the preferred basis for levying an *ad valorem tariff* (page 5).

IOM
International Organization for Migration (page 149).

IP
Intellectual property (page 142).

IPE
International political economy (page 149).

IPRs
Intellectual property rights (page 142).

IRS
Increasing returns to scale (page 138) = IRTS.

IRTS
Increasing returns to scale (page 138).

IS curve
In the *IS-LM model* (see below), the curve representing the combinations of national income and interest rate at which aggregate demand equals supply for goods. It is normally downward sloping because a rise in income increases output by more than aggregate demand (through consumption), while a rise in the interest rate reduces aggregate demand through investment.

ISI
Import substituting industrialization (page 136).

IS-LM model
A Keynesian macroeconomic model, popular especially in the 1960s, in which national income and the interest rate were determined by the intersection of two curves, the *IS curve* (see above) and the *LM curve* (page 165).

IS-LM-BP diagram
See *IS-LM-BP model* (below).

IS-LM-BP model
A particular version of the *Mundell-Fleming model* (page 183) that extends the *IS-LM model* (see above) by including in the *diagram* (page 308) a third line, called the *BP curve* (page 25), representing the *balance of payments* (page 17) and/or the *exchange market* (page 94).

Iso-price curve
A curve along which price is (or prices are) constant, most commonly in *factor-price space* (page 104) where it shows the

combinations of prices of *factors* (page 101) consistent with zero profit in producing a good at a specified price of the good.

Isocost line

A line along which the cost of something — usually a combination of two *factors* (page 101) of production — is constant. Since these are usually drawn for given prices, which are therefore constant along the line, an isocost line is usually a straight line, with slope equal to the ratio of the (factor) prices.

Isoquant

A curve representing the combinations of *factor* (page 101) inputs that yield a given level of output in a *production function* (page 220).

Israel-US Free Trade Area

A *free trade area* (page 113) between the United States and Israel that was initiated in 1985.

ITA

International Trade Administration (page 150)

ITC

International Trade Commission (page 150).

ITO

International Trade Organization (page 150).

IWE

Integrated world economy (page 142).

J-curve

The dynamic path followed by the balance of trade in response to a devaluation, which typically causes the trade balance to worsen before it improves, tracing a path that looks like a letter "J".

Joint venture

An undertaking by two parties for a specific purpose and duration, taking any of several legal forms. Two corporations, for example, perhaps from two different countries, may undertake to provide a product or service that is distinct, in kind or location, from what the companies do on their own.

Jones Act

A U.S. law that prohibits foreign ships from transporting goods or people between one U.S. location and another. Such a restriction on *cabotage* (page 29) is an example of a barrier to *trade in a service* (page 274).

Jones' hat algebra

See *hat algebra* (page 125).

Jubilee 2000

A movement advocating the cancellation of debts that burden developing countries, intended to occur in the year 2000.

JV

Joint venture (page 153).

Kaldor-Hicks criterion

The criterion that, for a change in policy or policy regime to be viewed as beneficial, the gainers should be able to compensate the losers and still be better off. The criterion does *not* require that the *compensation* (page 43) actually be paid, which, if it did, would make this the same as the *Pareto criterion* (page 204). Due to *Kaldor (1939)* (page 376), *Hicks (1940)* (page 375).

Kaleidoscope comparative advantage

A variant of *fragmentation* (page 112) due to *Bhagwati and Dehejia (1994)* (page 372).

Keiretsu

A group, or network, of manufacturing and other companies in Japan, usually centered around a bank and including a trading company. Keiretsus are characterized by cross-ownership of shares, strategic coordination, and preference for transactions within the network.

Kemp-Wan theorem

The proposition, due to *Kemp and Wan (1976)* (page 377), that any group of countries can form a *customs union* (page 60) that is *Pareto improving* (page 204) for the world, so long as non-distorting lump-sum transfers within the union are possible. This is accomplished by setting the vector of *common external tariffs* (page 41) so as to leave world prices unchanged.

Kennedy Round

The sixth *round* (page 239) of multilateral trade negotiations that was held under *GATT* (page 116) auspices, commencing 1964 and completed 1967. It was the first to move beyond negotiating only tariff reductions into such trade rules as *anti-dumping* (page 10).

Keynesian

Referring to models of the aggregate economy based on ideas stemming from *Keynes (1936)* (page 377). Keynesian models depart from *neoclassical* (page 187) assumptions primarily by allowing for *disequilibrium* (page 71) in labor markets, with aggregate employment and output being determined instead by *aggregate demand* (page 8).

Kuznets curve

An inverse U-shaped relationship between per capita income and inequality, suggesting that inequality is low in very poor countries, rises as they develop, and then ultimately falls as income rises still further. Hypothesized by *Kuznets (1955)* (page 377).

Labeling

A requirement to label imported goods with information about how they were produced. This is often suggested as an alternative to trade restrictions as a means to pursue particular trade-related objectives involving, for example, *environment* (page 87) or *labor standards* (page 156).

Labor abundant
A country is labor abundant if its *endowment* (page 86) of labor is large compared to other countries. Relative labor abundance can be defined by either the *quantity definition* (page 224) or the *price definition* (page 215).

Labor augmenting
Said of a *technological change* (page 268) or *technological difference* (page 268) if one production function produces the same as if it were the other, but with a larger quantity of labor. Same as *factor augmenting* (page 101) with labor the augmented factor. Also called *Harrod neutral* (page 125).

Labor force
The number of available workers in a country, defined as the sum of those who are employed and those who are classed as *unemployed* (page 283).

Labor intensive
Describing an industry or sector of the economy that relies relatively heavily on inputs of labor, usually relative to capital but sometimes to human capital or skilled labor, compared to other industries or sectors. See *factor intensity* (page 102).

Labor productivity
The value of output per unit of labor input. The reciprocal of the *unit labor requirement* (page 284).

Labor right
See *labor standard* (below).

Labor saving
A *technological change* (page 268) or *technological difference* (page 268) that is *biased* (page 22) in favor of using less labor, compared to some definition of *neutrality* (page 189).

Labor scarce
A country is labor scarce if its *endowment* (page 86) of labor is small compared to other countries. Relative labor scarcity can be defined by either the *quantity definition* (page 224) or the *price definition* (page 215).

Labor standard
Any of many conditions of workers in the workplace that are viewed as important for their wellbeing, and minimum levels

of which are advocated by labor rights activists and have been
agreed to by many of the countries that are members of the *ILO*
(page 132).

Labor standards argument for protection
    The view that trade restrictions (*trade sanctions* (page 277))
    should be used as a tool to improve *labor standards* (page 156),
    limiting imports, for example, from countries that do not en-
    force such labor rights as freedom of association and collective
    bargaining.

Labor theory of value
    The theory that the value of any produced good or service
    is equal to the amount of labor used, directly and indirectly,
    to produce it. Sometimes said to underlie the *Ricardian model*
    (page 237) of international trade.

Labor using
    A *technological change* (page 268) or *technological difference*
    (page 268) that is *biased* (page 22) in favor of using more la-
    bor, compared to some definition of *neutrality* (page 189).

Laffer curve
    An inverse-U-shaped curve representing tax revenue as a func-
    tion of the tax rate, attributed to Arthur Laffer. Although the
    idea that a rise in tax rate can reduce tax revenue is mostly
    based on induced reduction of work effort, for some types of
    taxes — especially corporate — movement of activity to another
    tax jurisdiction or country can have the same effect.

LAFTA
    Latin American Free Trade Association (page 158).

Lagging indicator
    A measurable economic variable that varies over the *business cy-
    cle* (page 28), reaching *peaks* (page 206) and *troughs* (page 281)
    somewhat later than other macroeconomic variables such as
    GDP (page 122) and *unemployment* (page 283). Contrasts with
    leading indicator (page 159).

Lagrangian
    A function constructed in solving economic models that include
    maximization of a function (the "objective function") subject
    to constraints. It equals the objective function minus, for each

constraint, a variable "Lagrange multiplier" times the amount by which the constraint is violated.

LAIA
Latin American Integration Association (see below).

Laissez faire
Free enterprise (page 112). The doctrine or system of government non-interference in the economy except as necessary to maintain *economic freedom* (page 79). Includes *free trade* (page 113).

Land reform
The process of changing the pattern of ownership of land in a country, usually by breaking up large holdings and distributing smaller parcels of land to a larger portion of the population. This can be done in various ways, including with or without compensation of the previous owners.

Large country
A country that is large enough for its international transactions to affect economic variables abroad, usually for its trade to matter for world prices. Contrasts with a *small open economy* (page 248).

Latin American Free Trade Association
A group of Latin American countries formed in 1960 with the aim of establishing a *free trade area* (page 113). This aim was never achieved, and LAFTA was replaced in 1980 with the *Latin American Integration Association* (see below).

Latin American Integration Association
An organization of Latin American countries that replaced the failed *LAFTA* (page 157). LAIA has the more limited goal of encouraging free trade but with no timetable for achieving it.

Laurel-Langley agreement
A trade agreement between the Philippines and the United States, signed in 1955 and expired in 1974, whereby Americans were given some of the same rights as Filipinos within the Philippines.

Laursen-Metzler effect
See *Harberger-Laursen-Metzler effect* (page 124).

Law of comparative advantage

The principle that, given the freedom to respond to market forces, countries will tend to export goods for which they have *comparative advantage* (page 42) and import goods for which they have comparative disadvantage, and that they will experience *gains from trade* (page 116) by doing so. *For more on the origin of this term, please see page 367.*

Law of demand

The observation that when price rises, quantity demanded falls. This is not necessary in theory, but it is *very* rarely violated in practice, including in demands for imports and exports, as well as demand for foreign exchange (barring effects on expectations).

Law of diminishing returns

The principle that, in any *production function* (page 220), as the input of one *factor* (page 101) rises holding other factors fixed, the *marginal product* (page 169) of that factor must eventually decline.

Law of one price

The principle that identical goods should sell for the same price throughout the world if trade were *free* (page 113) and *frictionless* (page 114).

LDC

For many years, the acronym LDC has stood for *less developed country* (page 161), which was more or less the same as *developing country* (page 67). However, in recent years LDC has also been used for *least developed country* (page 160), which has a narrower and more formal definition.

Leading indicator

A measurable economic variable that varies over the *business cycle* (page 28), reaching *peaks* (page 206) and *troughs* (page 281) somewhat earlier than other macroeconomic variables such as *GDP* (page 122) and *unemployment* (page 283), and therefore useful for forecasting them. Contrasts with *lagging indicator* (page 157).

Learning by doing

Refers to the improvement in *technology* (page 268) that takes place in some industries, early in their history, as they learn by experience, so that *average cost* (page 16) falls as accumulated output rises. See *infant industry protection* (page 140), *dynamic economies of scale* (page 77).

Learning curve

A relationship representing either *average cost* (page 16) or *average product* (page 16) as a function of the accumulated output produced. Usually reflecting *learning by doing* (see above), the learning curve shows cost falling, or average product rising.

Least developed country

A country designated by the *UN* (page 282) as least developed based on criteria of low per capita *GDP* (page 122), weak human resources (life expectancy, calorie intake, etc.), and a low level of economic diversification (share of manufacturing and other measures). As of 2003 there are 50 LDCs.

Lender of last resort

An institution that has the capacity and willingness to make loans when no one else can. Within a country, the *central bank* (page 35) may play that role, since it can create money. Some have argued that the *IMF* (page 132) or other institution should play that role internationally, to avert *financial crises* (page 106).

Leontief composite

A composite of two or more goods or factors that includes them in fixed proportions, analogous to the *Leontief technology* (page 161).

Leontief paradox

The finding of *Leontief (1954)* (page 378) that U.S. imports embodied a higher ratio of capital to labor than U.S. exports. This was surprising because it was thought that the U.S. was *capital abundant* (page 30), and the *Heckscher-Ohlin theorem* (page 126) would then predict that U.S. exports would be relatively *capital intensive* (page 32).

Leontief production function

See *Leontief technology* (page 161).

Leontief technology

A production function in which no substitution between inputs is possible: $F(V) = \min_i(V_i/a_i)$, where V is a vector of inputs V_i, and a_i are the constant per unit input requirements. *Isoquants* (page 153) are L-shaped.

Lerner diagram

The *diagram* (page 313) which, drawn for given prices and technology, uses *unit-value isoquants* (page 285) of two or more goods to deduce *patterns of specialization* (page 206) and *factor prices* (page 103) as they depend on goods prices and *factor endowments* (page 102). Due *originally* (page 369) to *Lerner (1952)* (page 378) and popularized by *Findlay and Grubert (1959)* (page 375).

Lerner paradox

The possibility, identified by *Lerner (1936)* (page 378), that a *tariff* (page 264) might worsen a country's *terms of trade* (page 269). This can happen only if the country spends a disproportionately large fraction of the tariff *revenue* (page 237) on the imported good, and it will not happen (from a *stable* (page 255) equilibrium) if the tariff revenue is *redistributed* (page 231). See *offer curve diagram* (page 196).

Lerner-Pearce diagram

This name is sometimes given (for years, by me at least) to the *Lerner diagram* (see above). In fact, *Pearce's (1952)* (page 380) diagram uses *unit isoquants* (page 284) rather than *unit value isoquants* (page 285) and is much more cumbersome.

Lerner Symmetry theorem

The proposition that a tax on all imports has the same effect as an equal tax on all exports, if the revenue is spent in the same way. The result depends critically on *balanced* (page 19) trade, as in a *real model* (page 229), so that a change in imports leads to an equal change in the value of exports. Due to *Lerner (1936)* (page 378).

Less developed country

Refers to any country whose per capita income is low by world standards. Same as **developing country**.

Letter of credit
A common means of payment in international trade, this is a written commitment by a bank to make payment to an exporter on behalf of an importer, under specified conditions.

Level playing field
The objective of those who advocate protection on the grounds the foreign firms have an unfair advantage. A level playing field would remove such advantages, although it is not usually clear what sorts of advantage (including *comparative advantage* (page 42)) would be permitted to remain. See *fairness argument for protection* (page 104).

Levy
1. To impose and collect a tax or tariff.
2. A tax or tariff.

Liability
An amount that is owed, in contrast to an *asset* (page 13). A liability may result from borrowing, from obligation to pay for a product or service received, etc.

Liberal
Associated with freedom and/or generosity. Thus in England to be liberal (or to be a liberal) is to favor free markets, including *free trade* (page 113). But in the U.S. it tends to mean favoring a generous, active government pursuing social and redistributive policies, with no implication for views on free trade.

Liberal trade
Free trade (page 113), or something approximating that. Thus a trade regime in which *tariffs* (page 264) are low or zero and in which *non-tariff barriers* (page 194) are largely absent.

Liberalism
The set of views associated with being *liberal* (see above), in the sense of freedom.

Liberalization
1. The process of making policies less constraining of economic activity.
2. Reduction of *tariffs* (page 264) and/or removal of *non-tariff barriers* (page 194).

LIBOR

London interbank offered rate (page 166).

Licensing

1. The requirement that importers and/or exporters get government approval prior to importing or exporting. Licensing may be *automatic* (page 15), or it may be **discretionary**, based on a *quota* (page 226), a *performance requirement* (page 208), or some other criterion.

2. Granting of permission, in return for a licensing fee, to use a *technology* (page 268). When done by firms in one country to firms in another, it is a form of *technology transfer* (page 268). See *compulsory licensing* (page 45).

Life cycle

See *product cycle* (page 220).

Life expectancy

The *expected value* (page 97) of the number of years a person has get to live at a given age or, if age is unspecified, at birth, based on the distribution of actual deaths in the population to which the person belongs. Life expectancy in a country is an important indicator of its level of development and wellbeing.

Light manufacturing

Sectors of the economy that produce manufactured goods without large amounts of *physical capital* (page 209), thus likely to be *labor intensive* (page 156).

Limit pricing

The act of setting a selling price just below the level at which other sellers would find it profitable to enter a market.

Linder hypothesis

The theory that a country's ability to export depends on domestic demand, so that countries that demand similar goods will trade more with each other than will countries with dissimilar demands. From *Linder (1961)* (page 378).

Linear regression model

A linear relationship between a dependent variable and one or more independent variables plus a *stochastic* (page 257) disturbance: $Y_i = b_0 + b_1 X_{1i} + \cdots + b_n X_{ni} + u_i$.

Linearly homogeneous

Homogeneous of degree 1 (page 128). Sometimes called **linear homogeneous**.

Linking scheme

A requirement that, in order to get an *import license* (page 134), the importer must buy a certain amount of the same product from local producers.

Liquid

Possessing *liquidity* (see below).

Liquid assets

The assets in a *portfolio* (page 211) that possess *liquidity* (see below), or the total value of those assets.

Liquidity

The capacity to turn assets into cash, or the amount of assets in a *portfolio* (page 211) that have that capacity. Cash itself (i.e., money) is the most **liquid** asset.

Liquidity crisis

A financial crisis that occurs due to lack of *liquidity* (see above). In *international finance* (page 147), it usually means that a government or central bank runs short of *international reserves* (page 149) needed to *peg its exchange rate* (page 207) and/or to service its foreign loans.

Liquidity trap

A situation in which expansionary *monetary policy* (page 179) fails to stimulate the economy. As used by *Keynes (1936)* (page 377), this meant interest rates so low that expectations of their increase made people unwilling to hold *bonds* (page 24). Today it usually means a *nominal* (page 191) *interest rate* (page 143) so near zero that lowering it further is impossible or ineffective.

Living wage

A *real* (page 228) *wage* (page 290) that is high enough for the worker and family to survive and remain healthy and comfortable, sometimes called meeting **basic needs**. Term is used in calling for higher wages in both developed and developing countries, where concepts of basic needs may be very different.

LM curve

In the *IS-LM model* (page 152), the curve representing combinations of income and interest rate at which demand for money equals the *money supply* (page 180) in the domestic *money market* (page 180). It is normally upward sloping because an increase in income increases demand for money while an increase in the interest rate reduces demand for money.

Loan

An amount, usually of money, conveyed by one to another in the expectation that it will be returned, perhaps with specified *interest* (page 143), at a later date. When the lender and borrower are in different countries with separate monetary and legal systems, loans bear extra *risk* (page 238).

Local content requirement

See *domestic content requirement* (page 74).

Local optimum

An *allocation* (page 9) that by some criterion is better than all those in its *neighborhood* (page 187).

Locational advantage

Any reason for a firm to locate production, or a stage of production, in a particular place, such as availability of a *natural resource* (page 186), *transport cost* (page 280), or *barriers to trade* (page 273). May explain why a country's firms succeed in trade, or why a *multinational firm* (page 183) locates there. (See *OLI* (page 197).)

Locomotive effect

The effect that economic expansion in one large country can have on other parts of the world economy, causing them to expand as well, as the large country demands more of their exports.

Logarithm

A particular mathematical transformation often used to express economic variables. Advantages: 1) If a variable grows at a constant percentage rate over time, the graph of its logarithm is a straight line. 2) A small change in the logarithm of a variable is approximately its percentage change.

Logrolling

The exchange of political favors, especially among legislators who agree to support each others' initiatives. Logrolling contributed importantly to the *Smoot-Hawley tariff* (page 248).

Lomé Convention

An agreement originally signed in 1975 committing the *EU* (page 89) to programs of assistance and preferential treatment for the *ACP countries* (page 4). The Lomé Convention was replaced by the *Cotonou agreement* (page 52) in June 2000.

London interbank offered rate

The *interest rate* (page 143) that the largest international banks charge each other for loans, usually of *Eurodollars* (page 90). In fact, LIBOR includes rates quoted each day for many currencies, excluding the euro, but it is the rate for dollar loans that is used as a benchmark for other transactions.

Long run

Referring to a long time horizon. This is not always well defined, but in trade models it usually means long enough for industries to vary the amounts of all factors they employ, and therefore for the factors to be mobile across industries. Contrasts with *short run* (page 245).

Long-term capital

In the *capital account* (page 30) of the *balance of payments* (page 17), long-term capital movements include *FDI* (page 105) and movements of *financial capital* (page 106) with maturity of more than one year (including *equities* (page 88)).

Lorenz curve

The graph of the percent of income owned by the poorest x percent of the population, for all x. Provides a picture of the income distribution within the population, and is used to construct the *Gini coefficient* (page 118).

Lost decade

There is, sadly, no single meaning for this term, as it has been applied to many episodes of economies that stagnated for most of a decade. Examples: Argentina and other Latin America in the 1980s; Japan in the 1990s; and the *least developed countries* (page 160) in the 1990s.

Louvre Accord

An agreement reached in 1987 among the central banks of France, Germany, Japan, U.S. and UK to stop the decline in the value of the US dollar that they had initiated at the *Plaza Accord* (page 209).

Love of variety

Preference for variety (page 213).

Ltd

The abbreviation used in the United Kingdom to represent a limited liability company, thus analogous to "Inc", for incorporated, in the United States.

Lump sum

Describes a tax or subsidy that does not distort behavior. By using a tax (or subsidy) in an amount (the lump sum) independent of any aspect of the payer's or recipient's behavior, it does not alter behavior. Non-distorting lump-sum taxes and subsidies do not exist, but they are a convenient fiction for theoretical analysis, especially of *gains from trade* (page 116).

M1

The smallest of several measures of the stock of money in an economy, this consisting primarily of *currency* (page 56) held by the public and *demand deposits* (page 65). Also includes several other very *liquid* (page 164) items: travelers checks and other accounts on which checks can be written.

M2

A measure of the stock of money in an economy that includes, in addition to all that is in *M1* (see above), savings deposits and other relatively *liquid* (page 164) assets such as small certificates of deposit and money market mutual funds.

Maastricht Treaty

The 1991 treaty among members of the *EU* (page 89) to work toward a monetary union, or common currency. This ultimately resulted in adoption of the *euro* (page 90) in 1999.

Macroeconomic

Referring to the variables or performance of an economy as a whole, or its major components, as opposed to that of individual industries, firms, or households.

Macroeconomic policy

Any policy intended to influence the behavior of important *macroeconomic* (see above) variables, especially *unemployment* (page 283) and *inflation* (page 141). Macroeconomic policies include *monetary* (page 179) and *fiscal* (page 107) policies, but also such things as *price controls* (page 215) and incentives for *economic growth* (page 79).

Made-to-measure tariff

A tariff set so as to raise the price of an imported good to the level of the domestic price, so as to leave domestic producers unaffected. Also called a *scientific tariff* (page 242).

Magnification effect

The property of the *Heckscher-Ohlin model* (page 126) that changes in certain exogenous variables lead to larger changes in the corresponding endogenous variables: goods prices as they affect factor prices in the *Stolper-Samuelson theorem* (page 258); factor endowments as they affect outputs in the *Rybczynski theorem* (page 239). Due to *Jones (1965)* (page 376).

MAI

Multilateral Agreement on Investment (page 182).

Managed float

An *exchange rate regime* (page 95) in which the rate is allowed to be determined in the *exchange market* (page 94) without an announced *par value* (page 204) as the goal of *intervention* (page 150), but the authorities do nonetheless intervene at their discretion to influence the rate.

Mandated countertrade

A requirement by government that importing firms engage in *countertrade* (page 52), as a means of increasing exports.

Manufactured good

A *good* (page 120) that is produced by *manufacturing* (see below).

Manufacturing

Production of *goods* (page 120) primarily by the application of labor and capital to raw materials and other intermediate inputs, in contrast to *agriculture* (page 8), mining, forestry, fishing, and *services* (page 244).

Maquiladora

A program for the temporary importation of goods into Mexico without duty, under the condition that they contribute — through further processing, transformation, or repair — to exports. The program was established in 1965, and expanded in 1989.

Marginal analysis

The determination of optimal behavior by comparing benefits and costs at the margin, that is, benefits and costs that result from small (i.e., marginal) changes. Optimality requires that marginal benefit equal marginal cost, since otherwise a rise or fall could increase benefit more than cost.

Marginal cost

The increase in cost that accompanies a unit increase in output; the partial derivative of the *cost function* (page 52) with respect to output.

Marginal product

In a *production function* (page 220), the marginal product of a *factor* (page 101) is the increase in output due to a unit increase in the input of the factor; that is, the partial derivative of the production function with respect to the factor. In a *competitive* (page 44) equilibrium, the equilibrium *price of any factor* (page 103) is its *marginal value product* (page 171) in every sector where it is employed.

Marginal profit

The amount by which a firm's *profit* (page 221) rises or falls when output increases by one unit; thus *marginal revenue* (page 170) minus *marginal cost* (see above).

Marginal propensity

The fraction of a change in income devoted to an activity, such as consumption, importing, or saving. See *propensity* (page 222).

Marginal propensity to consume

The fraction of a change in income (or perhaps *disposable income* (page 71)) spent on consumption. Contrasts with *average propensity to consume* (page 16).

Marginal propensity to import

The fraction of a change in income (or perhaps *disposable income* (page 71)) spent on imports. Contrasts with *average propensity to import* (page 16).

Marginal propensity to save

The fraction of a change in income (or perhaps *disposable income* (page 71)) that is saved.

Marginal rate of substitution

In a *production function* (page 220) or a *utility function* (page 287), the ratio at which one argument (input) substitutes for another along an *isoquant* (page 153) or *indifference curve* (page 139).

Marginal rate of technical substitution

More complete name for the *marginal rate of substitution* (see above) between *factors* (page 101) in a *production function* (page 220), sometimes used to distinguish it from the analogous concept in a *utility function* (page 287).

Marginal rate of transformation

The increase in output of one good made possible by a one-unit decrease in the output of another, given the technology and *factor endowments* (page 102) of a country; thus the absolute value of the slope of the *transformation curve* (page 279).

Marginal returns

1. Loosely, the extra that you get in return for doing more of something.

2. *Marginal product* (page 169).

Marginal revenue

The amount by which a firm's revenue increases when it expands output by one unit, taking into account that to sell one more unit it may need to reduce price on all units.

Marginal revenue product

The additional revenue generated by the extra output from employing one more unit of a *factor* (page 101) of production. In a competitive industry this equals the *marginal value product* (see below), but with *imperfect competition* (page 133) it is smaller, due to the implied price reduction. Determines factor prices in competitive factor markets.

Marginal utility

In a *utility function* (page 287), the increase in utility associated with a one-unit increase in consumption of one good; or the partial derivative of the utility function.

Marginal value product

The value of the *marginal product* (page 169) of a *factor* (page 101) in an industry; that is, the price of the good produced times the marginal product. Determines factor prices when all markets are competitive.

Marginalism

1. The belief that *marginal analysis* (page 169) provides a useful theory of economic behavior.

2. The belief that economic value reflects *marginal utility* (see above).

Marine Mammal Protection Act

The 1972 U.S. law prohibiting the "taking" (harassing, hunting, capturing, or killing) of marine mammals, and also prohibiting the import of any marine mammal product or any fish that has been associated with the taking of marine mammals. See *tuna-dolphin case* (page 281).

Market

1. The interaction between *supply* (page 261) and *demand* (page 65) to determine the *market price* (page 173) and corresponding quantity bought and sold.

2. The determination of economic *allocations* (page 9) by decentralized, voluntary interactions among those who wish to buy and sell, responding to freely determined *market prices* (page 173).

Market access

The ability of firms from one country to sell in another.

Market adjustment
The process by which the economy moves to a new *market equilibrium* (see below) when conditions change.

Market balance
Equality of supply and demand.

Market clearing
Equality of supply and demand. A **market-clearing condition** is an equation (or other representation) stating that supply equals demand. A **market-clearing price** is a price that causes supply and demand to be equal.

Market dynamics
The process by which *market adjustment* (see above) takes place. Common examples include *Walrasian* (page 290) and *Marshallian* (page 174).

Market economy
A country in which most economic decisions are left up to individual consumers and firms interacting through *markets* (page 171). Contrasts with *central planning* (page 36) and *nonmarket economy* (page 193).

Market equilibrium
Equality of supply and demand. See *equilibrium* (page 87).

Market failure
Any *market imperfection* (see below), but especially the complete absence of a market due to incomplete or *asymmetric information* (page 14).

Market imperfection
Any departure from the ideal benchmark of *perfect competition* (page 207), due to *externalities* (page 100), taxes, *market power* (page 173), etc.

Market mechanism
The process by which a market solves a problem allocating resources, especially that of deciding how much of a good or service should be produced, but other such problems as well. The market mechanism is an alternative, for example, to having such decisions made by government.

Market power

1. Ability of a firm or other market participant to influence price by varying the amount that it chooses to buy or sell.

2. Ability of a country to influence world prices by altering its trade policies.

Market price

The price at which a *market* (page 171) *clears* (page 39).

Market rate

The *interest rate* (page 143) or *exchange rate* (page 94) at which a *market* (page 171) *clears* (page 39).

Market structure

The way that suppliers and demanders in an industry interact to determine price and quantity. There are four main idealized market structures that have been used in trade theory: *perfect competition* (page 207), *monopoly* (page 180), *oligopoly* (page 197), and *monopolistic competition* (page 180).

Market value

See *factor cost* (page 102).

Marketing board

A form of *state trading enterprise* (page 256), a marketing board typically buys up the domestic supply of a good and sells it in the international market.

Markup

1. The amount (percentage) by which price exceeds marginal cost. A profit-maximizing seller facing a price *elasticity* (page 83) of demand η will set a markup equal to $(p - c)/p = 1/\eta$. One effect of international trade that increases competition is to reduce markups.

2. In *WTO* (page 293) terminology, sometimes used for the extent to which an *applied tariff* (page 11) exceeds the *bound rate* (page 25).

Marshall-Lerner condition

The condition that the sum of the elasticities of demand for exports and imports exceed one (in absolute value); that is, $\eta_X + \eta_M > 1$, where η_X, η_M are the *demand elasticities* (page 65) for a country's exports and imports respectively, both defined to be positive for downward sloping demands. Under certain assumptions, this is the condition for a *depreciation* (page 66) to *improve the trade balance* (page 136), for the *exchange market* (page 94) to be *stable* (page 255), and for international *barter* (page 20) exchange to be *stable* (page 255).

Marshall Plan

A U.S. program to assist the economic recovery of certain European countries after World War II. Also called the **European Recovery Program**, it was initiated in 1947 and it dispersed over $12 billion before it was completed in 1952.

Marshallian adjustment

A market *adjustment mechanism* (page 5) in which quantity rises when *demand price* (page 65) exceeds *supply price* (page 262) and falls when supply price exceeds demand price.

Marxist

Referring to the writings of Karl Marx and to a body of economic thought based, more or less loosely, on those writings.

Material injury

The *injury* (page 141) requirement of the *AD* (page 4) and *CVD* (page 60) statutes, understood to be less stringent than *serious injury* (page 244) but otherwise apparently not precisely defined.

Maximum price system

Similar to a *minimum price system* (page 177), except that the price specified is the highest, rather than the lowest, permitted for an imported good.

Maximum revenue tariff

A tariff set to collect the largest possible revenue for the government.

Meade geometry

The geometric technique introduced by *Meade (1952)* (page 378) of deriving a country's *offer curve* (page 196) from its *transformation curve* (page 279) and *community indifference curves* (page 42) by first constructing a set of *trade indifference curves* (page 275).

Mean

The arithmetic average of the values of an economic or statistical variable. For a variable x with values x_i, $i = 1, \ldots, n$, the mean is $\text{mean}(x) = \Sigma_{i=1 \ldots n}(x_i/n)$.

Measure of economic welfare

An aggregate figure that adjusts *GDP* (page 122) in an attempt to measure a country's economic wellbeing rather than its production, with adjustments for leisure, environmental degradation, etc.

Mercantilism

An economic philosophy of the 16th and 17th centuries that international commerce should primarily serve to increase a country's financial wealth, especially of gold and foreign currency. To that end, exports are viewed as desirable and imports as undesirable unless they lead to even greater exports.

Merchandise trade

Exports and imports of *goods* (page 120). Contrasts with trade in *services* (page 244).

MERCOSUR

A *common market* (page 41) among Argentina, Brazil, Paraguay and Uruguay, known as the "Common Market of the South" ("Mercado Comun del Sur"). It was created by the Treaty of Asunción on March 26, 1991, and added Chile and Bolivia as associate members in 1996 and 1997.

METI

Ministry of Economy, Trade and Industry (page 177).

Metzler paradox

The possibility, identified by *Metzler (1949)* (page 378), that a *tariff* (page 264) may lower the domestic *relative price* (page 233) of the imported good. This will happen if it drives the world price down by even more than the size of the tariff, as it may do if the foreign demand for the importing country's export good is *inelastic* (page 140).

MEW

Measure of economic welfare (see above).

MFA
Multifiber arrangement (page 182).
MFN
Most favored nation (page 181).
MFN rate
MFN tariff (see below).
MFN status
The status given by the U.S. to some non-members of the *GATT* (page 116)/*WTO* (page 293) whereby they are charged *MFN tariffs* (see below) even though they are eligible for higher tariffs. See *PNTR* (page 210).
MFN tariff
The tariff level that a member of the *GATT* (page 116)/*WTO* (page 293) charges on a good to other members.
Microeconomic
Referring to the behavior of and interactions among individual economic agents, especially firms and consumers, and especially in *markets* (page 171). Contrasts with *macroeconomic* (page 168).
Middle product
A good that has undergone some *processing* (page 219) and that requires further processing before going to final consumers; an *intermediate good* (page 144). *Sanyal and Jones (1982)* (page 381) introduced the term, observing that almost all international trade is of middle products, and they provided a model based on that assumption.
MIGA
Multilateral Investment Guarantee Agency (page 183).
Migration
The permanent relocation of people from one country to another. See *emigration* (page 85), *immigration* (page 132).
Millennium Round
The name suggested by the *European Union* (page 357) for the *trade round* (page 277) that they and others hoped would be initiated at the *Seattle Ministerial* (page 242) in 1999. That ministerial ended without agreement to start a new round.

Mill's test

One of two conditions needed for *infant industry protection* (page 140) to be welfare-improving, this requires that the protected industry become, over time, able to compete internationally without protection. See also *Bastable's test* (page 21).

Minimum efficient scale

The smallest output of a firm consistent with minimum *average cost* (page 16). In small countries, in some industries the level of demand in *autarky* (page 15) is not sufficient to support minimum efficient scale.

Minimum import price

See *minimum price system* (below).

Minimum price system

Specification of the lowest price permitted for an import. Prices below the minimum may trigger a *tariff* (page 264), hence a *variable levy* (page 288), or *quota* (page 226). See *maximum price system* (page 174). These have several names: **basic import price**, **minimum import price**, **reference price**, and **trigger price**.

Minister of International Trade

Title, in many but not all countries, of the *trade minister* (page 275).

Ministerial

A meeting of ministers. In the context of the *GATT* (page 116) and *WTO* (page 293), it is a meeting of the *trade ministers* (page 275) from the member countries (including, from the U.S., *USTR* (page 287)).

Ministry of Economy, Trade and Industry

The Japanese government ministry that deals with economic issues, including the vitality of the private sector, external economic relations, energy policy, and industrial development.

Ministry of International Trade and Industry

The Japanese government ministry that deals with trade and industrial policies. Established in 1949 as the Ministry of Commerce and Industry, MITI was renamed *METI* (page 175) as of January 6, 2000.

Missing trade
See *mystery of the missing trade* (page 184).

MITI
Ministry of International Trade and Industry (page 177).

Mixed economy
An economy in which some production is done by the private sector and some by the state, in *state-owned enterprises* (page 256).

Mixing regulation
1. Specification of the proportion of domestically produced *content* (page 48) in products sold on the domestic market.
2. Specification of an amount of domestically produced product that must be bought by an importer for given quantities of imports, under a *linking scheme* (page 164).

MNC
Multinational corporation (page 183).

MNE
Multinational enterprise (page 183).

Modality
Method or procedure. *WTO* (page 293) documents speak of modalities of negotiations, i.e., how the negotiations are to be conducted.

Mode of supply
The method by which suppliers of internationally *traded services* (page 274) deliver their service to buyers. The four modes usually identified are: *cross-border supply* (page 55), *consumer movement* (page 47), *producer presence* (page 219), and *movement of natural persons* (page 181).

Model
A stylized simplification of reality in which behavior is represented by variables and by assumptions about how they are determined and interact. Models enable one to think consistently and logically about complex issues, to work out how changes in an economic system matter, and (sometimes) to make predictions about economic performance.

Monetary approach
A framework for analyzing *exchange rates* (page 94) and the *balance of payments* (page 17) that focuses on supply and

demand for money in different countries. A *floating exchange rate* (page 108) is assumed to equate supply and demand and thus to reflect relative growth rates of money supplies and determinants of demand. Under a *pegged exchange rate* (page 207), the *balance of payments surplus* (page 18) or deficit equals the excess demand or supply, respectively, for a country's money.

Monetary base

Usually, the currency and central bank deposits that together provide the base for the money supply under fractional reserve banking. Also defined as the central bank assets the acquisition of which creates this monetary base by injecting domestic money into the economy. The latter definition usually includes *international reserves* (page 149) and *domestic credit* (page 74). By either definition, the monetary base changes as a result of *open market operations* (page 199) and *exchange market intervention* (page 94).

Monetary independence

The ability of a country to determine its own *monetary policy* (see below), as opposed to allowing the money supply to be determined by the *exchange market intervention* (page 94) required to maintain a *fixed exchange rate* (page 108).

Monetary integration

The adoption of a *common currency* (page 41) by two or more countries.

Monetary policy

The use of the *money supply* (page 180) and/or the *interest rate* (page 143) to influence the level of macroeconomic activity and other policy objectives including the *balance of payments* (page 17) or the *exchange rate* (page 94).

Monetary union

Two or more countries sharing a *common currency* (page 41).

Monetize

1. To turn anything into money.

2. To convert government debt into currency.

Money income

Nominal (page 191) income; contrasts with *real* (page 228) income

Money market

The money market, in macroeconomics and international finance, refers to the equilibration of demand for a country's domestic money to its *money supply* (see below). Both refer to the quantity of money that people in the country hold (a stock), not to the quantity that people both in and out of the country choose to acquire during a period in the *exchange market* (page 94), mostly for the purpose of then using it to buy something else.

Money overhang

A money supply that is larger than people want to hold at prevailing prices. This was said to be a major cause of *inflation* (page 141) in Russia after the fall of the Soviet Union, which left an excess of money in circulation.

Money supply

There are several formal definitions, but all include the quantity of currency in circulation plus the amount of *demand deposits* (page 65). The money supply, together with the amount of real economic activity in a country, is an important determinant of its price level and its *exchange rate* (page 94).

Monopolistic

Having some power to set price.

Monopolistic competition

A *market structure* (page 173) in which there are many sellers each producing a *differentiated product* (page 68). Each can set its own price and quantity, but is too small for that to matter for prices and quantities of other producers in the industry.

Monopoly

A *market structure* (page 173) in which there is a single seller.

Monopoly argument

The monopoly argument for a tariff is the same as the *optimal tariff argument* (page 200). It gets its name from the fact that a country using a tariff to *improve the terms of trade* (page 136) is acting much like a monopoly firm, restricting its sales to get a better price.

Monopsony

A *market structure* (page 173) in which there is a single buyer. Term introduced in *Robinson (1932)* (page 380).

Monotonic
Changing in one direction only; thus either strictly rising or strictly falling, but not reversing direction.

Moral hazard
The tendency of individuals, firms, and governments, once insured against some contingency, to behave so as to make that contingency more likely. A pervasive problem in the insurance industry, it also arises internationally when international financial institutions assist countries in financial trouble.

Most favored nation
The principle, fundamental to the *GATT* (page 116), of treating imports from a country on the same basis as that given to the most favored other nation. That is, and with some exceptions, every country gets the lowest tariff that any country gets, and reductions in tariffs to one country are provided also to others.

Mothballing
The preservation of a production facility without using it to produce, but keeping the machinery in working order and supplies available. This may be preferable — if the facility's operating costs are high and the aim is to have it available in time of war — to having it produce in peacetime under a *subsidy* (page 260) or *import protection* (page 135). See *national defense argument* (page 185).

Movement of natural persons
One of four *modes of supply* (page 178) under the *GATS* (page 116), this involving the temporary movement across national borders of *natural persons* (page 186) employed by or associated with a firm in order to participate in the firm's business. Also called *temporary producer movement* (page 269).

MPC
Marginal propensity to consume (page 170).

MRS
Marginal rate of substitution (page 170).

MRT
Marginal rate of transformation (page 170).

Multi-cone equilibrium

A free-trade equilibrium in the *Heckscher-Ohlin model* (page 126) in which prices are such that all goods cannot be produced within a single country, and instead there are multiple *diversification cones* (page 72). This, or a *two cone equilibrium* (page 281), will arise if countries' *factor endowments* (page 102) are sufficiently dissimilar compared to *factor intensities* (page 102) of industries. Contrasts with *one cone equilibrium* (page 198).

Multifactor model

A model with more than two *factors* (page 101). In the context of *trade theory* (page 277) this is likely to mean a *Heckscher-Ohlin model* (page 126) with more than two factors.

Multifiber arrangement

An agreement (*OMA*) (page 197) among developed country importers and developing country exporters of textiles and apparel to regulate and restrict the quantities traded. It was negotiated in 1973 under *GATT* (page 116) auspices as a temporary exception to the rules that would otherwise apply, and was superseded in 1995 by the *ATC* (page 14).

Multifunctionality

Refers to the purposes that an industry may serve in addition to producing its output. Most often applied to agriculture by countries that wish to subsidize it, arguing that subsidies are needed to serve these other purposes, such as rural viability, land conservation, cultural heritage, etc.

Multilateral

Among a large number of countries. Contrasts with *bilateral* (page 23) and *plurilateral* (page 210).

Multilateral agreement

An agreement among a large number of countries.

Multilateral Agreement on Investment

An agreement to liberalize rules on international direct investment that was negotiated in the *OECD* (page 196) but never completed or adopted because of adverse public reaction to it. Preliminary text of the agreement was leaked to the Internet in April 1997, where many groups opposed it. Negotiations were discontinued in November 1998.

Multilateral Investment Guarantee Agency

One of the five institutions that comprise the *World Bank* (page 293) Group, MIGA helps encourage foreign investment in developing countries.

Multinational corporation

A corporation that operates in two or more countries. Since it is headquartered in only one country but has production or marketing facilities in others, it is the result of previous *FDI* (page 105).

Multinational enterprise

A firm, usually a corporation, that operates in two or more countries. In practice the term is used interchangeably with *multinational corporation* (see above).

Multiple equilibria

Refers to a system in which there is more than one equilibrium, most commonly a *market* (page 171) in which a *backward bending* (page 16) supply curve crosses a demand curve more than once, at prices each of which is a *market clearing price* (page 172).

Multiplier

In Keynesian macroeconomic models, the ratio of the change in an *endogenous variable* (page 85) to the change in an *exogenous variable* (page 96). Usually means the multiplier for government spending on income. In the simplest Keynesian model of a closed economy, this is $1/s$, where s is the *marginal propensity to save* (page 170). See *open economy multiplier* (page 199).

Multistage production

Another term for *fragmentation* (page 112). Used by *Dixit and Grossman (1982)* (page 374).

Mundell-Fleming model

An open-economy version of the *IS-LM model* (page 152) that allows for international trade and international capital flows. Due to *Mundell (1962, 1963)* (page 379) and *Fleming (1962)* (page 375).

Mutatis mutandis

Latin phrase meaning, approximately, "allowing other things to change accordingly." Used as a shorthand for indicating the effect of one economic variable on another, within a system in which other variables that matter will also change as a result. Contrasts with *ceteris paribus* (page 36).

Mutual recognition

The acceptance by one country of another country's certification that a satisfactory standard has been met for ability, performance, safety, etc.

Mystery of the missing trade

The empirical observation, by *Trefler (1995)* (page 382), that the amount of trade is far less than predicted by the *HOV* (page 130) version of the *Heckscher-Ohlin model* (page 126). More precisely, the *factor content of trade* (page 102) is far less than the differences between countries in their *factor endowments* (page 102).

NAFTA

North American Free Trade Agreement (page 195).

NAFTA TAA

See *trade adjustment assistance* (page 272).

NAIRU

The level of the *unemployment rate* (page 283) at which prices rise at the same rate that they are expected to rise, and thus at which (since expectations needn't change) the rate of inflation does not then rise or fall. Stands for **N**on-**A**ccelerating **I**nflation **R**ate of **U**nemployment.

Narrow money

M1 (page 167).

Nash

Used as an adjective applied to a strategy in a *game* (page 116), this means that it is part of a *Nash equilibrium* (see below).

Nash equilibrium

An equilibrium in *game theory* (page 116) in which each player's action is optimal given the actions of the other players. E.g., in a *tariff-and-retaliation game* (page 264), with each country able to improve its *terms of trade* (page 269) with a tariff, zero tariffs are not Nash, since each can do better by raising its tariff. A Nash equilibrium, with positive tariffs, is likely to be inferior to free trade for both.

Nation

As used in international economics, a nation is almost invariably a country, or occasionally a similar entity (e.g., Hong Kong) with a single, usually independent government.

National

1. (adj.) Of, relating to, or belonging to a *nation* (see above).

2. (n.) A person who is a citizen or long-term resident of a nation.

National Bureau of Economic Research

A non-profit, non-partisan organization based in Cambridge, MA, that assembles economic data and sponsors economic research. Its **Business Cycle Dating Committee** also is traditionally responsible for identifying the beginnings and ends of *recessions* (page 229).

National debt

Although this term looks like it should mean the amount that a country owes to foreigners, in practice it is used instead to refer to the amount that a nation's government owes to anybody, including its own citizens. Thus it is the total of a national government's outstanding government *bonds* (page 24).

National defense argument for protection

The argument that imports should be restricted in order to sustain a domestic industry so that it will be available in case of trade disruption due to war. This is a *second best argument* (page 243), since there are a variety of ways of providing for defense at lower economic cost, including production *subsidies* (page 260), *mothballing* (page 181), and *stockpiling* (page 257).

National exhaustion

See *exhaustion* (page 96).

National income

The income generated by a country's production, and therefore the total income of its *factors of production* (page 103). Except for some adjustments that don't usually enter theoretical models, NI is the same as *GDP* (page 117).

National Income and Product Accounts

The statistics collected by the *Bureau of Economic Analysis* (page 28) on aggregate economic activity in the United States.

National sovereignty

See *sovereignty* (page 251).

National treatment

The principle of providing foreign producers and sellers the same treatment provided to domestic firms.

Natural person

This term appears in the *GATS* (page 116) where it deals with the international movement of employees of firms that are providing services in another country. Persons are called "natural" to distinguish them from "juridical persons," such as partnerships or corporations, which are given certain rights of persons under the law.

Natural resource

Anything that is provided by nature, such as deposits of minerals, quality of land, old-growth forests, fish populations, etc. The availability of particular natural resources is an important determinant of *comparative advantage* (page 42) and trade in products that depend on them. Natural resources are *primary factors* (page 217) of production.

Natural trade

Trade that is either *free* (page 113) or *restricted* (page 235), but that is not artificially encouraged by *subsidies* (page 260) or other stimulants.

Natural trading bloc

A *trading bloc* (page 278) consisting of *natural trading partners* (see below).

Natural trading partner

A country with whom another country's trade is likely to be large, because of low *transport* (page 280) or other *trade costs* (page 273) between them. Term introduced by *Wonnacott and Lutz (1989)* (page 383) and used extensively by *Frankel (1997)* (page 375).

NBER

National Bureau of Economic Research (page 185).

NDP
Net domestic product (page 188).

Necessity test
A procedure to determine whether a trade restriction intended to serve some purpose is necessary for that purpose.

Negative externality
A harmful *externality* (page 100); that is, a harmful effect of one economic agent's actions on another. Considered a *distortion* (page 72) because the first agent has inadequate incentive to curtail the action. Examples are pollution from factories (a *production externality* (page 220)) and smoke from cigarettes (a *consumption externality* (page 48)).

Negative list
In an international agreement, a list of those items, entities, products, etc. to which the agreement will *not* apply, the commitment being to apply the agreement to everything else. Contrasts with *positive list* (page 212).

Neighborhood
In mathematical Euclidean space, a small set of points surrounding and including a particular point. Thus, for an economic variable, such as an *allocation* (page 9), the neighborhood of a particular allocation includes all those allocations that are sufficiently similar to it.

Neighborhood production structure
A structure of technology for a general equilibrium model due to *Jones and Kierzkowski (1986)* (page 376). With an arbitrary but equal number of goods and factors, each factor produces two (different) goods, each good uses two (different) factors, in a way that yields more unambiguous results than one normally finds in *high-dimension* (page 127) trade models without *specific factors* (page 252).

Neoclassical
A collection of assumptions customarily made by mainstream economists starting in the late 19th century, including profit maximization by firms, utility maximization by consumers, and market equilibrium, with corresponding implications for determination of factor prices and the distribution of income. Contrasts

with *classical* (page 39), *Keynesian* (page 155), and *Marxist* (page 174).

Neoclassical ambiguity

In the *specific factors model* (page 253), the fact that the effect of a change in relative prices on the real wage of the mobile factor cannot be known *a priori*, since the wage rises relative to one price and falls relative to the other.

Neoclassical economics

Most of modern, mainstream economics based on *neoclassical* (page 187) assumptions. Tends to ascribe inevitability, if not necessarily desirability, to market outcomes.

Neoclassical growth model

A model of *economic growth* (page 79) in which income arises from *neoclassical production functions* (see below) in one or more sectors, displaying *diminishing returns* (page 68) to saving and capital accumulation. Due to *Solow (1956)* (page 381) and *Swan (1956)* (page 382).

Neoclassical production function

A *production function* (page 220) with the properties of *constant returns to scale* (page 47) and smoothly *diminishing returns* (page 68) to individual *factors* (page 101).

Neoliberalism

A view of the world that favors social justice while also emphasizing economic growth, efficiency, and the benefits of free markets.

NES

Not Elsewhere Specified. This abbreviation, "nes," appears frequently in classifications, of goods and of industries for example, to encompass all other items in a category that have not been included explicitly.

Net domestic product

Gross domestic product (page 122) minus *depreciation* (page 66). This is the most complete measure of productive activity within the borders of a country, though its accuracy suffers from the difficulty of measuring depreciation.

Net economic welfare

Same as *MEW* (page 175).

Net exports

Exports minus imports; same as the *balance of trade* (page 18).

Net foreign asset position

The value of the assets that a country owns abroad, minus the value of the domestic assets owned by foreigners. Equals *balance of indebtedness* (page 17).

Net foreign factor income

The income of a country's *factors* (page 101) earned abroad minus the income paid to foreign-owned factors domestically.

Net international reserves

International reserves (page 149) minus reserves that have been borrowed from the *IMF* (page 132) and other governments.

Net national product

Gross national product (page 122) minus *depreciation* (page 66). This is the most complete measure of productive activity by a country's *nationals* (page 185), though its accuracy suffers from the difficulty of measuring depreciation.

Net output

The output of a product that is available for final users, after deducting amounts of it used up as an *intermediate input* (page 144) in producing itself and other products. Contrasts with *gross output* (page 122).

Net present value

Same as *present value* (page 214), being sure to include (negative) payments as well as (positive) receipts.

Network

A set of connections among a multiplicity of separate entities sharing a common characteristic. Networks of firms or individuals in different countries are thought to facilitate trade.

Neutral

1. Said of a *technological change* (page 268) or *technological difference* (page 268) if it is not *biased* (page 22) in favor of using more or less of one *factor* (page 101) than another. This can be defined in several different ways that are not normally equivalent: *Hicks neutral* (page 127), *Harrod neutral* (page 125), and *Solow neutral* (page 250).

2. Said of economic growth if it expands actual or potential output of all goods at the same rate, not being biased in favor of one over another. In the *Heckscher-Ohlin model* (page 126) neutral growth will occur if all *factor endowments* (page 102) grow at the same rate or if there is *Hicks neutral* (page 127) technological progress at the same rate in all industries.

3. Said of a trade regime if the structure of *protection* (page 222) favors neither exportables nor importables. See *bias* (page 22).

NEW

Net economic welfare (page 188).

New bancor

A proposed non-national world currency to be used for payment and reserve purposes, to be issued by the *IMF* (page 132) and intended to maintain a fixed purchasing power in the dollar and euro countries.

New economic geography

The study of the location of economic activity across space, particularly a strand of literature begun by *Krugman (1991a)* (page 377) using *agglomeration economies* (page 7) to help explain why industries cluster within particular countries and regions.

New economy

This term was used in the late 1990's to suggest that *globalization* (page 119) and/or innovations in information technology had changed the way that the world economy works. Conjectures included changes in productivity, the inflation-unemployment tradeoff, the business cycle, and the valuation of enterprises.

New international economic order

A set of proposals put forward during the 1970s by developing countries through *UNCTAD* (page 283) to promote their interests by improving their *terms of trade* (page 269), increasing development assistance, developed-country tariff reductions, and other means.

New trade theory

Models of trade that, especially in the 1980s, incorporated aspects of *imperfect competition* (page 133), *increasing returns* (page 138), and *product differentiation* (page 220) into both *general equilibrium* (page 117) and *partial equilibrium* (page 205) models of trade and trade policy. Many contributed to this literature, but the most prominent was Krugman, starting with *Krugman (1979a)* (page 377).

Newly industrializing country

Refers to a group of countries previously regarded as developing (page 159) that then achieved high rates and levels of economic growth.

Newly industrializing economy

Newly industrializing country (see above).

News

Unexpected information. In an *efficient market* (page 83), as the *exchange market* (page 94) is supposed to be, price reflects all available information. It can change, therefore, only in response to news.

NGO

Non-governmental organization (page 193).

NIC

Newly industrializing country (see above).

NIE

Newly industrializing economy (see above).

NIEO

New international economic order (page 190).

NIPA

National Income and Product Accounts (page 186).

NNP

Net national product (page 189).

Nominal

1. In the form most directly observed or named, in contrast to a form that has been adjusted or modified in some fashion.

2. As measured in terms of money, usually in contrast to *real* (page 228).

Nominal anchor

The technique of fixing a *nominal* (see above) variable in an economy as a means of reducing *inflation* (page 141). For example, by firmly *pegging* (page 207) the *nominal exchange rate* (see below), a central bank or government reduces its own ability to expand the *money supply* (page 180).

Nominal exchange rate

The actual *exchange rate* (page 94) at which currencies are exchanged on an *exchange market* (page 94). Contrasts with *real exchange rate* (page 228).

Nominal interest rate

The *interest rate* (page 143) actually observed in the market, in contrast to the *real interest rate* (page 229).

Nominal rate of protection

The protection afforded an industry directly by the *tariff* (page 264) and/or *NTB* (page 195) on its output, ignoring effects of other trade barriers on the industry's inputs. Contrasts with the *ERP* (page 88).

Nominal return

The earnings on an asset or other investment, comparable to a *nominal interest rate* (see above), thus not adjusted for *inflation* (page 141).

Nominal tariff

The *nominal protection* (see above) provided by a tariff; that is, the tariff itself. Contrasts with *effective tariff* (page 82).

Nominal wage

The *wage* (page 290) of labor in units of currency, not adjusted for *inflation* (page 141), and thus not in terms of the goods that it will buy. Contrasts with *real wage* (page 229).

Non-actionable subsidy

A *subsidy* (page 260) that is not subject to *countervailing duties* (page 52) under the rules of the *WTO* (page 293). These include *non-specific subsidies* (page 193), subsidies for industrial research, *regional aids* (page 231), and some *environmental subsidies* (page 87).

Non-automatic licensing

Import *licensing* (page 163) that is discretionary, based on an import quota, or performance related.

Non-governmental organization

A not-for-profit organization that pursues an issue or issues of interest to its members by lobbying, persuasion, and/or direct action. In the arena of international economics, NGOs play an increasing role defending human rights and the environment, and fighting poverty.

Non-market-clearing

A situation or economic model in which a market or markets do not *clear* (page 39), perhaps because something prevents prices from adjusting to discrepancies between supply and demand.

Non-market economy

A country in which most major economic decisions are imposed by government and by *central planning* (page 36) rather than by free use of *markets* (page 171). Contrasts with a *market economy* (page 172).

Non-specific subsidy

A *subsidy* (page 260) that is available to more than a single specific industry and is therefore *non-actionable* (page 192) under *WTO* (page 293) rules.

Non-convexity

The property of an economic model or system that the sets representing technology, preferences, or constraints are not mathematically *convex* (page 50). Because convexity is needed for proof that competitive equilibrium is efficient and well-behaved, non-convexities may imply *market failures* (page 172).

Non-distorted

Without *distortions* (page 72). Many propositions in trade theory are strictly valid, often only implicitly, only in non-distorted economies.

Non-distorting lump sum

Redundant appellation for a *lump-sum* (page 167) tax or subsidy.

Non-economic objectives argument for protection

The view that a restriction on imports may serve a purpose outside of conventional economic models. Unless that purpose is itself the restriction of trade, then this is a *second-best argument* (page 243), since changes in output, consumption, etc. can be achieved at lower economic cost in other ways.

Non-homothetic

Any function that is not *homothetic* (page 129), but usually applied to consumer *preferences* (page 213) that include goods whose shares of expenditure rise (and others that fall) with income.

Non-production worker

A worker not directly engaged in production. In empirical studies of skilled and unskilled labor, data on non-production workers are often taken to represent skilled labor.

Non-prohibitive tariff

A *tariff* (page 264) that is not *prohibitive* (page 222).

Non-sterilization

Refers to *exchange market intervention* (page 94) that is done without *sterilizing* (page 257) its effects on the domestic *money supply* (page 180).

Non-tariff barrier

Any policy that interferes with exports or imports other than a simple *tariff* (page 264), prominently including *quotas* (page 226) and *VERs* (page 289).

Non-tariff measure

Any policy or official practice that alters the conditions of international trade, including ones that act to increase trade as well as those that restrict it. The term is therefore broader than *non-tariff barrier* (see above), although the two are usually used interchangeably.

Non-tradable

1. Not capable of being traded among countries.
2. A good or service that is non-tradable, with **non-tradables** referring to an aggregate of such goods and services.

Non-tradable good

A good that, by its nature, is *non-tradable* (see above).

Non-traded good

A good that is not traded, either because it cannot be or because trade barriers are too high. Except when *services* (page 244) are being distinguished from goods, they are often mentioned as examples of non-traded goods, or at least they were until it became common to speak of *trade in services* (page 274).

Non-violation

In *WTO* (page 293) terminology, this is shorthand for a complaint that a country's action, though not a violation of WTO rules, has **nullified** or **impaired** a member's expected benefits from the agreement.

Normal good

A good the demand for which rises with income if relative prices do not change. Contrasts with *inferior good* (page 140).

Normal value

Price charged for a product on the domestic market of the producer. Used to compare with export price in determining *dumping* (page 76).

Normative

Refers to value judgments as to "what ought to be," in contrast to *positive* (page 211) which is about "what is."

North American Free Trade Agreement

The agreement to form a *free trade area* (page 113) among the United States, Canada, and Mexico that went into effect January 1, 1994.

North-South model

An economic model in which two countries, North and South, represent *developed* (page 67) and *less developed* (page 161) countries respectively.

NTB

Non-tariff barrier (page 194).

NTM

Non-tariff measure (page 194).

Nullification

See *non-violation* (above).

Numeraire

The unit in which prices are measured. This may be a currency, but in *real models* (page 229), such as most trade models, the numeraire is usually one of the goods, whose price is then set at one. The numeraire can also be defined implicitly by, for example, the requirement that prices sum to some constant.

OAS
Organization of American States (page 202).
OBM
Obsolescing bargain model (see below).
Obsolescing bargain model
A model of interaction between a *multinational enterprise* (page 183) and a *host country* (page 130) government, which initially reach a bargain that favors the MNE but where, over time as the MNE's fixed assets in the country increase, the bargaining power shifts to the government. Due to *Vernon (1971)* (page 382).
OECD
Organisation for Economic Co-operation and Development (page 201).
OEEC
Organisation for European Economic Co-operation (page 201).
Offer curve
A curve showing, for a two-good model, the quantity of one good that a country will export (or "offer") for each quantity of the other that it imports. Also called the *reciprocal demand curve* (page 230), it is convenient for representing both exports and imports in the same curve and can be used for analyzing *tariffs* (page 264) and other changes.
Offer curve diagram
A *diagram* (page 322) that combines the *offer curves* (see above) of two countries (or one country and the rest of the world) to determine equilibrium *relative prices* (page 233).
Official rate
The *par value* (page 204) of a *pegged exchange rates* (page 207).
Official reserve transactions
Transactions by a central bank that cause changes in its *official reserves* (page 197). These are usually purchases or sales of

its own currency in the *exchange market* (page 94) in exchange for foreign currencies or other foreign-currency-denominated assets. In the *balance of payments* (page 17) a purchase of its own currency is a *credit* (page 54) $(+)$ and a sale is a *debit* (page 61) $(-)$.

Official reserves

The reserves of foreign-currency-denominated assets (and also gold and *SDRs* (page 242)) that a central bank holds, sometimes as backing for its own currency, but usually only for the purpose of possible future *exchange market intervention* (page 94).

Offset requirement

As a condition for importing into a country, a requirement that foreign exporters purchase domestic products and/or invest in the importing country.

Ohlin definition

The *price definition* (page 215) of *factor abundance* (page 101). In contrast to the *quantity definition* (page 224), the price definition incorporates differences in demands as well as supplies. Due to *Ohlin (1933)* (page 379).

OIM

French acronym of *International Organization for Migration* (page 149).

OLI paradigm

A framework for analyzing the decision to engage in *FDI* (page 105), based on three kinds of advantage that FDI may provide in comparison to exports: Ownership, Location, and *Internalization* (page 145). Due to *Dunning (1979)* (page 374).

Oligopoly

A *market structure* (page 173) in which there are a small number of sellers, at least some of whose individual decisions about price or quantity matter to the others.

Oligopsony

A *market structure* (page 173) in which there are a small number of buyers.

OMA

Orderly marketing arrangement (page 201).

OMO

Open market operation (page 199).

One cone equilibrium

A free-trade equilibrium in the *Heckscher-Ohlin model* (page 126) in which prices are such that all goods can be produced within a single country, and there is only one *diversification cone* (page 72). This will arise if countries' *factor endowments* (page 102) are sufficiently similar compared to *factor intensities* (page 102) of industries. Contrasts with *multi-cone equilibrium* (page 182).

One-dollar-one-vote yardstick

A characterization of the *Kaldor-Hicks* (page 154) *welfare criterion* (page 292) normally used in evaluating *trade policies* (page 276) and more generally in *cost-benefit analysis* (page 51), based on a sum of monetary values including *consumer* (page 48) and *producer surplus* (page 219).

One-way arbitrage

The use, by a potential supplier or demander in a market, of a different market or markets to accomplish the same purpose, taking advantage of a discrepancy among their prices. With transaction costs, this enforces smaller price discrepancies than would be permitted by conventional *arbitrage* (page 11). Due to *Deardorff (1979)* (page 374).

One-way option

Refers to the situation of a *speculator* (page 253) on an *exchange market* (page 94) with a *pegged exchange rate* (page 207). If there is doubt about the viability of the peg, the speculator can sell the currency *short* (page 245) knowing that there is only one direction (one way) that the currency is likely to move. Therefore there is little *risk* (page 238) associated with such speculation.

OPEC

Organization of Petroleum Exporting Countries (page 202).

Open economy

An economy that permits transactions with the outside world, at least including trade of some goods. Contrasts with *closed economy* (page 39).

Open-economy multiplier

The simple Keynesian *multiplier* (page 183) for a *small open economy* (page 248). Equals $1/(s+m)$, where s is the *marginal propensity to save* (page 170) and m is the *marginal propensity to import* (page 170).

Open market operation

The sale or purchase of government bonds by a central bank, in exchange for domestic currency or central-bank deposits. This changes the *monetary base* (page 179) and therefore the domestic *money supply* (page 180), contracting it with a bond sale and expanding it with a bond purchase.

Open markets

Markets that are free of restrictions on who can buy and sell.

Open position

An obligation to take or make delivery of an asset or currency in the future without *cover* (page 53), that is, without a matching obligation in the other direction that protects from effects of change in the price of the asset or currency. Aside from simple ownership and debt, an open position can be acquired or avoided using the *forward market* (page 111).

Open regionalism

Regional economic *integration* (page 142) that is not discriminatory against outside countries; typically, a group of countries that agrees to reduce trade barriers on an *MFN* (page 176) basis. Adopted as a fundamental principle, but not defined, by *APEC* (page 11) in 1989. *Bergsten (1997)* (page 372) offers five definitions, ranging from open membership to global liberalization and trade facilitation.

Openness

The extent to which an economy is *open* (page 198) to trade, and sometimes also to inflows and outflows of *international investment* (page 148).

Openness coefficient

The *coefficient* (page 40) on any variable measuring *openness* (see above) in a regression, often a *regression* (page 232) explaining *economic growth* (page 79). Thus an estimate of the importance of openness for growth.

Openness index
1. Any measure of *openness* (page 199).
2. The ratio of a country's trade (exports plus imports) to its *GDP* (page 122).

Opportunity cost
The cost of something in terms of opportunity foregone. The opportunity cost to a country of producing a unit more of a good, such as for export or to replace an import, is the quantity of some other good that could have been produced instead.

Optimal
Best, by whatever criterion decisions are being made; thus yielding the highest level of *utility* (page 287), *profit* (page 221), economic *welfare* (page 291), or whatever objective is being pursued.

Optimal currency area
The optimal grouping of regions or countries within which exchange rates should be held fixed. *First* (page 368) defined (as "**optimum** currency areas") by *Mundell (1961)* (page 379).

Optimal output
1. For a firm this usually means the output of the good that it produces that, when sold, maximizes *profit* (page 221).
2. For a country, this usually means the combination of different goods (and services) that it can produce that is worth the most at world prices, perhaps adjusted for any *externalities* (page 100).

Optimal tariff
The level of a *tariff* (page 264) that maximizes a country's *welfare* (page 291). In a *non-distorted* (page 193) *small open economy* (page 248), the optimal tariff is zero. In a *large country* (page 158) it is positive, due to its effect on the *terms of trade* (page 269).

Optimal tariff argument
An argument in favor of levying a tariff in order to *improve the terms of trade* (page 136). The argument is valid only in a *large country* (page 158), and then only if other countries do not *retaliate* (page 236) by raising tariffs themselves. Even then, this is a *beggar thy neighbor* (page 21) policy, since it lowers *welfare* (page 291) abroad. See *Johnson (1954)* (page 376).

Optimum
1. The best. Usually refers to a most preferred choice by consumers subject to a budget constraint, a profit maximizing choice by firms or industry subject to a technological constraint, or in *general equilibrium* (page 117), a complete *allocation* (page 9) of factors and goods that in some sense maximizes *welfare* (page 291).
2. As an adjective, same as *optimal* (page 200).

Optimum optimorum
The best of the best, or the *global optimum* (page 118). This term is used, when there are several allocations each of which is *locally optimal* (page 165), to refer to the best among these.

Option
A contract that permits one party to buy from (or sell to) the other party something at a prespecified price during a prespecified period of time, leaving the choice of whether to do this or not (whether to "**exercise**" the option) up to the first party, which buys the option. Options exist for many *assets* (page 13), including *foreign exchange* (page 109).

Orderly marketing arrangement
An agreement among a group of exporting and importing countries to restrict the quantities traded of a good or group of goods. Since the impetus normally comes from the importers protecting their domestic industry, an OMA is effectively a multi-country *VER* (page 289).

Organisation for Economic Co-operation and Development
An international organization of developed countries that "provides governments a setting in which to discuss, develop and perfect economic and social policy." As of January 2006, it had 30 *member countries* (page 358).

Organisation for European Economic Co-operation
An international organization established in 1948 as the recipient institution of aid through the Marshall Plan. In 1961 it was replaced by the *OECD* (page 196).

Organization of American States

An international organization of the countries of the Western Hemisphere, fostering cooperation among them and advancing their common interests. It has 35 member states, although the government of one of them, Cuba, is excluded from participating.

Organization of Petroleum Exporting Countries

A group of countries that includes many, but not all, of the largest exporters of oil. Its major purpose is to regulate the supply of petroleum and thereby to stabilize (often raise) its price. The international oil *cartel* (page 34). As of January 2006, it had 11 *member countries* (page 359).

Origin principle

The principle in international taxation that *value added taxes* (page 287) be kept only by the country where production takes place. Under the origin principle, value added taxes are not collected on imports and not rebated on exports. Contrasts with the *destination principle* (page 67).

Origin rule

See *rules of origin* (page 239).

Output augmenting

Said of a *technological change* (page 268) or *technological difference* (page 268) if one production function produces a scalar multiple of the other. Also called *Hicks neutral* (page 127).

Output gap

The amount by which a country's output, or *GDP* (page 122), falls short of what it could be given its available resources. A positive output gap is considered to exist when a country's *unemployment rate* (page 283) is greater than the *NAIRU* (page 184).

Outsourcing

1. Performance outside a firm or plant of a production activity that was previously done inside.

2. Manufacture of inputs to a production process, or a part of a process, in another location, especially in another country.

3. Another term for *fragmentation* (page 112).

Outward oriented strategy

Export promotion (page 99).

Over-invoicing

The provision of an *invoice* (page 151) that reports the price as higher than is actually being paid.

Overvalued currency

The situation of a currency whose value on the *exchange market* (page 94) is higher than is believed to be sustainable. This may be due to a *pegged* (page 207) or *managed* (page 168) rate that is above the market-clearing rate, or, under a *floating rate* (page 108), it may be due to *speculative* (page 253) capital inflows. Contrasts with *undervalued currency* (page 283).

Overdraft facility

In the *IMF* (page 132), an arrangement permitting countries to draw more foreign currency from it than they have deposited. The right to do so is a *special drawing right* (page 251) and, when used, is transferred to the country whose currency is withdrawn.

Overhang

See *debt overhang* (page 62) and *money overhang* (page 180).

Overshooting

See *exchange rate overshooting* (page 95).

Pacific Rim

A collective term for the countries that border on the Pacific Ocean.

Panel

A three-person committee assembled by the *WTO* (page 293) to hear evidence in disputes between members, as part of the WTO *dispute settlement mechanism* (page 71). Panels are also used to settle disputes under *NAFTA* (page 184).

Par

1. Equality. See *at par* (page 14).

2. Official value. See *par value* (page 204).

Par value

The central value of a *pegged exchange rate* (page 207), around which the actual rate is permitted to fluctuate within set bounds.

Para tariff

A charge on imports that is not included in a country's tariff schedule, such as a **statistical tax**, **stamp fee**, etc.

Paradox

As used in economics, it seems to mean something unexpected, rather than the more extreme normal meaning of something seemingly impossible. Some paradoxes are just theoretical results that go against what one thinks of as normal. Others, like the *Leontief paradox* (page 160), are empirical findings that seem to contradict theoretical predictions.

Parallel import

Trade that is made possible when the owner of *intellectual property* (page 142) causes the same product to be sold in different countries for different prices. If someone else imports the low-price good into the high-price country, that is a parallel import.

Parent

In a firm that has one or more *subsidiaries* (page 260), especially a *multinational corporation* (page 183), the portion of the firm that owns and ultimately controls the others.

Pareto criterion

The criterion that for change in an economy to be viewed as socially beneficial it should be *Pareto improving* (see below).

Pareto efficient

Same as *Pareto optimal* (see below).

Pareto improving

Making no one worse off and making at least one person better off.

Pareto optimal

Having the property that no *Pareto improving* (see above) change is possible.

Paris club

A group of *creditor countries* (page 55) that meets regularly but informally in Paris to seek ways of helping debtor countries to manage their debts through coordinated *rescheduling* (page 234) and other means.

Parity
   1. Equality. Same as *par* (page 203). See also *interest parity* (page 143) and *purchasing power parity* (page 223).
   2. Official value, or *par value* (page 204).

Parsimonious
   Stingy. Although in normal language, this has a negative connotation, when applied to a model or an explanation in economics it tends to be positive, meaning that it relies on as simple a structure as possible.

Partial
   Favoring one person or side over another; not impartial.

Partial equilibrium
   Equality of supply and demand in only a subset of an economy's markets — usually just one — taking variables from other markets as given. Partial equilibrium models are appropriate for products that constitute only a negligibly small part of the economy. They are used routinely (not always appropriately) for analysis of trade policies in single industries. Contrasts with *general equilibrium* (page 117).

Pass-through
   The extent to which an exchange rate change is reflected in the prices of imported goods. With **full pass-through**, a currency *depreciation* (page 66), which increases the price of foreign currency, would increase the prices of imported goods by the same amount, and vice versa. With no pass-through, prices of imports remain constant. See *pricing to market* (page 217).

Patent
   The legal right to the proceeds from, and control over the use of, an invented product or process, granted for a fixed period of time, usually 20 years. Patent is one form of *intellectual property* (page 142) that is subject of the *TRIPS* (page 281) agreement.

Path dependent
   The property that where you get to depends on how you got there. That is, if the equilibrium that will ultimately be

reached by a system depends on the values of variables that occur away from equilibrium, then the equilibrium is path dependent.

Patriotism argument for protection
The view that one is helping one's country by buying domestically produced goods instead of imports. In a *non-distorted* (page 193) economy, this is not correct, since the country can do better producing where it has a *comparative advantage* (page 42) rather than using scarce resources where it does not.

Pattern of specialization
Which goods a country produces and which it does not produce.

Pattern of trade
See *trade pattern* (page 276).

Pauper labor argument
The view that a country loses by importing from another country that has low wages, presumably by lowering wages at home. This view ignores the fact that low wages are due to low productivity, and that the high-wage home country, with high productivity, will have *comparative advantage* (page 42) in some products and will *gain from trade* (page 116).

Payment at sight
Written as one of the terms of payment in a *letter of credit* (page 162), this means that the payment will be made immediately when the completion of the trade is documented, as opposed to after some specified delay.

Payments deficit
Balance of payments deficit (page 18).

Payments imbalance
Imbalance (page 132) in the *balance of payments* (page 17), normally including both *current* (page 58) and *capital accounts* (page 30).

Peak
The point in the *business cycle* (page 28) when an economic expansion reaches its highest point before turning down. Contrasts with *trough* (page 281).

Peg

1. To maintain a *pegged exchange rate* (see below); thus to set a currency's value within a narrow range.

2. The *par value* (page 204) of a *pegged exchange rate* (see below).

3. The regime of a *pegged exchange rate* (see below).

Pegged exchange rate

A regime in which the government or central bank announces an official (**par value**) of its currency and then maintains the actual market rate within a narrow band above and below that by means of *exchange market intervention* (page 94).

Per capita

Per person.

Per capita income

Income per person, usually measured as *GDP* (page 122) divided by population.

Per capita output

The value of an economy's output per person, *GDP* (page 122) divided by population and thus the same as *per capita income* (see above).

Perfect capital mobility

1. The absence of any barriers to international *capital movements* (page 33).

2. The requirement that, in equilibrium, rates of return on capital (*interest rates* (page 143)) must be the same in different countries.

Perfect competition

An idealized *market structure* (page 173) in which there are large numbers of both buyers and sellers, all of them small, so that they act as *price takers* (page 216). Perfect competition also assumes *homogeneous products* (page 129), *free entry* (page 112) and *exit* (page 112), and *complete information* (page 44). Most international trade theory prior to the *New Trade Theory* (page 190) assumed perfect competition.

Perfect foresight

Exact knowledge of the future. Under perfect foresight, for example, the *forward rate* (page 112) would exactly equal the *spot rate* (page 254) that later prevails when the forward contract matures.

Perfect substitute

A good that is regarded by its demanders as identical to another good, so that the *elasticity of substitution* (page 84) between them is infinite.

Perfectly competitive

Refers to an economic agent (firm or consumer), group of agents (industry), model, or analysis that is characterized by *perfect competition* (page 207). Contrasts with *imperfectly competitive* (page 133).

Perfectly elastic

Refers to a supply or demand curve with a *price elasticity* (page 215) of infinity, implying that the supply or demand curve as usually drawn is horizontal. A *small open economy* (page 248) faces perfectly elastic demand for its exports and supply of its imports, and a foreign *offer curve* (page 196) that is a straight line from the origin.

Perfectly mobile capital

Perfect capital mobility (page 207).

Performance requirement

A requirement that an importer or exporter achieve some level of performance, in terms of exporting, *domestic content* (page 74), etc., in order to obtain an import or export *license* (page 163).

Performance target

In the international economic context, this is likely to refer to one of several targets specified by the *IMF* (page 132) as a *condition* (page 46) for a loan to a *developing country* (page 67).

Peril point

The point beyond which *tariff* (page 264) reduction in an industry would cause it serious injury. The U.S. *Tariff Commission* (page 264) was required to determine peril points for U.S. industries as a constraint on negotiations in early *GATT* (page 116) *Rounds* (page 239).

Periphery

This is something that is on the edge. It therefore is used to refer to countries that are located far from the center of the world's economic activity.

Permanent normal trading relations

The granting of permanent *MFN status* (page 176) to a country that is not a member of the *WTO* (page 293). It is "normal" in the sense that most countries *are* WTO members and therefore have MFN status (or better) automatically.

Permit

A license issued by government granting permission to engage in some activity, such as to export, import, or invest.

Petrodollar

Refers to the profits made by oil exporting countries when the price rose during the 1970s, and their preference for holding these profits in U.S. dollar-denominated assets, either in the U.S. or in Europe as *Eurodollars* (page 90). A portion of these were in turn lent by banks to oil-importing developing countries that used them to buy oil.

Physical capital

The same as "*capital* (page 30)," without any adjective, in the sense of plant and equipment. The word "physical" is used only for clarity, to distinguish it from *human capital* (page 130) and *financial capital* (page 106).

Phytosanitary

Pertaining to the health of plants. See *sanitary and phytosanitary regulations* (page 240).

Piecemeal tariff reform

The reduction of only one tariff (or a subset of tariffs) by a country that has additional tariffs on other products.

Platform

See *export platform* (page 99).

Plaza Accord

An agreement reached in 1985 among the central banks of France, Germany, Japan, US, and UK to bring down the value of the U.S.

dollar, which had *appreciated* (page 11) substantially since 1980. By the time of the *Louvre Accord* (page 167), two years later, the dollar had fallen 30%.

Plurilateral

Among several countries — more than two, which would be *bilateral* (page 23), but not a great many, which would be *multilateral* (page 182).

Plurilateral agreement

The plurilateral agreements of the *WTO* (page 293) contrast with the larger multilateral agreements in that the former are signed by only those member countries that choose to do so, while all members are party to the multilateral agreements.

PNTR

Permanent normal trading relations (page 209).

Point elasticity

See *elasticity* (page 83).

Policy

A deliberate act of government that in some way alters or influences the society or economy outside the government. Includes, but is not limited to, taxation, regulation, expenditures, and legal requirements and prohibitions, including in each case those which affect international transactions.

Political economy

1. Early name for the discipline of economics.

2. A field within economics encompassing several alternatives to *neoclassical economics* (page 188), including *Marxist* (page 174) economics. Also called **radical political economy**.

3. A field within economics that concerns the interactions between political processes and economic variables, especially economic policies.

Political economy of protection

The study of reasons, especially political ones, that countries choose to use *protection* (page 222). Includes models of voting, lobbying, and campaign contributions as these lead policy makers to erect tariffs.

Pollution haven

A country that, because of its weak or poorly enforced environmental regulations, attracts industries that pollute the environment.

Porter's Diamond

The four determinants of *competitive advantage* (page 44) of nations, as identified by *Porter (1990)* (page 380): factor conditions; demand conditions; related and supporting industries; and firm strategy, structure, and rivalry.

Portfolio

The entirety of the financial assets (and usually also liabilities) that an economic agent or group of agents owns.

Portfolio approach

An approach to explaining exchange rates that stresses their role in changing the proportions of different currency-denominated assets in portfolios. The exchange rate adjusts to equate these proportions to desired levels.

Portfolio capital

Financial assets, including stocks, bonds, deposits, and currencies.

Portfolio flow

The sale or purchase of financial assets across countries.

Portfolio investment

The acquisition of *portfolio capital* (see above). Usually refers to such transactions across national borders and/or across currencies.

Positive

Refers to "what is," in contrast to *normative* (page 195) which involves value judgments as to "what ought to be." The word is not, in this use, the opposite of either "negative" or "harmful."

Positive externality

A beneficial *externality* (page 100); that is, a beneficial effect of one economic agent's actions on another. Considered a *distortion* (page 72) because the first agent has inadequate incentive to act. Examples are the attractiveness of well-kept farms for the tourism industry (a *production externality* (page 220)) and reduced contagion of disease due to vaccines (a *consumption externality* (page 48)).

Positive list

In an international agreement, a list of those items, entities, products, etc. to which the agreement *will* apply, with no commitment to apply the agreement to anything else. Contrasts with *negative list* (page 187).

Positive sum game

A *game* (page 116) in which the payoffs to the players may add up to more than zero, so that it may be possible for all players to gain. Contrasts with *zero sum game* (page 295). Due to the *gains from trade* (page 116), trade and trade policy may be thought of as positive sum games.

Poverty datum line

Same as *poverty line* (see below).

Poverty line

The level of annual income below which a household is defined to be living in poverty. This is defined differently by different governments and institutions and, in spite of the great importance of its intent, is not in fact as meaningful as one might wish.

Poverty reduction and growth facility

The *IMF's* (page 132) low-interest lending facility for poor countries, established in 1999 and intended to be more favorable to reducing poverty and promoting growth than previous policies.

PPF

Production possibility frontier (page 220).

PPP

Purchasing power parity (page 223).

PPP exchange rate

Purchasing power parity exchange rate (page 223).

Prebisch-Singer hypothesis

The idea that the relative prices of *primary products* (page 217) would decline over the long term, and therefore that *developing countries* (page 67) that were led by *comparative advantage* (page 42) to specialize in them would find their prospects for *development* (page 67) diminished. Due to *Prebisch (1950)* (page 380) and *Singer (1950)* (page 381).

Precautionary principle
The view that when science has not yet determined whether a new product or process is safe or unsafe, policy should prohibit or restrict its use until it is known to be safe. Applied to trade, this has been used as the basis for prohibiting imports of *GMOs* (page 119), for example.

Predation
The use of aggressive (i.e., low) pricing to put a competitor out of business, with the intent, once they are gone, of raising prices to gain monopoly profits.

Predatory dumping
Dumping (page 76) for the purpose of driving competitors out of business and then raising price. This is the one motivation for dumping that most economists agree would be undesirable, like predatory pricing (see *predation* above) in other contexts.

Predatory pricing
Predation (see above).

Preference for variety
The increased utility that people experience when they have access to a larger number of *differentiated product* (page 68) varieties. In reality this may reflect their ability to find products more closely suited to their own particular needs, but as modeled in the *Dixit-Stiglitz utility function* (page 73), they are better off consuming small quantities of each of a larger number of products.

Preferences
1. In trade policy, this refers to special advantages, such as lower-than-*MFN* (page 176) tariffs, accorded to another country's exports, usually in order to promote that country's development. See *GSP* (page 123).
2. In trade theory, this refers to the attitudes of consumers toward different goods, as represented by a utility function. Some propositions in trade theory use the assumption of *identical* (page 132) and/or *homothetic* (page 129) preferences.

Preferential duty
A *tariff* (page 264) lower than the *MFN* (page 176) tariff, levied against imports from a country that is being given favored

treatment, as in a *preferential trading arrangement* (see below) or under the *GSP* (page 123).

Preferential trading arrangement

1. An agreement among a group of two or more countries to levy lower (or zero) tariffs against each other than they levy against outsiders. Includes *FTAs* (page 114), *customs unions* (page 60), and *common markets* (page 41). Encouragement to use this term instead of the more misleading FTA has come from Jagdish Bhagwati, as in *Bhagwati and Panagariya (1996)* (page 372).

2. *Frankel (1997)* (page 375) uses PTA for an arrangement where internal tariffs are reduced but not zero, reserving FTA for a *trading bloc* (page 278) with zero internal tariffs.

Present value

The value today of a stream of payments and/or receipts over time in the future and/or the past, converted to the present using an interest rate. If X_t is the amount in period t and r the interest rate, then present value at time $t = 0$ is $V = \Sigma_t \, (X_t)/(1 + r)^t$.

Pre-shipment inspection

Certification of the value, quality, and/or identity of traded goods done in the exporting country by specialized agencies or firms on behalf of the importing country. Traditionally used as a means to prevent over- or *under-invoicing* (page 283), it is now being used also as a security measure.

Preston curve

The relationship between a country's *life expectancy* (page 163) and its real per capita income. Named after *Preston (1975)* (page 380).

PRGF

Poverty reduction and growth facility (page 212).

Price ceiling

A government-imposed upper limit on the price that may be charged for a product. If that limit is binding, it implies a situation of *excess demand* (page 93) and shortage.

Price competition

Competition among firms by reducing price, as opposed to by changing characteristics of the product.

Price control

Intervention by a government to set the price in a market or limit its movement, thus attempting to override the *market mechanism* (page 172).

Price definition

A method of defining relative *factor abundance* (page 101) based on ratios of factor prices in autarky: Compared to country B, country A is abundant in factor X relative to factor Y iff $w_X^A/w_Y^A < w_X^B/w_Y^B$, where w_I^J is the autarky price of factor I in country $J, I = X, Y, J = A, B$. This is also known as the "*Ohlin definition* (page 197)," since it is the one used by *Ohlin (1933)* (page 379).

Price discrimination

The sale by a firm to buyers at two different prices. When this occurs internationally and the lower price is charged for export, it is regarded as *dumping* (page 76).

Price elastic

Having a *price elasticity* (see below) greater than one (in absolute value).

Price elasticity

The *elasticity* (page 83) of supply or demand with respect to price.

Price floor

A government-imposed lower limit on the price that may be charged for a product. If that limit is binding, it implies a situation of *excess supply* (page 93), which the government may need to purchase itself to keep price from falling.

Price index

A measure of the average prices of a group of goods relative to a base year. A typical price index for a vector of quantities q and prices p^b, p^g in the base and given years respectively would be $I = 100\Sigma p^g q/\Sigma p^b q$.

Price inelastic

Having a *price elasticity* (see above) of less than one (in absolute value).

Price level

The overall level of prices in a country, as usually measured empirically by a *price index* (page 215), but often captured in theoretical models by a single variable.

Price line

A straight line representing the combinations of variables, usually two goods, that cost the same at some given prices. The slope of a price line measures *relative prices* (page 233), and changes in prices can therefore be represented by changing the slope of, or rotating, a price line. A steeper line means a higher relative price of the good measured on the horizontal axis.

Price mechanism

Same as *market mechanism* (page 172).

Price specie flow mechanism

Same as *specie flow mechanism* (page 252).

Price stabilization

1. Intervention in a market in order to reduce fluctuations in price. This has sometimes been attempted by means of a *buffer stock* (page 27) in markets for *primary products* (page 217).

2. The use of *macroeconomic policies* (page 168) to reduce *inflation* (page 141).

Price support

Government action to increase the price of a product, usually by buying it. May be associated with a *price floor* (page 215).

Price system

Same as *market mechanism* (page 172).

Price taker

An economic entity that is too small relative to a market to affect its price, and that therefore must take that price as given in making its own decisions. Applies to all buyers in sellers in markets that are *perfectly competitive* (page 208). Applies also to a country if it is a *small open economy* (page 248).

Price undertaking

A commitment by an exporting firm to raise its price in an importing-country market, as a means of settling an *anti-dumping suit* (page 10) and preventing an *anti-dumping duty* (page 10).

Pricing to market

The practice of an exporting firm holding fixed (or not fully adjusting) the price it charges in the export market when its costs or exchange rate change. See *pass-through* (page 205). Seminal treatment was *Krugman (1987)* (page 377).

Primary budget surplus

The primary *budget surplus* (page 27) (or deficit) of a government is the surplus excluding interest payments on its outstanding debt.

Primary commodity

Primary product (see below).

Primary factor

An input that exists as a stock providing services that contribute to production. The stock is not used up in production, although it may deteriorate with use, providing a smaller flow of services later. The major primary factors are labor, *capital* (page 30), *human capital* (page 130) (or *skilled labor* (page 247)), land, and sometimes *natural resources* (page 186).

Primary input

Same as *primary factor* (see above).

Primary product

A good that has not been processed and is therefore in its natural state, specifically products of agriculture, forestry, fishing, and mining.

Primary surplus

The government *budget surplus* (page 27), not including net *interest* (page 143) payments on the *government debt* (page 120).

Prime rate

The interest rate that a country's largest banks announce for loans to their best customers. In practice, their most creditworthy customers get a rate lower than this.

Principal

1. The initial amount of a loan, thus not including *interest* (page 143).

2. The person or other entity on whose behalf an *agent* (page 7) acts, in the *principal-agent theory* (page 218).

Principal-agent theory

The theory of interaction between an *agent* (page 7) and the *principal* (page 217) for whom they act, the point being to structure incentives so that the agent will act to benefit the principal. Can be used, for example, to analyze government as agent for society, or *international institutions* (page 148) as agents for governments.

Principal supplier

The country that has the largest share of imports of a good into a particular importing country, among those exporters subject to *MFN* (page 176) tariffs. It is customary in tariff negotiations, and to some extent mandated by *WTO* (page 293) rules, that countries negotiate with their principal suppliers.

Prisoners' dilemma

A strategic interaction in which two players both gain individually by not cooperating, but leading to a *Nash equilibrium* (page 184) in which both are worse off than if they cooperated. Important especially for explaining why countries may choose *protection* (page 222) even though all lose as a result. See *tariff-and-retaliation game* (page 264).

Private benefit

The benefit to an individual economic agent, such as a consumer or firm, from an event, action, or policy change. Contrasts with *social benefit* (page 249).

Private cost

The cost to an individual economic agent, such as a consumer or firm, from an event, action, or policy change. Contrasts with *social cost* (page 249).

Privatization

The conversion of a government-owned enterprise to private ownership.

Probability density

For a continuous *random variable* (page 227), a function whose integral over any set is the probability of the variable being in that set.

Probability distribution

A specification of the probabilities for each possible value of a *random variable* (page 227).

Processed good

A good that has been transformed in some way by a production activity, in contrast to a *raw material* (page 227).

Procurement

See *government procurement* (page 120).

Procurement officer

A government official responsible for purchasing goods and services and for deciding among alternative suppliers.

Producer presence

A *mode of supply* (page 178) of a *traded service* (page 274) in which the producer establishes a presence in the buyer's country by *FDI* (page 105) and/or permanent relocation of workers.

Producer subsidy equivalent

1. *Producer support estimate* (see below).

2. This ought logically to measure the extent to which existing policies serve to *subsidize* (page 260) producers, defined as the *ad valorem* (page 5) subsidy that, if paid directly to producers per unit of production, would lead to the same level of output as existing policies.

Producer support estimate

Introduced by the *OECD* (page 196) to quantify support in agriculture, it measures "transfers from consumers and taxpayers to agricultural producers as a result of measures [of] support," expressed as percentage of gross farm receipts. Also called *producer subsidy equivalent* (see above). See also *CSE* (page 56).

Producer surplus

The difference between the revenue of producers and production cost, measured as the area above the supply (or marginal cost) curve and below price, out to the quantity supplied, and net of fixed cost and losses at low output. If input prices are constant, this is profit; if not, it includes gains to input suppliers, such as labor. Normally useful only as the *change in producer surplus* (page 37).

Product

A good or service that is produced.

Product cycle

The life cycle of a new product, which first can be produced only in the country where it was developed, then as it becomes standardized and more familiar, can be produced in other countries and exported back to where it started. Due to *Vernon (1966)* (page 382).

Product differentiation

See *differentiated product* (page 68).

Product life cycle

See *product cycle* (above).

Product price equalization

The equalization of the price of a homogeneous good (or perhaps service, though that is less likely) across countries as a result of *free trade* (page 113). Full product price equalization can be expected, other than by accident, only if all *trade costs* (page 273) are zero.

Production externality

An *externality* (page 100) arising from production.

Production factor

Factor of production (page 103).

Production function

A function that specifies the output in an industry for all combinations of inputs.

Production possibilities schedule

A table reporting various combinations of outputs that are possible for an economy, given its *technology* (page 268) and *factor endowments* (page 102). Thus the data on which the *production possibility frontier* (see below) is based.

Production possibility curve

See *production possibility frontier* (below).

Production possibility frontier

A diagram showing the maximum output possible of one good for various outputs of another (or several others), given technology and factor endowments. Also called a *transformation curve* (page 279) or **production possibility curve**.

Production worker

A worker directly engaged in production. In empirical studies of skilled and unskilled labor, data on production workers are often taken to represent unskilled labor.

Productivity

Output per unit input, usually measured either by *labor productivity* (page 156) or by *total factor productivity* (page 271).

Productivity of labor

See *labor productivity* (page 156).

Profit

1. The net gain from an activity.

2. For a firm: revenue minus cost.

Profit maximizing

The level of a variable or behavior that maximizes the profit of a firm.

Profit remittance

In a *multinational corporation* (page 183), the return of part of the *profit* (see above) earned by a *subsidiary* (page 260) in one country to the *parent* (page 204) in another.

Profit shifting

The use of government policies to alter the outcome of international oligopolistic competition so as to increase the profits of domestic firms at the expense of foreign firms. This is a key element of *strategic trade policy* (page 258).

Prohibited subsidy

A *subsidy* (page 260) that is forbidden under the rules of the *WTO* (page 293). These include subsidies that are specifically designed to distort international trade, such as *export subsidies* (page 99) or subsidies that require use of domestic rather than imported inputs.

Prohibition

Denial of the right to import or export, applying to particular products and/or particular countries. Includes *embargo* (page 84).

Prohibitive tariff
A *tariff* (page 264) that reduces imports to zero.

Propensity
The extent to which an economic agent is inclined to use income for a particular purpose, such as the (marginal or average) propensity to import, or propensity to consume, measured as the fraction of income (or of a change in income, if marginal) devoted to the activity.

Prospective analysis
Ex ante analysis (page 93).

Protection
1. Without any adjective, or as "import protection," this refers to restriction of imports by means of *tariffs* (page 264) and/or *NTBs* (page 195), and thereby intended to insulate domestic producers from competition with imported goods.
2. As "IP protection," or "intellectual property protection," this refers to enforcement of *intellectual property* (page 142) rights by granting patents, copyrights, and trademarks and by prosecuting those who violate them.

Protectionism
Advocacy of protection. The word has a negative connotation, and few advocates of protection in particular situations will acknowledge being **protectionists**.

Protocol of accession
Legal document specifying the procedures for a country to join an international agreement or organization, including the rights and responsibilities that accompany such *accession* (page 4).

PSE
Producer support estimate (page 219).

PTA
Preferential trading arrangement (page 214).

Public good
A good that is provided for users collectively, use by one not precluding use of the same units of the good by others.

Public procurement
Government procurement (page 120).

Punitive tariff

A high *tariff* (page 264) the purpose of which is to inflict harm on a foreign exporter as punishment for some previous behavior.

Purchasing power

The amount of goods that money will buy, usually measured (inversely) by the *CPI* (page 54).

Purchasing power parity

1. The equality of the prices of a bundle of goods (usually the *CPI* (page 54)) in two countries when valued at the prevailing exchange rate. Called **absolute PPP**.

2. The equality of the rates of change over time in the prices of a bundle of goods in two countries when valued at the prevailing exchange rate. Called **relative PPP**. Implies that the rate of *depreciation* (page 66) of a currency must equal the difference between its *inflation rate* (page 141) and the inflation rate in the currency to which it is being compared.

Purchasing power parity exchange rate

An exchange rate calculated to yield absolute *purchasing power parity* (see above). Useful for making comparisons of *real* (page 228) values (wages, GDP) across countries with different currencies. Since *absolute purchasing power parity* (page 3) is rarely correct, this contrasts with the *nominal exchange rate* (page 192).

Purchasing power parity theory

A theory of the *exchange rate* (page 94) that the rate will adjust to achieve *purchasing power parity* (see above), in either its absolute or its relative form.

Pure competition

Same as *perfect competition* (page 207).

Pure exchange economy

A theoretical economy in which goods are not produced, but exist as endowments, and are then traded among consumers.

QR
Quantitative restriction (see below).

Quad
Refers both to the *quadrilateral meetings* (see below) and to the participants in those meetings, the U.S., Canada, *EU* (page 89), and Japan.

Quadrilateral meetings
Meetings that occur occasionally involving the *trade ministers* (page 275) of the U.S., Canada, *EU* (page 89), and Japan to discuss trade policy issues.

Qualitative
1. Referring only to the characteristics of something being described, rather than exact numerical measurement.
2. Indicative only of relative sizes or magnitudes, rather than their numerical values. A qualitative comparison would say whether one thing is larger, smaller, or equal to another, without specifying the size of any difference. As opposed to **quantitative**.

Quantitative
Expressed in numerical values. See *qualitative* (above).

Quantitative restriction
A restriction on trade, usually imports, limiting the quantity of the good or service that is traded; a *quota* (page 226) is the most common example, but *VERs* (page 289) usually take the form of QRs. QRs on traded services are more likely to restrict the number or activities of foreign service providers than the services themselves, since the latter are hard to monitor and measure.

Quantity definition
A method of defining relative *factor abundance* (page 101) based on ratios of factor quantities: Compared to country B, country A is abundant in factor X relative to factor Y iff $X^A/Y^A > X^B/Y^B$,

where I^J is the quantity of factor I with which country J is *endowed* (page 86), $I = X, Y, J = A, B$.

Quantity quota

A *quota* (page 226) specifying quantity, in units, weight, volume, etc. of a good.

Quantity theory of money

The classic theory of the price level and therefore of *inflation* (page 141), building on the *equation of exchange* (page 87) and the additional assumption that *velocity of money* (page 288) is constant. Together, these imply that the rate of inflation equals the rate of growth of money minus the rate of growth of real output.

Quarter

One of the four three-month periods into which the calendar year is divided for the reporting of economic data.

Quartile

One of four segments of a distribution that has been divided into quarters. For example, the second-from-the-bottom quartile of an income distribution refers to those with incomes above the bottom 25% of the population and below the top 50%.

Quasi-fiscal

Having to do with financial transactions of units that are not included in a government's budget but that have some of the same effects as *fiscal policy* (page 107). Most often mentioned as having quasi-fiscal effects are *central banks* (page 35).

Quasi-linear utility

A *utility function* (page 287) of the form $U(x_0, x_1, \ldots, x_n) = x_0 + \Sigma_i u^i(x_i)$, where $u^i(\cdot)$ are strictly *concave* (page 45) functions. This is useful for generating demand functions for goods x_i that depend only on their own prices in terms of the numeraire x_0.

Quid pro quo FDI

FDI in response to the threat of protection. Done by a firm that exports into the domestic market, the motive is to create jobs there and lessen the threat that its exports will be restricted. Due to *Bhagwati (1985)* (page 372).

Quintile
One of five segments of a distribution that has been divided into fifths. Analogous to *quartile* (page 225).

Quota
1. A government-imposed restriction on quantity, or sometimes on total value.
2. An **import quota** specifies the maximum amount of an import per year, typically administered with *import licenses* (page 134) that may be sold or directly allocated, to individuals or firms, domestic or foreign. May be *global* (page 118), *bilateral* (page 23), or *by country* (see below).
3. An *IMF quota* (page 132).

Quota by country
A *quota* (see above) that specifies the total amount to be imported (or exported) and also assigns specific amounts to each exporting (or importing) country.

Quota rent
The economic *rent* (page 233) received by the holder of the right (or *license* (page 135)) to import under a *quota* (see above). Equals the domestic price of the imported good, net of any tariff, minus the world price, times the quantity of imports.

R&D
Research and development (page 234).

Race to the bottom
The idea that, if one country provides a *competitive advantage* (page 44) to its firms by lax regulation (of the environment, for example), then competing firms in other countries will demand even weaker regulation by their governments, and regulation will be reduced to minimal levels everywhere.

Radical political economy

See *political economy* (page 210).

Random variable

An economic or statistical variable that takes on multiple (or a continuum of) values, each with some probability that is specified by a *probability distribution* (page 219) (or *probability density function* (page 218)).

Rate of interest

Interest rate (page 143).

Rate of return

The percentage of an asset's value that the owner of the asset earns, usually per year.

Ration

1. In the presence of excess demand (for a good, etc.), to allocate among demanders by some means other than the price they are willing to pay.

2. The quantity of a rationed good allocated to one demander.

Ration foreign exchange

To *ration* (see above) access to scarce foreign currency under a *pegged exchange rate* (page 207) with an *overvalued currency* (page 203). Usually done by means of *import licensing* (page 134). See *exchange control* (page 93).

Rational expectations

In forming opinion about future events, the use of all available information to assess the probabilities of the possible states of the world. More simply, expectations that are as correct as is possible with available information.

Raw material

A good that has not been transformed by production; a *primary product* (page 217).

Ray

A straight line drawn from the origin of a diagram. In the *Heckscher-Ohlin model* (page 126), two rays are used to define a *diversification cone* (page 72).

RCA

Revealed comparative advantage (page 236).

Reaction curve

The graph of a *reaction function* (see below).

Reaction function

The function specifying the choice of a *strategic variable* (page 259) by one economic agent as a function of the choice of another agent. Most familiar: specifying output choices of firms in a *Cournot* (page 53) *duopoly* (page 76).

Real

1. Expressed in terms of the amounts of goods and services that something is worth at market prices.

2. *Adjusted for inflation* (page 5).

3. Referring only to real economic variables as opposed to *nominal* (page 191), or monetary ones, as in *real models* (page 229).

4. Used with "appreciation" or "depreciation," refers to the *real exchange rate* (see below). Thus a **real appreciation** means that the *nominal* (page 191) value of a country's currency has increased by more than its relative price level may have decreased, so that the prices of its goods relative to foreign goods have increased.

5. The name of one unit of the Brazilian currency. One real equals 100 centavos. Pronounced "ray-all".

Real effective exchange rate

The *effective exchange rate* (page 82) adjusted for the rates of *inflation* (page 141) in each country.

Real exchange rate

1. The *nominal exchange rate* (page 192) adjusted for inflation. Unlike most other *real* (see above) variables, this adjustment requires accounting for price levels in two currencies. The real exchange rate is: $R = EP^*/P$ where E is the nominal domestic-currency price of foreign currency, P is the domestic price level, and P^* is the foreign price level.

2. The real price of foreign goods; i.e., the quantity of domestic goods needed to purchase a unit of foreign goods. Equals the reciprocal of the *terms of trade* (page 269). Equivalent to definition 1.

3. The relative price of *traded goods* (page 278) in terms of *nontraded goods* (page 194).

Real GDP

The real counterpart to *nominal* (page 191) *GDP* (page 122), obtained by valuing output in a given year at prices from another year, called the *base year* (page 20).

Real interest rate

The *nominal interest rate* (page 192) adjusted for *inflation* (page 141), to get the percentage yield an asset holder receives in terms of real resources. Equals the nominal interest rate minus the rate of inflation.

Real model

An economic model without money. Most *general equilibrium* (page 117) models of trade are real models. This includes the *Ricardian model* (page 237), the *Heckscher-Ohlin model* (page 126), and the models of the *new trade theory* (page 190).

Real money balances

The *real* (page 228) value of the amount of *money* (page 179) held by a person, household, or firm, or the amount in circulation in the economy.

Real national income

National income (page 185) *adjusted for inflation* (page 5).

Real terms

Same as *real* (page 228). A "wage expressed in real terms" is just the real wage.

Real trade

A shorthand term for most of the theory of international trade, which consists largely of *real models* (see above). Contrasts with *international finance* (page 147).

Real wage

The wage of labor — or more generally the price of any *factor* (page 101) — relative to an appropriate *price index* (page 215) for the goods and services that the worker (or factor owner) consumes.

Recession

A significant decline in economic activity. In the U.S., recession is approximately defined as two successive *quarters* (page 225) of falling *GDP* (page 122), as judged by *NBER* (page 186).

A recession in one country may be caused by, or may itself cause, recession in another country with which it trades.

Reciprocal demand

The concept that, in international trade, it is not just supply and demand that interact, but demand and demand. That is, a trading equilibrium is a reciprocal equilibrium in which one country's demand for another country's products (and willingness to pay for them with its own) matches with the other country's demands for the products of the first.

Reciprocal demand curve

An *offer curve* (page 196). So called to emphasize that a country exports in order, reciprocally, to get imports in return.

Reciprocal dumping

The sale by firms from two countries into each others' markets for prices below what each charges at home. So called because the exports of both firms meet the price-discrimination definition of *dumping* (page 76). *Brander and Krugman (1983)* (page 373) introduced the term and showed that this is likely to happen in an international *duopoly* (page 76) with transport costs.

Reciprocal trade agreement

Agreement between two countries to open their markets to each other's exports, usually by each reducing *tariffs* (page 264). Early *trade rounds* (page 277) under the *GATT* (page 116) consisted mostly of reciprocal trade agreements, extended to other *contracting parties* (page 49) by the *MFN* (page 176) requirement.

Reciprocal Trade Agreements Act of 1934

US legislation in 1934 in which Congress delegated the setting of *tariffs* (page 264) to the President, who was then authorized to negotiate *reciprocal trade agreements* (see above).

Reciprocity

A principle that underlies *GATT* (page 116) negotiations, that countries exchange comparable *concessions* (page 46).

Reciprocity conditions

In the production structure of the *Heckscher-Ohlin model* (page 126), the fact that the effect of a small change in any factor endowment on output of any good is equal to the effect of a small change in the price of that good on the price of that factor. That is, the matrices of *Rybczynski derivatives* (page 239) and *Stolper-Samuelson derivatives* (page 257) are the same. Also called **Samuelson's reciprocity conditions**, from *Samuelson (1953)* (page 380).

Red box

A category of *subsidies* (page 260) that is forbidden under *WTO* (page 293) rules. This terminology is used in the *agriculture agreement* (page 9), where however there is no red box. Presumably equivalent to *prohibited subsidies* (page 221).

Redistributed tariff revenue

Refers to a common assumption that tariff *revenue* (page 237) is given to consumers as transfer payments (*not* in proportion to what they paid by importing) to be spent like any other income. Since in *general equilibrium* (page 117) the effects of a tariff depend on how the revenue is spent, this is a useful neutral assumption.

Redundant tariff

A tariff that, if changed, will not change the quantity of imports, either because the tariff is *prohibitive* (page 222), or because some other policy such as a *quota* (page 226) or an *embargo* (page 84) is limiting quantity.

Re-export

The *export* (page 97) without further processing or transformation of a good that has been *imported* (page 134). See *entrepot trade* (page 86).

Reference price

See *minimum price system* (page 177).

Reflation

Expansionary *monetary* (page 179) or *fiscal policy* (page 107).

Regional aid

A *subsidy* (page 260) directed at a geographic region within a country to assist its development. Such subsidies are *non-actionable* (page 192) under *WTO* (page 293) rules.

Regional integration

The formation of closer economic linkages among countries that are geographically near each other, especially by forming *preferential trade agreements* (page 214).

Regional policy

In a trade context, this usually refers to a *regional aid* (page 231).

Regional trade

Trade among countries that are geographically close together, especially on the same continent.

Regionalism

The formation or proliferation of *preferential trading arrangements* (page 214).

Registered exports and imports

If a country regulates what can be traded, then "registered" means legal. In contrast, **unregistered** exports and imports are *smuggled* (page 248) in some fashion.

Regression analysis

The statistical technique of finding a straight line that approximates the information in a group of data points. Used throughout empirical economics, including in both international trade and finance.

Regression model

See *linear regression model* (page 163).

Regressor

In a *linear regression model* (page 163), an independent — or right-hand-side — variable. That is, one of the variables that is being used to explain another.

Regulation

Any government effort to influence the performance of the economy or the behavior of economic agents, especially firms, within it. Conflicts sometimes arise between domestic regulations and international commerce or commitments.

Relative demand

The ratio of the demand for one good to the demand for another, most useful in representing general equilibrium in a two-good economy, where relative price adjusts to equate relative supply and relative demand.

Relative factor prices

The ratio of the price of one *factor* (page 101) to the price of another. In a two-factor model with *constant returns to scale* (page 47), this alone determines the ratio of factors employed in a sector.

Relative price

The price of one thing (usually a good) in terms of another; i.e., the ratio of two prices. The relative price of good X in terms of good Y is p_X/p_Y.

Relative supply

The ratio of the supply of one good to the supply of another, most useful in representing general equilibrium in a two-good economy, where relative price adjusts to equate relative supply and relative demand.

Remedy

In a *trade dispute* (page 274) in the *WTO* (page 293) or other forum, the measure recommended by the *dispute settlement* (page 71) *panel* (page 203) to resolve the dispute, usually a measure that will bring the offending country into compliance with WTO (or other) rules.

Remittances

Payments from one country to another that are not payment *for* anything (goods, services, assets, the use of capital, etc.), such as charitable contributions, gifts to family members, and government aid.

Remuneration

Payment in return for services rendered.

Rent

1. Economic rent: The premium that the owner of a resource receives over and above its *opportunity cost* (page 200).

2. The payment to the owner of land or other property in return for its use.

Rent seeking

The using up of real resources in an effort to secure the rights to economic *rents* (see above) that arise from government policies. In international economics the term usually refers to efforts to obtain *quota rents* (page 226). Term *introduced* (page 370) by *Krueger (1974)* (page 377).

Rental price

The payment per unit time for the services of a unit of a *factor of production* (page 103), such as land or capital.

Rentier

A person whose income comes mainly from rent on land or, more broadly, from assets rather than labor. (Pronounced "Ron' Tee Yay".)

Reparations

Payment or other compensation provided by a government to a group of people or to another country to compensate for loss or damage that it has caused. Internationally, reparations have been paid after a war by the losers to the winners, most notably by Germany after World War I.

Repatriation

To return something, especially money or profit, to the country of its owner or its origin.

Repo

Repurchase agreement (see below).

Repurchase agreement

An agreement to sell a security for a specified price and to buy it back later at another specified price. A repo is essentially a secured loan.

Reschedule

To renegotiate the terms of a loan, reducing payments by extending them over time and/or forgiving a portion of the principal. Debt rescheduling has been a primary means of dealing with international *debt crises* (page 62).

Research and development

The use of resources for the deliberate discovery of new information and ways of doing things, together with the application of that information in inventing new products or processes.

Reserve asset

Any *asset* (page 13) that is used as *international reserves* (page 149), including a national *currency* (page 56), precious metal such as gold, or *SDRs* (page 242).

Reserve currency

A currency that is used as *international reserves* (page 149), often because it is an *intervention currency* (page 151). See also *seigniorage* (page 243).

Reserve ratio

The ratio of a *commercial bank's* (page 40) *reserves* (see below) to its *deposits* (page 66).

Reserves

1. *International reserves* (page 149) of a government or *central bank* (page 35).

2. Amounts held by *commercial banks* (page 40) in their vaults or on deposit with the central bank as backing for *deposits* (page 66).

Resource

1. An input to be used in an activity, especially production.

2. A *natural resource* (page 186).

Restricted trade

Trade that is restrained in some fashion by *tariffs* (page 264), *transport costs* (page 280), or *NTBs* (page 195).

Restriction on trade

See *trade restriction* (page 277).

Restrictive business practice

Action by a firm or group of firms to restrict entry by other firms, that is, to prevent other firms from selling their product or in their market. This is a restraint of competition and would normally be illegal under *competition policy* (page 44).

Restructure

To alter the terms of repayment of a *debt* (page 61), usually by extending repayment over a longer period of time, perhaps at a lower interest rate.

Results-based trade policy

The use of trade policies targeted to specific indicators of economic performance. For example, in the early 1990s, the U.S. insisted on achieving specified market shares in trade with Japan.

Retaliation
1. The use of an increased trade barrier in response to another country increasing its trade barrier, either as a way of undoing the adverse effects of the latter's action or of punishing it.
2. The formal procedure permitted under the *GATT* (page 116) whereby a country may raise discriminatory tariffs above *bound levels* (page 264) against a GATT member that has violated GATT rules and not provided *compensation* (page 43).

Retrospective analysis
Ex post analysis (page 93).

Return
The amount that is earned by someone who holds an *asset* (page 13), usually expressed as a percentage of what it cost to acquire the asset. The return includes *interest* (page 143), *dividends* (page 72), and *capital gains and losses* (page 32), the latter due to both changes in the price of the asset and, for international holdings, changes in *exchange rates* (page 94).

Return to capital
Same as the *rental price* (page 234) of capital. Since capital can only be measured in monetary units, the rental price is, say, dollars per dollar's worth of capital per unit time, and it therefore has the form of a rate of return like an interest rate.

Returns to scale
Same as *increasing returns to scale* (page 138).

Revealed comparative advantage
Balassa's (1965) (page 371) measure of relative export performance by country and industry, defined as a country's share of world exports of a good divided by its share of total world exports. The index for country i good j is $RCA_{ij} = 100(X_{ij}/X_{wj})/(X_{it}/X_{wt})$ where X_{ab} is exports by country a (w = world) of good b (t = total for all goods).

Revealed preference
The use of the value of expenditure to "reveal" the preference of a consumer or group of consumers for the bundle of goods they purchase compared to other bundles of equal or smaller value. Used by *Samuelson (1939)* (page 380) and *Ohyama (1972)* (page 379), especially, to examine the *gains from trade* (page 116).

Revenue

Referring to a tariff, the money collected by the government. Equals the size of the tariff times the quantity of imports. An analysis of the effects of a tariff needs to account for the revenue, and in a *general equilibrium* (page 117) model it must specify whether and how the revenue is spent.

Revenue argument for a tariff

The use of a *tariff* (page 264) to raise revenue for the government. Many other kinds of tax cause smaller distortions and are therefore preferable to tariffs for this purpose. However, a tariff is one of the easiest taxes to collect, and it is therefore common in the early stages of a country's development.

Revenue deficit

1. In general use, this seems to be essentially the same as a *budget deficit* (page 27), but with attention given to the low level of revenue rather than to the high level of expenditure.

2. More precisely, this means a larger deficit (or smaller surplus) than had been budgeted for.

Revenue seeking

The use of real resources in an effort to secure a share of the disposition of tariff revenues. Term due to *Bhagwati and Srinivasan (1980)* (page 373).

Reverse engineering

The process of learning how a product is made by taking it apart and examining it.

Ricardian model

The classic model of international trade introduced by David Ricardo to explain the pattern of and the gains from trade in terms of *comparative advantage* (page 42). It assumes perfect competition and a single factor of production, labor, with constant requirements of labor per unit of output that differ across countries.

Ricardo point

On the world *PPF* (page 212) of a two-country, 2-good *Ricardian model* (see above), the point at which each country is specialized in production of a different good; the kink of the world PPF.

Ricardo-Viner model

A *specific factors model* (page 253) with a single specific factor in each industry and one mobile factor, named after two of the many who used this as the standard model of trade prior to the *Heckscher-Ohlin model* (page 126). It extends the simple *Ricardian model* (page 237) by allowing the *marginal product* (page 169) of labor to fall with output. It was revived by *Jones (1971)* (page 376), *Samuelson (1971)* (page 381), then merged with HO by *Mayer (1974)* (page 378), *Mussa (1974)* (page 379), and *Neary (1978)* (page 379).

Rio Summit

The United Nations Conference on Environment and Development, held 3–14 June 1992 in Rio de Janeiro, Brazil. 172 governments participated, including 108 heads of state. Also called the **Earth Summit**.

Risk

1. *Uncertainty* (page 282) associated with a transaction or an asset.

2. The probability of loss. Differs from definition 1 because "uncertainty" includes probability of gain as well.

Risk aversion

Desire to avoid uncertainty. Risk aversion is usually quantified by the mathematical *expected value* (page 97) that one is willing to forego in order to get greater certainty.

Risk free rate

The *interest rate* (page 143) on a riskless, or safe, asset, usually taken to be a short-term U.S. government security.

Risk premium

1. The higher expected return (in the sense of mathematical *expected value* (page 97)) that an uncertain asset must pay in order for *risk averse* (see above) investors to be willing to hold it.

2. The difference between the *interest rate* (page 143) on a risky asset and that on a safe one.

3. In *exchange markets* (page 94) the difference between the *forward rate* (page 112) and the *expected* (page 97) future *spot rate* (page 254).

Rollback
    1. The phasing out of measures that are not consistent with an agreement.
    2. In the *Uruguay Round* (page 286), the agreement to remove all *GATT* (page 116)-inconsistent trade-restricting and trade-distorting measures by the time negotiations were completed. See *standstill* (page 256).

ROO
    Rule of origin (see below).

Round
    See *trade round* (page 277).

Rule of law
    A legal system in which rules are clear, well-understood, and fairly enforced, including property rights and enforcement of contracts.

Rules-based trade policy
    Institutional arrangements in which national trade policies are governed by internationally agreed-upon rules, as in the *GATT* (page 116) and *WTO* (page 293).

Rules of origin
    Rules included in a *FTA* (page 114) specifying when a good will be regarded as produced within the FTA, so as to cross between members without tariff. Typical *ROOs* (see above) are based on percentage of *value added* (page 287) or on changes in *tariff heading* (page 265).

Run on a currency
    The short-term *capital outflows* (page 33) that occur when a *pegged exchange rate* (page 207) regime is thought to be running out of *reserves* (page 235) and is thus expected (and therefore forced) to *devalue* (page 67).

Rybczynski derivative
    The effect of a small change in a single factor endowment on the output of a good.

Rybczynski theorem
    The property of the *Heckscher-Ohlin model* (page 126) that, at constant prices, an increase in the *endowment* (page 86) of one

factor (page 101) increases the output of the industry that uses that factor *intensively* (page 143) and reduces the output of the other (or some other) industry. Due to *Rybczynski (1955)* (page 380).

SA8000
A system of international labor standards and mechanisms for compliance and certification overseen by the non-profit *Social Accountability International* (page 249) with participation by corporations, unions, and *NGOs* (page 191).

Safeguard protection
Import *protection* (page 222) provided under the *safeguards clause* (see below).

Safeguards clause
Article XIX of the *GATT* (page 116) that permits countries to restrict imports if they cause injury. Restrictions must be for a limited time and non-discriminatory. See *escape clause* (page 88).

SAI
Social Accountability International (page 249).

Sanction
1. To approve or give permission for an action, as when an international organization sanctions the use of particular economic policies.
2. A coercive measure used by a nation or group of nations against another as a penalty for violating international law or international norms. Usually plural: sanctions.

Sanitary and phytosanitary regulations
Government standards to protect health, of humans, plants, and animals. SPS measures are subject to rules in the *WTO* (page 293) to prevent them from acting as *NTBs* (page 195).

SAP

  Structural adjustment program (page 259).

Satisficing

  Seeking or achieving a satisfactory outcome, rather than the best possible. Contrasts with the optimizing behavior usually assumed in economics and *trade theory* (page 277). Alternative models based on satisficing are spreading within economics, but not yet much in international.

Say's law

  The proposition that "supply creates its own demand." The idea is clearest in a *barter economy* (page 20), where the act of supplying one thing is, intrinsically, the act of demanding something else. Named for Jean Baptiste Say, although he never stated it in this form.

Scale economies

  Increasing returns to scale (page 138).

Scarce

  Available in small supply; opposite of *abundant* (page 3). Usually meaningful only in relative terms, compared to demand and/or to supply at another place or time. See *factor abundance* (page 101), *factor scarcity* (page 104).

Scarce factor

  The factor in a country's *endowment* (page 86) with which it is least well endowed, relative to other factors, compared to other countries. May be defined by *quantity* (page 224) or by *price* (page 215).

Scarcity rent

  An economic *rent* (page 233) that is due to something being *scarce* (see above).

Schedule

  1. A list. See *tariff schedule* (page 266).

  2. A graph of a list of data; thus also a curve. See *demand schedule* (page 65).

Schengen agreement

  An agreement (later, convention) signed in 1985 to remove all frontier controls and permit free movement of persons between the participating countries. In 1999 it was incorporated into the *European Union* (page 357). Currently (2006), the participants include all 15 countries that were in the EU prior to its 2004 enlargement, except Ireland and the UK, plus Iceland and Norway.

Scientific tariff

A *made-to-measure tariff* (page 168).

Scitovszky indifference curve

An indifference curve for a group of individuals representing the minimum needed to keep all of them at given levels of utility. A well-behaved family of such indifference curves is defined holding utilities of all but one individual constant and varying only the one. These are useful in discussing the *gains from trade* (page 116). Due to *Scitovszky (1942)* (page 381).

SDR

Special drawing right (page 251).

SDRM

Sovereign debt restructuring mechanism (page 250).

Seasonal quota

A restriction on the quantity of imports of a good for a specified period of the year.

Seasonal tariff

A tariff that is levied at different rates at different times of the year, usually on agricultural products, being highest at the time of the domestic harvest.

Seattle Ministerial

The *ministerial* (page 177) meeting of the *WTO* (page 293) that was held in Seattle in November, 1999. It attracted a large group of protesters and ended without agreement among the participating countries.

Second best

Refers to what is the optimal policy when the true optimum (the **first best**) is unavailable due to constraints on policy choice. The **theory of second best** says that a policy that would be optimal without such constraints (such as a zero tariff in a small country) may not be second-best optimal if other policies are constrained. See *Lipsey and Lancaster (1956)* (page 378).

Second-best argument for protection

1. Any argument for protection that can be countered by pointing to a different and less distortionary policy that would achieve the same desired result at lower economic cost.

2. An argument for protection to partially correct an existing distortion in the economy when the first-best policy for that purpose is not available. For example, if domestic production generates a *positive externality* (page 211) and a production *subsidy* (page 260) to *internalize* (page 145) it is not available, then a tariff may be second-best optimal.

Second theorem of welfare economics

The proposition of *welfare economics* (page 292) that any *Pareto-optimal* (page 204) *allocation* (page 9) can be attained by a *competitive* (page 44) *general equilibrium* (page 117).

Secondary tariffs

Any charges imposed on imports in addition to the statutory tariff, such as an *import surcharge* (page 136).

Section 201

The *escape clause* (page 88) of the U.S. Trade Act of 1974.

Section 301

The provision of U.S. trade law that permits private parties to seek redress through the U.S. government if their commercial interests have been harmed by illegal or unfair actions of foreign governments.

Securities

Stocks (page 257), *bonds* (page 24), and other tradable *financial assets* (page 106).

Seigniorage

The difference between what money can buy and its cost of production. Therefore, seigniorage is the benefit that a government or other monetary authority derives from the ability to create money. In international exchange, if one country's money is willingly held by another, the first country derives these seigniorage benefits. This is the case of a *reserve currency* (page 235).

Selective

Applied to a trade policy, this means one that affects only some countries, not all, in contrast to *MFN* (page 176) policy.

Selectivity is an important concern in the use of *safeguards* (page 240), which countries often would prefer to make selective but are required by *GATT* (page 116) *Article XIX* (page 12) to be non-discriminatory.

Self-sufficiency

Provision by one's self of all of one's own needs. In international trade this means either not trading at all (*autarky* (page 15)), or importing only non-necessities.

Self-sufficiency argument for protection

The view that a country is better off providing for its own needs than depending on imports. It may be based on fear that war or foreign governments will interrupt imports. This is a *second-best argument* (page 243), since many policies could provide for that contingency without sacrificing all the *gains from trade* (page 116).

Sensitive

In trade negotiations and agreements, countries often identify lists of particular **sensitive products** or **sensitive sectors** that they regard as especially vulnerable to import competition and that they wish to exempt from trade liberalization.

Serious injury

The *injury* (page 141) requirement of the *escape clause* (page 88), understood to be more stringent than *material injury* (page 174) but otherwise apparently not rigorously defined.

Service

1. A product that is not embodied in a physical good and that typically effects some change in another product, person, or institution. Contrasts with *good* (page 120). *Trade in services* (page 274) is the subject of the *GATS* (page 116).

2. To make the scheduled payments on a *debt* (page 61), usually including both interest and amounts towards repayment of the principal. See *debt service* (page 62).

SEZ

Special economic zone (page 251).

Shadow exchange rate

1. The *shadow price* (page 245) of *foreign exchange* (page 109).

2. What the market *exchange rate* (page 94) would be in the absence of various *market imperfections* (page 172).

Shadow price

The implicit value or cost associated with a constraint. That is, the increased value that will be achieved by relaxing the constraint by one unit. When *foreign exchange* (page 109) is rationed, the shadow price of foreign exchange becomes the relevant *exchange rate* (page 94) for decisions.

Shallow integration

Reduction or elimination of *tariffs* (page 264), *quotas* (page 226), and other barriers to trade in goods at the border, such as trade-limiting *customs procedures* (page 59). Contrasts with *deep integration* (page 63).

Shelf life

The length of time that a good can be stored while still remaining useful enough to sell. Important for both perishable goods and goods that may become obsolete for reasons of technology or fashion. Relevant for international trade when, for example, *customs procedures* (page 59) cause delays.

Shock

1. An unexpected change.

2. Any change in an *exogenous variable* (page 96) (although strictly speaking, models often fail to deal adequately with the complications of an exogenous change being expected).

Short

1. Used with "sell" or "sale," this means that the seller does not currently have the thing being sold, but intends to acquire it on the market prior to making delivery.

2. Used by itself as a verb, it means to sell short, as "to short a currency," meaning to sell it *forward* (page 111) in anticipation that its value on the *spot market* (page 254) will fall.

Short run

Referring to a short time horizon, usually one in which some aspects of behavior that would vary over a longer time do not have time to do so. In trade models, it usually means that the employment of some factors of production is fixed. Contrasts with *long run* (page 166).

Short-term

1. Happening within the *short run* (page 245), or within a matter of months.

2. In the case of *bonds* (page 24) or *capital flows* (page 32), this refers to financial assets with a maturity of less than one year.

Short-term capital flow

A *capital flow* (see above) that is *short-term* (see above); of interest because such capital flows are likely to be very *liquid* (page 164) and therefore easily reversed and sources of *instability* (page 142) in *exchange markets* (page 94).

Shrimp-Turtle case

A case filed in the *WTO* (page 293) against the United States for restricting imports of shrimp from countries whose shrimp were caught by means that endangered sea turtles. The WTO ruled against the U.S., enraging many environmentalists.

Shuttle trade

The trade accomplished by individuals and groups traveling to other countries, buying goods, and bringing them home, often in their luggage, to resell. An important source of imports for Russia in the 1990s, some people traveling abroad several times a month for this purpose.

Silver standard

A monetary system in which the value of a currency is defined in terms of silver. If two currencies are both on a silver standard, then the *exchange rate* (page 94) between them is approximately determined by their two prices in terms of silver.

Singapore issues

The issues on which it was agreed to form working groups at the Singapore Ministerial: *trade and investment* (page 272), *competition policy* (page 44), transparency in *government procurement* (page 120), and *trade facilitation* (page 274).

Singapore Ministerial

The first ministerial meeting of the *WTO* (page 293), held in Singapore in 1996. It did not attempt to launch a round of trade negotiations, but it agreed to form working groups on several *Singapore issues* (page 246).

Single European Act

Treaty, signed in Luxembourg and The Hague and entering into force 1 July 1987, completing the **Single Market**. See *Europe 1992* (page 90).

Single market

Removal of the remaining barriers among the countries of the *European Union* (page 357), permitting the free movement of goods, persons, services, and capital; also known as *Europe 1992* (page 90).

Single undertaking

A term, in *trade negotiations* (page 275), for requiring participants to accept or reject the outcome of multiple negotiations in a single package, rather than selecting among them.

Skill

The abilities acquired by workers through education, training, and experience that permit them to be more productive. Essentially the same as *human capital* (page 130).

Skill biased

A *technological change* (page 268) or *technological difference* (page 268) that is *biased* (page 22) in favor of using more skilled labor, compared to some definition of *neutrality* (page 189).

Skill intensive

Describing an industry or sector of the economy that relies relatively heavily on inputs of skilled labor, usually relative to unskilled labor, compared to other industries or sectors. See *factor intensity* (page 102).

Skilled labor

Labor with a high level of *skill* (see above) or *human capital* (page 130). Identified empirically as labor earning a high wage, with a high level of education, or in an occupational category associated with these; sometimes crudely proxied as *non-production workers* (page 194).

Slicing up the value chain

Term for *fragmentation* (page 112) used by *Krugman (1996)* (page 377).

Slump

A decline in performance, either of a firm as a slump in sales or profits, or of a country as a slump in output or employment.

SMAC function

An acronym for the *CES function* (page 36) based on the names of the four authors who introduced it in *Arrow et al. (1961)* (page 371).

Small country assumption

The assumption in an economic model that a country is too small to affect world prices, incomes, or interest rates.

Small open economy

An economy that is small enough compared to the world markets in which it participates that (as a good approximation) its policies do not alter world prices or incomes. The country is thus a *price taker* (page 216) in world markets. The term is normally applied to a country as a whole, although it is sometimes used in the context of only a single product.

Smoot-Hawley tariff

The *Tariff Act of 1930* (page 264), this raised average U.S. tariffs on *dutiable imports* (page 76) to 53% and provoked *retaliation* (page 236) by other countries.

Smuggle

To take a good across a national border illegally. If the good itself is legal, the purpose is usually to avoid paying a tariff or to circumvent some other trade barrier.

Snake

An arrangement in which currencies were *pegged* (page 207) to each other but left free to *float* (page 108) as a group against the U.S. dollar. Named for the graph that the limits of variation of a currency would follow over time.

Snake in the tunnel

An arrangement used briefly in Europe after the collapse of the *Bretton Woods System* (page 26) in which European currencies were permitted to vary ±1% against each other (see *snake* above) but ±2.25% against the dollar (the **tunnel**).

Social Accountability International

A U.S.-based non-profit organization that develops and implements the *SA8000* (page 240) international workplace standards.

Social benefit

The benefit to society as a whole from an event, action, or policy change. Includes *externalities* (page 100) and deducts any benefits that are transfers from others, in contrast to *private benefit* (page 218).

Social capital

The *networks* (page 189) of relationships among persons, firms, and institutions in a society, together with associated norms of behavior, trust, cooperation, etc., that enable a society to function effectively.

Social cost

The cost to society as a whole from an event, action, or policy change. Includes negative *externalities* (page 100) and does not count costs that are transfers to others, in contrast to *private cost* (page 218).

Social dumping

Export of a good from a country with weak or poorly enforced *labor standards* (page 156), reflecting the idea that the exporter has costs that are artificially lower than its competitors in higher-standards countries, constituting an unfair advantage in international trade.

Social indifference curve

A curve showing the combinations of goods that, when available to a country, yield the same level of *social welfare* (see below).

Social welfare function

A function mapping allocations of goods to the individuals in an economy to a level of welfare for the economy as a whole. If it depends only on the levels of utility of the individuals rather than separately on the allocations, then it is a *Bergsonian social welfare function* (page 22).

SOE

  1. *State-owned enterprise* (page 256).

  2. *Small open economy* (page 248).

Soft currency

A *currency* (page 56) that is not widely accepted in exchange for other currencies, in contrast to a *hard currency* (page 124).

Softwood lumber dispute

A *trade dispute* (page 274) between the U.S. and Canada that has extended over many years. Canada's forest land is mostly owned by provincial governments, which charge a "stumpage fee" for lumber companies to harvest trees. The U.S. claims that this fee is too low and constitutes an illegal *subsidy* (page 260).

Sole importing agency

An entity, either private or government, that has been granted by government the exclusive right to import certain goods.

Solow model

The *neoclassical growth model* (page 188). Also called the **Solow-Swan model**.

Solow neutral

A particular specification of *technological change* (page 268) or *technological difference* (page 268) that is *capital augmenting* (page 31).

Solow residual

A measure of technological progress equal to the difference between the rate of growth of output and the weighted average of the rates of growth of capital and labor, with factor income shares as weights. Due to *Solow (1957)* (page 381). Also called the growth of *total factor productivity* (page 271). Used to compare sources of growth across countries.

Sound money

A currency that is responsibly managed so as to avoid excessive *inflation* (page 141).

Source country

See *FDI* (page 105).

Sovereign debt restructuring mechanism

A framework proposed by the *IMF* (page 132) for permitting countries facing *financial crises* (page 106) to *restructure* (page 235) their debts in an orderly manner and minimally disruptive manner, analogous to bankruptcy for a private debtor.

Sovereign spread

The *spread* (page 254) on the debt of a sovereign government, and thus a measure of the riskiness of lending to it and the cost to it of borrowing.

Sovereignty

A country or region's power and ability to rule itself and manage its own affairs. Some feel that memberships in international organizations such as the *WTO* (page 293) are a threat to their sovereignty.

Spaghetti bowl

Term frequently used by Bhagwati for the tangle of relationships created by multiple overlapping *preferential trading arrangements* (page 214).

Spatial arbitrage

Arbitrage (page 11) on price differences in different locations.

Special and differential treatment

The *GATT* (page 116) principle that developing countries be accorded special privileges, exempting them from some requirements of developed countries. It also permits *tariff preferences* (page 265) among developing countries and by developed countries in favor of developing countries, as under the *GSP* (page 123).

Special drawing right

Originally intended within the *IMF* (page 132) as a sort of international money for use among central banks pegging their exchange rates, the SDR is a transferable right to acquire another country's currency. Defined in terms of a basket of currencies, today it mainly plays the role of a unit of international account.

Special economic zone

These exist in several countries, including especially China, and their characteristics vary. Typically they are regions designated for economic development oriented toward inward *FDI* (page 105) and exports, both fostered by special policy incentives that may include being an *EPZ* (page 87).

Special entry procedure

An administrative procedure that is required as a condition of entry for an imported good, such as transport by the importing country's national fleet, or entry through a specific port or *customs station* (page 60).

Special safeguard

As part of the *Agreement on Agriculture* (page 8) of the *WTO* (page 293), a special provision for providing *safeguard protection* (page 240) to specified agricultural products that had been subject to *tariffication* (page 266).

Specialization

1. Producing more than you need of some things, and less of others, hence "specializing" in the first. In international trade, this is just the opposite of *self-sufficiency* (page 244).

2. Doing less than everything, as when a country produces fewer different goods than it consumes. In a *2x2x2* (page 281) trade model, this means a country produces just one good. With many goods and countries, it means a country has some goods that it does not (and cannot competitively) produce. Also may be called *complete specialization* (page 44).

Specie

Coins, normally including only those made of precious metal.

Specie flow mechanism

Under the *gold standard* (page 119), the mechanism by which international payments would adjust. A country with high *inflation* (page 141) would export less, import more, and thus lose *specie* (see above), i.e., gold. With the *money supply* (page 180) fixed to the quantity of gold, the resulting monetary contraction would reduce prices. Due to David Hume.

Specific commitment

Under the *GATS* (page 116), the identification of a category of *services* (page 244) in which a country will apply *national treatment* (page 186) and assure *market access* (page 171) for foreign service providers.

Specific factor

A *factor of production* (page 103) that is unable to move into or out of an industry. The term is used to describe factors that would not be of any use in other industries and also — more loosely — factors that could be used elsewhere but do not, in the short run, have the time or resources needed to move. See *specific-factors model* (below). The term seems to come from *Haberler (1937)* (page 375).

Specific-factors model

A model (diagram on page 331) in which some or all factors are *specific factors* (page 252). The most common version is the *Ricardo-Viner model* (page 238), with one specific factor (often capital or land) in each industry plus another factor (often labor) that is mobile between them. But an extreme form of the model, the *Cairnes-Haberler model* (page 29), has all factors specific.

Specific tariff

A *tariff* (page 264) specified as an amount of currency per unit of the good.

Specificity

The property that a policy measure applies to one or a group of enterprises or industries, as opposed to all industries.

Specificity rule

The principle that the optimal policy for correcting a *distortion* (page 72) is one that deals most directly, or specifically, with that distortion.

Speculation

The purchase or sale of an asset (or acquisition otherwise of an *open position* (page 199)) in hopes that its price will rise or fall respectively, in order to make a profit. See *destabilizing speculation* (page 66) and *stabilizing speculation* (page 255).

Speculative attack

In any asset market, the surge in sales of the asset that occurs when investors expect its price to fall. A common phenomenon in the *exchange market* (page 94), especially under an *adjustable pegged* (page 5) exchange rate.

Speculator

Anyone who engages in *speculation* (see above), May include those who transfer their assets into different forms (or curren cies) in order to avoid a prospective *capital loss* (page 33).

Splintering

Another term for *fragmentation* (page 112). Used by *Bhagwati (1984)* (page 372).

Spoke

See *hub and spoke integration* (page 130).

Sporadic dumping

Intermittent dumping (page 144).

Spot

On the *spot market* (see below).

Spot market

A market for exchange (of currencies, in the case of the *exchange market* (page 94)) in the present (as opposed to a *forward* (page 111) or *futures market* (page 114) in which the exchange takes place in the future).

Spot rate

The *exchange rate* (page 94) on the *spot market* (see above). Also called the **spot exchange rate**.

Spread

1. The difference between the price one must pay to buy something, such as a currency, and the price one receives for selling it.
2. The difference between the interest rate on a bond and the *risk free rate* (page 238); thus the *risk premium* (page 238) on the bond.

SPS

Sanitary and phytosanitary (page 240).

SST

Stolper-Samuelson theorem (page 258).

Stability and Growth Pact

The 1997 agreement among the countries participating in the *EMU* (page 85) to coordinate their fiscal policies in a way that would limit budget deficits and debt.

Stabilization policy

The use of *monetary* (page 179) and *fiscal policies* (page 107) to *stabilize* (page 255) *GDP* (page 122), aggregate employment, and prices.

Stabilize

To reduce the size of fluctuations in an economic variable over time. Examples include stabilizing *exchange rates* (page 94) by *exchange market intervention* (page 94); stabilizing the price of a *commodity* (page 41) by operation of a *buffer stock* (page 27); and stabilizing *GDP* (page 122) by macroeconomic *stabilization policy* (page 254).

Stabilizing speculation

Speculation (page 253) that decreases the movements of the price in the market where the speculation occurs. See *destabilizing speculation* (page 66). *Friedman (1953)* (page 375) provided a classic argument that speculation on a *floating exchange rate* (page 108) would be stabilizing.

Stable

1. Of an equilibrium, that the dynamic adjustment away from equilibrium converges to the equilibrium.

2. Of an economic variable, not subject to large or erratic fluctuations.

Stackelberg equilibrium

A *game theoretic* (page 116) equilibrium in which one player acts as a leader and another as a follower, the leader setting strategy taking account of the follower's optimal response. Contrasts with *Nash equilibrium* (page 184) in which both players take the other's strategy as given.

Stamp fee

See *para tariff* (page 204).

Standard

Rule and/or procedure specifying characteristics that must be met for a product to be sold in a country's domestic market, typically to protect health and safety. When a standard puts foreign producers at a disadvantage, it may constitute an *NTB* (page 195).

Standard error

A common measure of the uncertainty associated with a numerical estimate. In a *regression analysis* (page 232), standard errors are often reported with (or below) the *coefficient* (page 40) estimates. As a rough rule of thumb, one can be 95% confident that the true coefficient is within ± 2 standard errors of the estimate.

Standard of living

Usually refers to a country's *per capita income* (page 207), but sometimes takes account also of additional conditions that matter for a person's or household's wellbeing, such as leisure or the quality of the environment.

Standstill

1. A commitment to refrain from introducing new measures that are not consistent with an agreement.

2. In the *Uruguay Round* (page 286), the agreement not to introduce new *GATT* (page 116)-inconsistent trade-restricting and trade-distorting measures during the negotiations. See *rollback* (page 239).

State bank

A bank owned by government, other than the *central bank* (page 35), and performing the same functions as a *commercial bank* (page 40). State banks are often directed by their governments to provide *credit* (page 54) to activities or persons favored by the government.

State-owned enterprise

A firm owned by government. Relations between SOEs and private firms on international markets raise special problems for *GATT* (page 116), since SOEs may not respond normally to market forces and their actions may reflect government policies.

State trading enterprise

An entity of government that is responsible for exporting and/or importing specified products. See *marketing board* (page 173).

Static gains from trade

The economic benefits from trade that arise in *static models* (page 257), including the efficiency gains from exploiting *comparative advantage* (page 42), the reduced costs from *scale economies* (page 241), reduction in *distortion* (page 72) from *imperfect competition* (page 133), and increased product *variety* (page 288). Contrasts with *dynamic gains from trade* (page 77).

Static model

An economic model that has no explicit time dimension. A static model abstracts from the process by which an equilibrium or an optimum might be reached only over time, as well as from the dependence of the variables in the model itself on a changing past or future. Contrasts with *dynamic model* (page 78).

Statistical tax

See *para tariff* (page 204).

Status quo

The current situation. A preference for the status quo means a reluctance to change.

Steady state

A type of *equilibrium* (page 87), especially in a *neoclassical growth model* (page 188), in which those variables that are not constant grow over time at a constant and common rate.

Sterilize

To use offsetting *open market operations* (page 199) to prevent an act of *exchange market intervention* (page 94) from changing the *monetary base* (page 179). With **sterilization**, any purchase of *foreign exchange* (page 109) is accompanied by an equal-value sale of domestic bonds, and vice versa.

Stochastic

Random; arising from a process that generates different values each with some probability.

Stock

A share in the ownership of a corporation.

Stockpiling

The storage of something in order to have it available in the future if the need for it increases. In international economics, stockpiling occurs for *speculative* (page 253) purposes; by governments to provide for *national security* (page 185); and by central banks managing *international reserves* (page 149).

Stolper-Samuelson derivative

In *general equilibrium* (page 117), the effect of a small change in the price of a single good on the price of a *factor of production* (page 103).

Stolper-Samuelson theorem

1. The proposition of the *Heckscher-Ohlin model* (page 126) that a rise in the *relative price* (page 233) of a good raises the *real wage* (page 229) of the *factor* (page 101) used *intensively* (page 143) in that industry and lowers the real wage of the other factor.

2. The further proposition (requiring addition assumptions) that protection raises the *real wage* (page 229) of a country's *scarce factor* (page 241) and lowers the real wage of its *abundant factor* (page 3). Due to *Stolper and Samuelson (1941)* (page 381).

Straight-line PPF

The *PPF* (page 212) that arises in the *Ricardian model* (page 237), or in the *HO model* (page 128) if the two sectors have the same *factor intensity* (page 102). It is a downward sloping straight line with, therefore, a constant *marginal rate of transformation* (page 170).

Strategic industry argument for a tariff

The view that an industry serves a special "strategic" purpose in an economy and needs to be *protected* (page 222) by a tariff to prevent it from disappearing. Views of what constitutes a strategic purpose are often vague and contradictory.

Strategic trade policy

The use of trade policies, including *tariffs* (page 264), *subsidies* (page 260), and even *export subsidies* (page 99), in a context of *imperfect competition* (page 133) and/or *increasing returns to scale* (page 138) to alter the outcome of international competition in a country's favor, usually by allowing its firms to capture a larger share of industry profits. The seminal contribution was *Brander and Spencer (1981)* (page 373).

Strategic trade policy argument for a tariff

In an example of *strategic trade policy* (see above), the use of a tariff to extract monopoly profits from a foreign monopolist, or to *shift profit* (page 221) from foreign to domestic competitors in an international oligopoly. The monopoly case seems to have originated with *Katrak (1977)* (page 377), but the classic treatment of the larger issue is *Brander and Spencer (1984)* (page 373).

Strategic variable

An economic variable that is chosen with regard to, and sometimes with a view to influencing, economic behavior by someone else. Most frequently refers to the choice of firms in an *oligopoly* (page 197).

Structural adjustment

The reallocation of resources (labor and capital) among sectors of the economy in response to changing economic circumstances, including trading conditions, or changes in policy.

Structural adjustment program

The list of budgetary and policy changes required by the *IMF* (page 132) and *World Bank* (page 293) in order for a *developing country* (page 67) to qualify for a loan. This "*conditionality* (page 46)" typically includes reducing barriers to trade and *capital flows* (page 32), tax increases, and cuts in government spending.

Structural impediments initiative

A 1990 agreement between the United States and Japan to reduce their *bilateral* (page 23) *trade imbalance* (page 274). Among other commitments, the U.S. promised to reduce its *budget deficit* (page 27) and encourage saving, while Japan promised to increase spending and facilitate entry of new businesses.

Structure of protection

The pattern of *protection* (page 222) across sectors of an economy: which sectors are highly protected and which not, perhaps in terms of *effective protection* (page 82), or — even better — in terms of their expansion and contraction that would occur if all protection were removed.

Stumbling block

The term that *Bhagwati (1991)* (page 372) used, together with **building block**, to address whether *PTAs* (page 222) help move the world toward or away from *multilateral* (page 182) *free trade* (page 113).

Subcontracting

Delegation by one firm of a portion of its production process, under contract, to another firm, including in another country. A form of *fragmentation* (page 112).

Subsidiary

A firm that is owned and ultimately controlled by another firm. Thus a *multinational corporation* (page 183) has a *parent* (page 204) in once country and one or more subsidiaries in others.

Subsidy

A payment by government, perhaps implicit, to the private sector in return for some activity that it wants to reward, encourage, or assist. Under *WTO* (page 293) rules, subsidies may be *prohibited* (page 221), *actionable* (page 4), or *non-actionable* (page 192).

Substitute

One good is a substitute for another if an increase in demand for one (or a fall in its price) causes a decrease in demand for the other.

Substitute in production

One good is a substitute for another in production if an increase in output of one (or a rise in its price) causes a decrease in output of the other.

Substitution effect

That portion of the effect of price on quantity demanded that reflects the changed tradeoff between the good and other alternatives. Contrasts with *income effect* (page 137).

Sunk cost

A cost that has already been incurred and cannot be reversed, which therefore cannot be avoided by current or future action. Sunk costs should therefore be irrelevant to current decisions.

Sunset clause

A provision within a piece of legislation providing for its expiration on a specified date unless it is deliberately renewed.

Sunset industry argument

The *argument* (page 12), in contrast to the *infant industry argument* (page 140), that a mature industry should be provided protection, either to help it restore its competitiveness, or to cushion its exit from the economy.

Super 301

A U.S. law authorizing *USTR* (page 287) to identify the most significant *unfair trade* (page 284) practices confronting U.S.

exports and to seek to eliminate them. In contrast to *Section 301* (page 243), this does not require a private party to initiate the action.

Superior good

A good the demand for which is *income elastic* (page 137).

Supernatural trading bloc

A *trading bloc* (page 278) among countries that are *natural trading partners* (page 186) but that, because its tariff preferences are too extreme or transport costs with the outside world are too low, reduces world welfare. Due to *Frankel (1997)* (page 375).

Supply

1. The act of offering a product for sale.

2. The quantity offered for sale.

3. The quantities offered for sale at various prices; the *supply curve* (see below).

Supply chain

The sequence of steps, often done in different firms and/or locations, needed to produce a *final good* (page 105) from *primary factors* (page 217), starting with processing of *raw materials* (page 227), continuing with production of perhaps a series of intermediate inputs, and ending with final assembly and *distribution* (page 72).

Supply curve

The graph of quantity supplied as a function of price, normally upward sloping, straight or curved, and drawn with quantity on the horizontal axis and price on the vertical axis. Supply curves for exports and for foreign exchange usually have the same qualitative properties as supply curves for labor, being potentially *backward bending* (page 16).

Supply elasticity

The *elasticity* (page 83) of a supply function, usually with respect to price.

Supply function

The mathematical function explaining the quantity *supplied* (see above) in terms of its various determinants, including price; thus the algebraic representation of the *supply curve* (see above).

Supply price

The price at which a given quantity is supplied; the supply curve viewed from the perspective of price as a function of quantity.

Supply side

Anything that contributes to supply, as opposed to demand, in a *market* (page 171) or, especially, in the aggregate economy; *aggregate supply* (page 8).

Supranational

Transcending nations, especially through organizations that encompass more than one nation, such as the *European Union* (page 357).

Surplus

In the *balance of payments* (page 17), or in any category of international transactions within it, the surplus is the sum of credits minus the sum of debits. Also called simply the "balance" for that category. Thus the *balance of trade* (page 18) is the same as the surplus on trade, or the trade surplus, and similarly for *merchandise trade* (page 175), *current account* (page 58), and *capital account* (page 30).

Sustainable development

Economic development (page 79) that is achieved without undermining the incomes, resources, or environment of future generations.

Swan diagram

A diagram illustrating the conflict between *internal balance* (page 144) and *external balance* (page 100) as they respond to its *fiscal deficit* (page 107) and its costs relative to the world (and thus its *exchange rate* (page 94)). Due to *Swan (1955)* (page 381).

Swap

1. In exchange markets, this is a simultaneous sale of a currency on the *spot market* (page 254) together with a purchase of the same amount on the *forward market* (page 111). By combining these two transactions into a single one, *transactions costs* (page 278) may be reduced.

2. An arrangement between *central banks* (page 35) whereby they each agree to lend their currency to the other.

Swap rate

The difference between the *spot* (page 254) and *forward* (page 111) *exchange rates* (page 94). Thus the price of a *swap* (page 262).

Sweatshop

A manufacturing workplace that treats its workers inhumanely, paying low wages, imposing harsh and unsafe working conditions, and demanding levels of performance that are harmful to the workers.

Swiss formula

A formula devised during the *Tokyo Round* (page 271) for reducing tariffs in a manner that would *harmonize* (page 124) them. The formula is $t_{new} = (t_{old} \times M)/(t_{old} + M)$, where the t's are the new and old tariffs, in percent, and M is a number that turns out to be the maximum possible new tariff. Somebody, presumably Swiss, was very clever!

TAA

Trade adjustment assistance (page 272).

Takeover

The acquisition by one firm of another.

Target

1. Any objective of economic policy.

2. The value of an economic variable that policy makers regard as ideal and use as the basis for setting policy. Contrasts with *instrument* (page 142).

3. The level of an *exchange rate* (page 94) that guides *exchange market intervention* (page 94) by a *central bank* (page 35) or *exchange stabilization fund* (page 96).

Tariff

A tax on trade, usually an **import tariff** but sometimes used to denote an *export tax* (page 100). Tariffs may be *ad valorem* (page 5) or *specific* (page 253).

Tariff Act of 1930

Smoot-Hawley tariff (page 248).

Tariff-and-retaliation game

The *game* (page 116) of countries setting tariffs knowing that by doing so they alter the *terms of trade* (page 269) to their own advantage. This is one very specific form of *trade war* (page 278).

Tariff binding

A commitment, under the *GATT* (page 116), by a country not to raise the tariff on an item above a specified level, called the **bound rate**.

Tariff classification

See *tariff heading* (page 265).

Tariff Commission

The name of what is today the *International Trade Commission* (page 150) as of its founding in 1916, until it was renamed the ITC in 1975.

Tariff equivalent

The level of tariff that would be the same, in terms of its effect, usually on the quantity of imports, as a given *NTB* (page 195).

Tariff escalation

In a country's *tariff schedule* (page 266), the tendency for tariffs to be higher on *processed goods* (page 219) than on the *raw materials* (page 227) from which they are produced. This causes the *effective rate of protection* (page 82) on these goods to be higher than the *nominal rate* (page 192) and puts *LDC* (page 159) producers of *primary products* (page 217) at a disadvantage.

Tariff factory

A production facility established by a foreign firm through *FDI* (page 105) in a country in spite of its higher production costs, in order to serve its market without paying a tariff.

Tariff heading

The descriptive name attached to a *tariff line* (see below), indicating the product to which it applies. Same as **tariff classification**.

Tariff items 806 & 807

Lines 806.30 and 807.00 of the U.S. tariff schedule, which permit goods that have been sent abroad for processing or assembly to be admitted subject to duty only on the *value added* (page 287) abroad.

Tariff jumping

The establishment of a production facility within a foreign country, through *FDI* (page 105) or *licensing* (page 163), in order to avoid a *tariff* (page 264).

Tariff line

A single item in a country's *tariff schedule* (page 266).

Tariff peak

In a *tariff schedule* (page 266), a single tariff or a small group of tariffs that are particularly high, often defined as greater than three times the average nominal tariff.

Tariff preference

A lower (or zero) tariff on a product from one country than is applied to imports from most countries. This violation of the *MFN* (page 176) principle is permitted in special cases, including some *preferential trade arrangements* (page 214) and the *GSP* (page 123).

Tariff protection

Protection (page 222) provided by a *tariff* (page 264).

Tariff quota

A *tariff rate quota* (see below).

Tariff rate quota

A combination of an import *tariff* (page 264) and an import *quota* (page 226) in which imports below a specified quantity enter at a low (or zero) tariff and imports above that quantity enter at a higher tariff. Also called a **tariff quota**.

Tariff redundancy

See *redundant tariff* (page 231).

Tariff revenue

See *revenue* (page 237).

Tariff schedule

The list of all of a country's tariffs, organized by product.

Tariff Schedule of the United States

The official product nomenclature for specifying tariffs in the United States used until 1988, when it was replaced with the *harmonized system* (page 125).

Tariff wall

A tariff, presumably a high one, perhaps in lots of industries. The term is used to highlight the difficulty foreign sellers have in getting their products past the tariff, often in the context of the incentive therefore provided for *FDI* (page 105). See *foreign investment argument for protection* (page 110).

Tariffication

Conversion of *NTBs* (page 195) to *tariffs* (page 264) at the level of their *tariff equivalents* (page 264). In the *Uruguay Round* (page 286), agricultural NTBs were **tariffied** and *bound* (page 24), the purpose being to replace unwieldy NTBs with tariffs that can then become the subject of negotiation.

Tariffs and retaliation

The process of one country raising its tariff to secure some advantage, to which another country responds by raising its tariff, the first raises its tariff still further, etc. See *retaliation* (page 236), *trade war* (page 278). Classic treatment is *Johnson (1954)* (page 376).

Tax base

The amount on which a taxpayer pays taxes, as for example their taxable income in the case of an income tax, or the taxable value of their property in the case of a property tax.

Tax break

Any provision of the tax code, such as a *tax credit* (page 267) or *tax deduction* (page 267), that reduces the amount of tax that a firm or individual will pay, perhaps in return for behavior that the government wishes to encourage.

Tax buoyancy

A measure of how rapidly the actual revenue from a tax rises (including that due to any change in the tax law) as the *tax base* (see page 266) rises. It is defined, like an *elasticity* (page 83), as $\%\Delta R/\%\Delta B$ where R is the *real* (page 228) revenue from the tax, B is the real tax base, and $\%\Delta$ is percent change. It differs from *tax elasticity* (see below) in not holding the tax law constant.

Tax credit

A provision of the tax code that specifies an amount by which a taxpayer's taxes will be reduced in return for some behavior.

Tax deduction

A provision of the tax code that specifies an amount by which a taxpayer's *tax base* (page 266) will be reduced in return for some behavior, resulting in a lowering of the amount of tax paid that depends on their tax rate.

Tax elasticity

The *elasticity* (page 83) of the *real* (page 228) revenue from a tax with respect to the real *tax base* (page 266), for a given tax law.

Tax rebate

The refund of a tax that has been overpaid. Some countries rebate certain taxes that have been paid on goods that are then exported.

TBT

Technical barrier to trade (see below).

Technical barrier to trade

A *technical regulation* (see below) or other requirement (for testing, labeling, packaging, marketing, certification, etc.) applied to imports in a way that restricts trade.

Technical inefficiency

See *X-efficiency* (page 294).

Technical progress

Same as *technological progress* (page 268).

Technical regulation

A requirement of characteristics (such as dimensions, quality, performance, or safety) that a product must meet in order to be sold on a country's market. See *standards* (page 255).

Technique

1. A specific method of production, using a particular combination of inputs.

2. A point on an *isoquant* (page 153).

Technique of analysis

A method used for displaying or manipulating economic models.

Technological change

A change in a *production function* (page 220) that alters the relationship between inputs and outputs. Normally it is understood to be an improvement in technology, or *technological progress* (see below), and it is of interest in international economics for its implications for trade and economic welfare.

Technological difference

A difference in production functions, usually for the same industry compared between two countries, such that one country has higher output for any given input than the other.

Technological progress

A *technological change* (see above) that increases output for any given input.

Technology

1. The complete set of knowledge about how to produce in an economy at a point in time, including *techniques* (see above) of production that are available but not economically viable.

2. The set of *production functions* (page 220) available to an economy.

3. Referring to industries that are experiencing, or recently have experienced, *technological progress* (see above).

Technology gap

The presence in a country of a technology that other countries do not have, so that it can produce and export a good whose cost might otherwise be higher than abroad.

Technology spillover

Same as *technology transfer* (see below), though usually not done intentionally by the transferor.

Technology transfer

The communication or transmission of a *technology* (see above) from one country to another. This may be accomplished in a variety of ways, ranging from deliberate *licensing* (page 163) to *reverse engineering* (page 237).

Temporary admission

Permission to import a good duty free for use as an input in producing for export. See *drawback* (page 75), *export processing zone* (page 99).

Temporary producer movement

A *mode of supplying* (page 178) a *traded service* (page 274) through the temporary movement of persons employed by the supplier into the buyer's country.

Tender

To offer a product for sale at a specified price, usually in response to a specific request from a potential purchaser. *Government procurement* (page 120), for example, that is not open to **international tendering** is a form of *non-tariff barrier* (page 194).

Tequila crisis

Refers to the economic and financial crisis that began in late 1994 when the Mexican peso devalued, causing disruption in the Mexican economy that then spread through other countries of Latin America.

Terms of trade

1. The *relative price* (page 233) of a country's exports compared to its imports. See *improve the terms of trade* (page 136).

2. Outside of the economics of international trade, this expression often refers more broadly to the policies, facilities, and other arrangements that characterize the trade between one country or group of countries and another.

Terms of trade argument

Same as the *optimal tariff argument* (page 200), which works by restricting the quantity of trade in order to *improve the terms of trade* (page 136).

Terms of trade effect

The effect of a tariff on the *terms of trade* (see above). By reducing the demand for imports, a tariff levied by a *large country* (page 158) causes the prices of those imported goods to fall on the world market relative to the country's exports, *improving* (page 136) its terms of trade.

Textbook Heckscher-Ohlin model

The *2x2x2 model* (page 281).

Textiles

Cloth. The textile sector is important for trade, along with *apparel* (page 11), because with some exceptions (synthetics) it is a very *labor intensive* (page 156) sector, and it is therefore a likely source of *comparative advantage* (page 42) for *developing countries* (page 67). See *textiles and apparel* (below).

Textiles and apparel

These largely *labor intensive* (page 156) sectors are often the first *manufactured* (page 169) exports of *developing countries* (page 67). Because of the threat to employment in *developed countries* (page 67), however, they have long been *protected* (page 222) there. This is only now changing under the *WTO's* (page 293) *ATC* (page 14).

TFP

Total factor productivity (page 271).

Theoretical proposition

A property of an economic model that is derived (deduced) from its assumptions. It usually takes the form of a prediction about something that would be true in the world if the world conformed to the model's assumptions, and perhaps also to additional assumptions specified in the proposition.

Theory of second best

See *second best* (page 242).

Third world

Refers to all *less developed countries* (page 161) as a group. Term originated during the Cold War, when the "first world" was the developed capitalist countries and the "second world" was the communist countries, although these terms were seldom used.

Tied aid

Aid (page 9) that is given under the condition that part or all of it must be used to purchase goods from the country providing the aid.

Tiger economy

Any one of several economies that have developed extremely rapidly over a period of years. Especially the *Four Tigers* (page 112), but also a number of others who began to grow more recently.

TNC

Transnational corporation (page 279).

Tobin tax

A small tax on international currency transactions, proposed by *James Tobin* (page 382) in 1978 to discourage *destabilizing* (page 66) short-term international *capital movements* (page 33). Advocates suggest a tax of 0.1–0.25% with revenue used for urgent global priorities. Others question enforceability.

Tokyo Round

The 7th *round* (page 239) of multilateral trade negotiations that took place under *GATT* (page 116) auspices, commencing 1973 and completed in 1979. This was the first *trade round* (page 277) to deal with *NTBs* (page 195), by negotiating the *Tokyo Round codes* (see below).

Tokyo Round codes

The codes of behavior negotiated in the Tokyo Round covering several *NTBs* (page 195), arising from *customs valuation* (page 60), *standards* (page 255), *government procurement* (page 120), etc. Participation was optional, each code covering only those countries that chose to sign.

TOT

Terms of trade (page 269).

Total factor productivity

A measure of the output of an industry or economy relative to the size of all of its primary factor inputs. The term, and its acronym TFP, often refers to the growth of this measure, as measured by the *Solow residual* (page 250). See also *Hicks neutral* (page 127) technical progress.

TPA

Trade Promotion Authority (page 276).

TPRM
Trade policy review mechanism (page 276).

Tradable
1. Capable of being traded among countries.
2. A good or service that is tradable, with **tradables** referring to an aggregate of such goods and services.

Trade
1. To *exchange* (page 93) one item for another, one person or firm providing an item (good, service, asset, etc.) to another person or firm, with the latter providing a different item to the first in return, as payment.
2. To *export* (page 97) and/or *import* (page 134).
3. The quantity or value of exports and/or imports.

Trade Act of 1974
Actually signed on January 3, 1975, this major piece of trade legislation not only renewed and revised the authority to negotiate trade agreements, it also dealt with an expanded list of issues including *tariff preferences* (page 265), *unfair trade* (page 284), the *escape clause* (page 88), and *adjustment assistance* (page 5), and it introduced *fast track* (page 105) authority.

Trade adjustment assistance
A program of *adjustment assistance* (page 5) for workers and firms in industries that have suffered from competition with imports. In the U.S., TAA began with the *Trade Expansion Act of 1962* (page 274), and it has been renewed and expanded since then, including as part of the *NAFTA* (page 184).

Trade and investment
The interactions between, and the rules and policies governing, international trade and *foreign direct investment* (page 109). One of the *Singapore Issues* (page 246).

Trade and transformation curve diagram
One of the most frequently used *diagrams* (pages 343–345) of trade theory, using a *transformation curve* (page 279) together with one or more *price lines* (page 216) and sometimes *community indifference curves* (page 42) to illustrate production, consumption, and trade and the effects on them of *tariffs* (page 264) and other *exogenous* (page 96) changes.

Trade and wages debate

The debate between and among trade economists and labor economists as to the reason for the increase in the relative wages of skilled labor, compared to unskilled labor, in the U.S. starting in the 1980s. A central issue was the importance of "trade" as a contributing cause.

Trade balance

Balance of trade (page 18).

Trade barrier

An artificial disincentive to export and/or import, such as a *tariff* (page 264), *quota* (page 226), or other *NTB* (page 195).

Trade bias

See *bias* (page 22) of a trade regime.

Trade bloc

Trading bloc (page 278).

Trade cost

Any cost incurred in order to engage in international trade, including *transport cost* (page 280), insurance, etc.

Trade creation

Trade that occurs between members of a *preferential trading arrangement* (page 214) that replaces what would have been production in the importing country were it not for the PTA. Associated with welfare improvement for the importing country since it reduces the cost of the imported good. Concept due to *Viner (1950)* (page 382).

Trade credit

1. An amount that is loaned to an exporter to be repaid when the exports are paid for by the foreign importer.

2. Credit extended by an exporter to an importer, permitting them to pay at some time after they take delivery.

Trade deficit

Imports minus exports of goods and services. See *deficit* (page 63).

Trade deflection

Entry, into a low-tariff member of a *free trade area* (page 113), of imports intended for a purchaser in its higher-tariff partner.

Trade dispute

Any disagreement between nations involving their international trade or trade policies. Today, most such disputes appear as cases before the *WTO* (page 293) *dispute settlement mechanism* (page 71), but prior to the WTO, some were handled by the *GATT* (page 116) while others were dealt with *bilaterally* (page 23), sometimes precipitating *trade wars* (page 278).

Trade diversion

Trade that occurs between members of a *preferential trading arrangement* (page 214) that replaces what would have been imports from a country outside in the PTA. Associated with welfare reduction for the importing country since it increases the cost of the imported good. Concept due to *Viner (1950)* (page 382).

Trade Expansion Act of 1962

The legislation authorizing US participation in the *Kennedy Round* (page 155), replacing the *Reciprocal Trade Agreements Act of 1934* (page 230). It also established *trade adjustment assistance* (page 272).

Trade facilitation

One of the *Singapore issues* (page 246), this refers in the *Doha Declaration* (page 73) to "expediting the movement, release and clearance of goods, including goods in transit." This includes *customs procedures* (page 59) and other practices that may add to the cost or time requirements of trade.

Trade flow

The quantity or value of a country's *bilateral trade* (page 23) with another country.

Trade imbalance

A *trade surplus* (page 277) or *trade deficit* (page 273).

Trade in services

The provision of a service to buyers within or from one country by a firm in or from another country. Because such transactions do not involve a physical product crossing borders, they were not regarded as "trade" and were not covered by *GATT* (page 116). In the mid-1980s they were recognized as a form of trade and were incorporated into the *WTO's* (page 293) *GATS* (page 116).

Trade indifference curve

In a diagram measuring quantities of exports and imports, a curve representing amounts of trade among which a freely trading country is indifferent, based on its *community indifference curves* (page 42) and its *transformation curve* (page 279). Due to *Meade (1952)* (page 378).

Trade integration

The process of increasing a country's participation in world markets through trade, accomplished by *trade liberalization* (see below).

Trade intensity index

For a group or *bloc* (page 24) of countries, usually in a *PTA* (page 222), the ratio of the bloc's share of intra-bloc trade to the bloc's share in world trade. If greater than one, this is said to suggest that the bloc displays *trade diversion* (page 274). Index seems to be due to *Frankel (1997)* (page 375).

Trade liberalization

Reduction of *tariffs* (page 264) and removal or relaxation of *NTBs* (page 195).

Trade minister

The government official, at the ministerial or cabinet level, primarily responsible for issues of international trade policy; the *Minister of International Trade* (page 177). In the U.S. that is the *USTR* (page 287).

Trade mission

1. An office or other facility maintained in one country by the government of another to help residents of both to engage in international trade between them.

2. A group of persons from business and government of a country that travels to another country to promote its exports.

Trade negotiation

A negotiation between pairs of governments, or among groups of governments, exchanging commitments to alter their trade policies, usually involving reductions in *tariffs* (page 264) and sometimes *non-tariff barriers* (page 194).

Trade pattern

What goods and services a country trades, with whom, and in what direction. Explaining the trade pattern is one of the major purposes of trade theory, especially which goods a country will export and which it will import. This may be done directly, as the *commodity pattern of trade* (page 41), in indirectly as the *factor content pattern of trade* (page 102).

Trade policy

Any *policy* (page 210) affecting international *trade* (page 272), including especially *tariffs* (page 264) and *non-tariff barriers* (page 194).

Trade policy review mechanism

The periodic review of the trade policies and practices of the member countries of the *WTO* (page 293), conducted and published by the WTO.

Trade Promotion Authority

New (in 2000) name being used for *fast track* (page 105).

Trade regime

The rules and practices prevailing in a country's *international trade* (page 149) relationships.

Trade-related intellectual property rights

This was the term used for bringing *intellectual property protection* (page 142) into the *Uruguay Round* (page 286) of trade negotiations under the pretense that only trade-related aspects of the issue would be included. In practice, that did not constrain the coverage of the resulting *agreement* (page 281).

Trade-related investment measure

Any policy applied to *foreign direct investment* (page 109) that has an impact on international trade, such as an *export requirement* (page 99). The *Uruguay Round* (page 286) included negotiations on TRIMs.

Trade remedy

Protection (page 222) provided by any of the following: *antidumping duties* (page 10), *countervailing duties* (page 52), or *safeguards protection* (page 240).

Trade restriction

Any policy that reduces the amount of exports or imports, such as a *tariff* (page 264), *quota* (page 226), or other *non-tariff barrier* (page 194).

Trade restrictiveness index

A theoretically consistent index of the restrictiveness of trade policy — both *tariffs* (page 264) and *NTBs* (page 195) — developed by *Anderson and Neary (1996)* (page 371).

Trade round

A set of multilateral negotiations, held under the auspices of the *GATT* and WTO, in which countries exchange commitments to reduce tariffs and agree to extensions of rules. Most recent were the *Kennedy* (page 155), *Tokyo* (page 271), *Uruguay* (page 286) and Doha (page 73) Rounds.

Trade sanction

Use of a trade policy as a *sanction* (page 240), most commonly an *embargo* (page 84) imposed against a country for violating human rights.

Trade share

This can mean a variety of things, but most commonly it refers either to *imports* (page 134) or *exports* (page 97) as a percentage of *GDP* (page 122).

Trade surplus

Exports minus imports of goods and services, or *balance of trade* (page 18). See *surplus* (page 262).

Trade theory

The body of economic thought that seeks to explain why and how countries engage in international trade and the welfare implication of that trade, encompassing especially the *Ricardian model* (page 237), the *Heckscher-Ohlin model* (page 126), and the *new trade theory* (page 190).

Trade triangle

In the *trade and transformation curve diagram* (page 272), the right triangle formed by the world price line and the production and consumption points, the sides of which represent the quantities exported and imported.

Trade war

Generally, a period in which each of two countries alternate in further restricting trade from the other. More specifically, the process of *tariffs and retaliation* (page 266).

Trade-weighted average tariff

The *average* (page 16) of a country's tariffs, weighted by value of imports. This is easily calculated as the ratio of total tariff revenue to total value of imports.

Trade-weighted exchange rate

The weighted average of a country's *bilateral exchange rates* (page 23) using *bilateral trade* (page 23) — exports plus imports — as weights. Also called an *effective exchange rate* (page 82).

Traded good

A good that is exported or imported or — sometimes — a good that *could be* exported or imported if it weren't for those pesky *tariffs* (page 264).

Trademark

A symbol and/or name representing a commercial enterprise, whose right to the exclusive use of that symbol is, along with *patents* (page 205) and *copyrights* (page 50), one of the fundamental *intellectual property rights* (page 142) that are the subject of the *WTO* (page 293) *TRIPS* (page 281) agreement.

Trading arrangement

An agreement between two or more countries concerning the rules under which trade among them will be conducted, either in a particular industry or more broadly.

Trading bloc

A group of countries that are somehow closely associated in international trade, usually in some sort of *PTA* (page 222).

Transaction cost

On the foreign exchange markets, this includes *broker's fees* (page 26) and/or the *bid/ask spread* (page 23).

Transaction value

The actual price of a product, paid or payable, used for *customs valuation* (page 60) purposes.

Transfer payment

Payment made by the government or private sector of one country to another as a gift or aid, not as payment for any good or service nor as an obligation. Also called a unilateral transfer.

Transfer price

Literally this only refers to the price charged on goods and services that are traded between subsidiaries of a *multinational corporation* (page 183). However, the term usually connotes the setting of such prices high or low so as to minimize the total taxes paid to different governments, in response to differences in *corporate tax* (page 51) rates.

Transfers

Transfer payments (see above).

Transformation curve

Same as *production possibility frontier* (page 220). The name comes from the idea that, by devoting resources to producing one good instead of another, it is as though one good is being transformed into another.

Transition

The process of converting from a *centrally planned* (page 36), *non-market economy* (page 193) to a *market economy* (page 172).

Translog function

The transcendental logarithmic production function, a flexible functional form due to *Christensen et al. (1973)* (page 373). With output Y and inputs X_i, it takes the form $\ln Y = \alpha_0 + \Sigma_i \alpha_i \ln X_i + 1/2 \, \Sigma_i \Sigma_j \beta_{ij} \ln X_i \ln X_j$.

Transnational corporation

1. Same as *multinational corporation* (page 183), though for some reason this term seems to be preferred by those who don't like them.

2. A corporation whose national identity is a matter of convenience only, and that will move its headquarters readily in response to incentives.

Transparency

The clarity with which a regulation, policy, or institution can be understood and anticipated. Depends on openness, predictability, and comprehensibility. Lack of transparency can itself be a *NTB* (page 195).

Transport cost

The cost of transporting a good, especially in international trade.

Transportation cost

See *transport cost* (above).

Treaty of Rome

The 1957 agreement among six countries of Western Europe to form the *European Economic Community* (page 91), which went into effect January 1, 1958.

Trend

The long-term movement of an economic variable, such as its average rate of increase or decrease over enough years to encompass several *business cycles* (page 28).

TRI

Trade restrictiveness index (page 277).

Triad

1. Europe, North America, and Japan.

2. The *EU* (page 89), the U.S., and Japan.

Triangular arbitrage

Arbitrage (page 11) among three currencies. For example (letting x/y be the currency x per unit of currency y exchange rate), if $\$/¥ > (\$/£)(£/¥)$, then an arbitrager can make a profit buying £ with \$; buying ¥ with those £; and then selling those ¥ for \$.

Triffin's dilemma

A flaw in the *dollar-based* (page 74) international monetary standard created by the *IMF* (page 132): To provide the growing *reserves* (page 235) that other central banks needed to sustain growing economies, the U.S. needed to run *balance of payments deficits* (page 18) that would undermine confidence in the dollar as a *reserve asset* (page 234). Due to testimony before Congress by Robert Triffin in 1960.

Trigger price

See *minimum price system* (page 177).

TRIMs

Trade-related investment measures (page 276).

TRIPs

Trade-related intellectual property rights (page 276).

TRIPs agreement

The agreement negotiated in the *Uruguay Round* (page 286) that incorporated issues of intellectual property into the *WTO* (page 293). It provides a set of minimum standards for *intellectual property protection* (page 142) to which all but the poorest member countries of the WTO must conform.

Trough

The point in the *business cycle* (page 28) when an economic contraction reaches its lowest level before turning up. Contrasts with *peak* (page 206).

TRQ

Tariff rate quota (page 265).

TSUS

Tariff Schedule of the United States (page 266).

Tuna-dolphin case

Actually a pair of cases, resulting from the U.S. ban on imports of tuna, under the *Marine Mammal Protection Act* (page 171), from countries that did not effectively prohibit tuna fishers from killing dolphins by catching them together with whole schools of tuna in large ("purse seine") nets. Cases filed under *GATT* (page 116) in 1991 and 1994 led to panel decisions against the U.S.

Tunnel

See *snake in the tunnel* (page 248).

Twin deficits

Refers to the *budget deficit* (page 27) and *trade deficit* (page 273) of a country (in spite of the fact that, although they are related, they are far from being the same or necessarily equal).

2x2x2 model

The *Heckscher-Ohlin model* (page 126) with 2 factors, 2 goods, and 2 countries.

Two cone equilibrium

A free-trade equilibrium in the *Heckscher-Ohlin model* (page 126) in which prices are such that all goods cannot be produced within a single country, and instead there are two *diversification cones* (page 72). This, or a *multi-cone equilibrium* (page 182), will arise if countries' *factor endowments* (page 102) are sufficiently dissimilar compared to *factor intensities* (page 102) of industries. Contrasts with *one cone equilibrium* (page 198).

Two-gap model
   A model of *economic development* (page 79) that focuses on two constraints: the need for savings to finance investment, and the need for foreign exchange to finance imports.

Two-ness
   The property of simple versions of many trade models that they have two of everything: goods, factors, and countries especially. An important issue addressed by *Jones (1977)* (page 376), who coined the term, and by *Jones and Scheinkman (1977)* (page 376) is the extent to which the results of these models depend on this two-ness.

UN
   United Nations (page 285).

Uncertainty
   Failure to know anything that may be relevant for an economic decision, such as future variables, details of a technology, or sales. In models, uncertainty usually appears as a *random variable* (page 227) and corresponding *probability density* (page 218) function. But in practice, most international models, especially of trade, assume *certainty* (page 36).

UNCITRAL
   United Nations Commission on International Trade Law (page 285).

Uncovered interest parity
   Equality of expected returns on otherwise comparable financial assets denominated in two currencies, without any *cover*

(page 53) against *exchange risk* (page 95). Uncovered interest parity requires approximately that $i = i^* + a$ where i is the domestic interest rate, i^* the foreign interest rate, and a the expected *appreciation* (page 11) of foreign currency at an annualized percentage rate.

UNCTAD
United Nations Conference on Trade and Development (page 285).

Under-invoicing
The provision of an *invoice* (page 151) that states price as less than is actually being paid. This might be done on an import in order to reduce the amount that will be collected by an *ad valorem tariff* (page 5). Or it might be done on an export to reduce apparent profit and thus taxes.

Undervalued currency
The situation of a currency whose value on the *exchange market* (page 94) is lower than is believed to be sustainable. This may be due to a *pegged* (page 207) or *managed* (page 168) rate that is below the market-clearing rate, or, under a *floating rate* (page 108), it may be due to *speculative* (page 253) capital outflows. Contrasts with *overvalued currency* (page 203).

Underdeveloped country
A synonym, not usually used today, for *less developed country* (page 161).

Underemployment
The employment of workers for fewer hours or in less desirable jobs than they would prefer and are qualified for.

Undertaking
See *price undertaking* (page 216).

Unemployment
A measure of the number of workers that want to work but do not have jobs.

Unemployment rate
The ratio of *unemployment* (see above) to the *labor force* (page 156) of a country.

Unequal exchange

Trade in which the labor used to produce a country's exports is more than the labor used to produce its imports, as in the exchange between low-wage developing countries and high-wage developed countries.

Unfair trade

1. Under the *GATT* (page 116) this refers only to exports that are *subsidized* (page 260) or *dumped* (page 76).

2. Under U.S. law, this also includes various actions that interfere with U.S. exports. See *Section 301* (page 243) and *Super 301* (page 260).

3. Also used to refer to almost any trade that the speaker objects to, sometimes including that based on low wages or weak regulations.

Unilateral transfer

Transfer payment (page 279).

Unit elastic

Having an elasticity equal to one. For a *price elasticity* (page 215) of *demand* (page 65), this means that expenditure remains constant as price changes. For an *income elasticity* (page 137) it means that expenditure share is constant. *Homothetic preferences* (page 129) imply unit income elasticities. Contrasts with *elastic* (page 83) and *inelastic* (page 140).

Unit isocost line

An *isocost line* (page 153) along which cost is equal to one unit of the *numeraire* (page 195), such as one dollar.

Unit isoquant

The *isoquant* (page 153) for a quantity equal to one unit of a good. The unit isoquant is useful for relating the price of a good to the prices of factors employed in its production.

Unit labor requirement

The amount of labor used per unit of output in an industry; the ratio of labor to output. In a *Heckscher-Ohlin model* (page 126) this varies along an *isoquant* (page 153) as different *techniques* (page 268) are chosen in response to different *factor prices* (page 103). But in a *Ricardian model* (page 237), these are the constant building blocks for defining *comparative advantage* (page 42) and determining behavior.

Unit of account

A basic function of money, providing a unit of measurement for defining, recording, and comparing value. That is, one dollar signifies not only a one dollar bill, but also a dollar's worth of money in other forms (deposits), of wealth in other forms than money, and of any good or service with a market value.

Unit tariff

Specific tariff (page 253).

Unit-value isoquant

The *isoquant* (page 153) for a quantity of a good worth one unit of value. This is meaningful only if the nominal price of the good is given, for some specified currency or *numeraire* (page 195). Unit-value isoquants are central to the *Lerner diagram* (page 369) for analyzing the *Heckscher-Ohlin model* (page 126).

United Nations

An organization of countries established in 1945 with 51 members, expanded to 191 countries as of January 2006. Its purpose is "to preserve peace through international cooperation and collective security."

United Nations Commission on International Trade Law

A legal body created in 1966 to formulate and harmonize national rules on international commercial transactions. It includes 36 member states elected by the UN General Assembly, representing various geographic regions and economic and legal systems. It differs from the *WTO* (page 293) in its more technical focus and its broad representation.

United Nations Conference on Trade and Development

An intergovernmental body established in 1964 within the United Nations, responsible for trade and development. Historically it has often been the international voice of developing countries.

United Nations organizations

The complex and extensive system of organizations that exist under the umbrella of the *United Nations* (see above). Several of these, like the *WTO* (page 293) and the *IMF* (page 132), play critical roles in the international economy.

United States Court of International Trade

The U.S. court in which matters involving international trade are adjudicated. These include determinations of the *customs service* (page 60) and findings of the *ITC* (page 153).

United States Customs Service

The agency of the U.S. government that monitors the border to prevent illegal goods from crossing it and to collect *tariffs* (page 264) — customs duties — on legal goods that are subject to them.

United States Trade Representative

The cabinet-level official of the U.S. government "responsible for developing and coordinating U.S. international trade, commodity, and direct investment policy, and leading or directing negotiations with other countries on such matters."

Unnatural trading bloc

A *trading bloc* (page 278) among countries that are not *natural trading partners* (page 186).

Unregistered exports and imports

See *registered exports and imports* (page 232).

Unskilled labor

Labor with a low level of *skill* (page 247) or *human capital* (page 130). Identified empirically as labor earning a low wage, with a low level of education, or in an occupational category associated with these; sometimes crudely proxied as *production workers* (page 221).

UPF

Utility possibility frontier (page 287).

Upstream subsidization

Export of a good one of whose inputs has been subsidized.

Uruguay Round

The *round* (page 239) of multilateral trade negotiations under the *GATT* (page 116) that commenced in 1986 and was completed in 1994 with the creation of the *WTO* (page 293). In addition it broke new ground by negotiating over *agriculture* (page 8), *textiles and apparel* (page 270), *services* (page 244), and *intellectual property* (page 142).

US-Central American Free Trade Agreement
A *free trade agreement* (page 113) signed in 2004 between the United States, the Dominican Republic, and a number of countries in Central America. As of January 2006, the agreement had been ratified by all but Costa Rica.

USTR
United States Trade Representative (page 286).

Utility function
A function that specifies the utility (wellbeing) of a consumer for all combinations of goods consumed (and sometimes other considerations). Represents both their *welfare* (page 291) and their *preferences* (page 213).

Utility possibility frontier
In a diagram with levels of individual utility on the axes, a curve showing the maximum attainable levels of utility in a given situation, such as *free trade* (page 113) or *autarky* (page 15). Used by *Samuelson (1962)* (page 380) to demonstrate the *gains from trade* (page 116).

Value added
The value of output minus the value of all *intermediate inputs* (page 144), representing therefore the contribution of, and payments to, *primary factors of production* (page 217).

Value added tax
A tax that is levied only on the *value added* (see above) of a firm. A VAT is usually subject to *border tax adjustment* (page 25).

Value marginal product
Marginal value product (page 171).

Value quota

A *quota* (page 226) specifying value — price times quantity — of a good.

Variable cost

The portion of a firm or industry's cost that changes with output, in contrast to *fixed cost* (page 108).

Variable levy

A tax on imports that varies over time so as to stabilize the domestic price of the imported good. Essentially, the tax is set equal to the difference between the target domestic price and the world price.

Variable returns to scale

The property of a *production function* (page 220) that *returns to scale* (page 236) may be increasing or *decreasing* (page 63), at different rates, at different levels of output.

Variance

A measure of how much an economic or statistical variable varies across values or observations. Its calculation is the same as that of the *covariance* (page 53), being the covariance of the variable with itself.

Variety

Refers to the multiplicity of *differentiated products* (page 68) that are available in some industries, a multiplicity that tends to become larger with trade.

VAT

Value added tax (page 287).

Vehicle currency

The currency used to *invoice* (page 151) an international trade transaction, especially when it is not the national currency of either the importer or the exporter.

Velocity of money

The rate at which money changes hands in an economy, usually defined by the *equation of exchange* (page 87).

Vent for surplus

The concept that a country — especially a *developing country* (page 67) — may be able to gain by exporting the products of factors that would not be employed at all without trade. This "vent for surplus" theory of trade was developed especially by *Myint (1958)* (page 379), who attributed the term to *Williams (1929)* (page 382) and before that to *Mill (1848)* (page 379) and the idea to *Smith (1776)* (page 381).

VER
Voluntary export restraint (see below).

Vertical integration
Production of different stages of processing of a product within the same firm.

Vertical intra-industry trade
Intra-industry trade (page 151) in which the exports and imports are at different stages of processing. Contrasts with *horizontal IIT* (page 130).

Vertical specialization
Another term for *fragmentation* (page 112). Used by *Hummels, Rapoport, and Yi (1998)* (page 376).

VIE
Voluntary import expansion (see below).

Vinerian
Associated with the work of economist Jacob Viner, as in the Vinerian concept of *trade diversion* (page 274).

Visible
In referring to international trade, used as a synonym for "*good* (page 120)." "Visibles trade" is trade in goods. Contrasts with *invisible* (page 151).

Volatility
The extent to which an economic variable, such as a price or an exchange rate, moves up and down over time.

Voluntary export restraint
A restriction on a country's imports that is achieved by negotiating with the foreign exporting country for it to restrict its exports.

Voluntary import expansion
The use of policies to encourage imports, in response to pressure from trading partners. Due to *Bhagwati (1987)* (page 372).

Voluntary restraint agreement
Same as a *VER* (page 289).
VRA
Voluntary restraint agreement, same as a *VER* (page 289).

Wage
The payment for the service of a unit of labor, per unit time. In trade theory, it is the only payment to labor, usually unskilled labor. In empirical work, wage data may exclude other compensation, which must be added to get the total cost of employment.

Wage-rental ratio
The ratio of the wage of labor to the *rental price* (page 234) of either capital or land, whichever is the other *factor* (page 101) in a two-factor *Heckscher-Ohlin model* (page 126). The ratio plays a critical role in this model since it determines the ratios of factors employed in both industries.

Waiver
An authorized deviation from the terms of a previously negotiated and legally binding agreement. Many countries have sought and obtained waivers from particular obligations of the *GATT* (page 116) and *WTO* (page 293).

Walras' law
The property of a *general equilibrium* (page 117) that if all but one of the markets are in equilibrium, then the remaining market is also in equilibrium, automatically. This follows from the *budget constraints* (page 27) of the market participants, and it implies that any one *market-clearing* (page 172) condition is redundant and can be ignored.

Walrasian adjustment
A market *adjustment mechanism* (page 5) in which price rises when there is excess demand and falls when there is excess supply. Strictly speaking, these excess supplies and demands are

those that would obtain without any history of disequilibrium, as with a *Walrasian auctioneer* (see below).

Walrasian auctioneer

A hypothetical entity that facilitates market adjustment in disequilibrium by announcing prices and collecting information about supply and demand at those prices without any disequilibrium transactions actually taking place.

WARP

Weak axiom of revealed preference (see below).

Warsaw Pact

A "treaty of friendship, co-operation, and mutual assistance" including the Soviet Union and its satellite states in Central Europe. Signed in 1955, it included *eight countries* (page 360).

Washington Consensus

A set of economic practices and reforms deemed by *international financial institutions* (page 147) (located in Washington, D.C.) to be helpful for *financial stability* (page 107) and *economic development* (page 79); often imposed as *conditions* (page 46) for economic assistance by these institutions. Phrase coined by *John Williamson (1990)* (page 382).

Water in the tariff

The extent to which a tariff is higher than necessary to be *prohibitive* (page 222).

Weak axiom of revealed preference

The assumption that a consumer who reveals strict preference for one bundle of goods over another will not, in other circumstances, reveal their preference for the second over the first. That is, if q^i, q^j are the vectors of goods purchased at prices p^i, p^j respectively, then $p^i q^i > p^i q^j \Rightarrow p^j q^i > p^j q^j$. Used in proving *correlation results* (page 51).

Wealth

The total value of the accumulated *assets* (page 13) owned by an individual, household, community, or country.

Welfare

Refers to the economic wellbeing of an individual, group, or economy. For individuals, it is conceptualized by a *utility function* (page 287). For groups, including countries and the world, it is a tricky philosophical concept, since individuals fare differently. In trade theory, an improvement in welfare is often inferred from an increase in *real national income* (page 229).

Welfare criterion

A basis, usually quantitative, for judging whether one state of the world or of an economy is better than another, for use in *welfare economics* (see below) and in evaluation of *policies* (page 210).

Welfare economics

The branch of economic thought that deals with economic *welfare* (page 291), including especially various propositions relating *competitive* (page 44) *general equilibrium* (page 117) to the efficiency and desirability of an *allocation* (page 9). See the *first* (page 107) and *second* (page 243) theorems of welfare economics.

Welfare proposition

In trade theory, this usually refers to any of several *gains from trade theorems* (page 116).

Welfare state

A set of government programs that attempt to provide economic security for the population by providing for people when they are unemployed, ill, or elderly.

Welfare triangle

In a *partial equilibrium* (page 205) market diagram, a triangle representing the net welfare benefit or loss from a policy or other change. In trade theory it often means the triangle or triangles representing the *deadweight loss* (page 61) due to a tariff.

Western Hemisphere Free Trade Area

Name sometimes proposed for a *preferential trading arrangement* (page 214) including most or all of the countries of the western hemisphere. Now called *FTAA* (page 114).

WHFTA

Western Hemisphere Free Trade Area (see above).

Willingness to pay

The largest amount of money that an individual or group could pay, along with a change in policy, without being made worse off. It is therefore a monetary measure of the benefit to them of the policy change. If negative, it measures its cost.

WIPO

World Intellectual Property Organization (see below).

Withholding tax

A tax on income that is levied at the source, thus diverted to the government before the recipient of the income ever sees it. Used in international tax treaties to assist tax collection.

Working party

A group that is delegated to study an issue. Used by the *WTO* (see below) as a first step in considering a new issue that may later become the subject of negotiations.

World Bank

A group of five closely associated international institutions providing loans and other development assistance to developing countries. The five institutions are *IBRD* (page 131), *IDA* (page 132), *IFC* (page 132), *MIGA* (page 176), and *ICSID* (page 131). As of January 2006, the largest of these, IBRD, had 184 member countries.

World Fact Book

An excellent source of information about the countries of the world, including basic economic data.

World Intellectual Property Organization

The United Nations organization that establishes and coordinates standards for *intellectual property protection* (page 142).

World price

The price of a good on the "world market," meaning the price outside of any country's borders and therefore exclusive of any trade taxes or subsidies that might apply crossing a border into a country but inclusive of any that might apply crossing out of a country.

World Trade Organization

A global international organization that specifies and enforces rules for the conduct of international trade policies and serves as a forum for negotiations to reduce barriers to trade. Formed in 1995 as the successor to the *GATT* (page 116), it had 149 member countries as of January 2006.

WTO

World Trade Organization (see above).

X-efficiency

The ability of a firm to get maximum output from its inputs. Failure to do so, called **X-inefficiency** or *technical inefficiency* (page 267), may be due to lack of incentives provided by competition. Improvement in X-efficiency is one hypothesized source of *gain from trade* (page 116). Term is due to *Leibenstein (1966)* (page 378).

Yield

The amount of return on an *investment* (page 151); the *interest rate* (page 143).

Zero degree homogeneous

Homogeneous of degree zero (page 128).

Zero profit

A situation in which profit in an industry is zero, usually as a result of *free entry and exit* (page 112). It may, if firms are not identical, refer only to the marginal firm. And it always means zero *excess profit* (page 93), not that all returns to capital invested in the industry are zero.

Zero substitution

An *elasticity of substitution* (page 84) of zero. In a *production function* (page 220), this means a *Leontief technology* (page 161).

Zero sum game

A *game* (page 116) in which the payoffs to the players add up to zero, so that a gain for one is necessarily equaled by loss to others. Contrasts with *positive sum game* (page 212).

(Key to some numerical terms)

11

Chapter 11 (page 37).

1992

Europe 1992 (page 90).

201

Section 201 (page 243).

301

Section 301 (page 243).

50 Years Is Enough

A U.S.-based coalition of organizations committed to the transformation of the *IMF* (page 132) and the *World Bank* (page 293). Its more formal name is U.S. Network for Global Economic Justice. Its demands include *debt cancellation* (page 61), end of *structural adjustment* (page 259), and payment of various *reparations* (page 234).

77

G-77 (page 116).

807 imports

Tariff items 806 & 807 (page 265).

Part II
Picture Gallery

1. Edgeworth Production Box

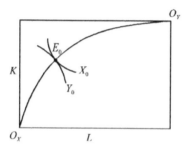

Fig. 1. Basic Edgeworth Production Box.

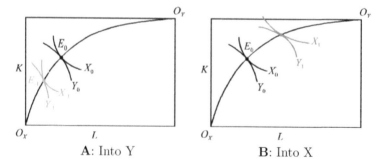

A: Into Y   **B**: Into X

Fig. 1.1. Factor Reallocation along Efficiency Locus (A and B).

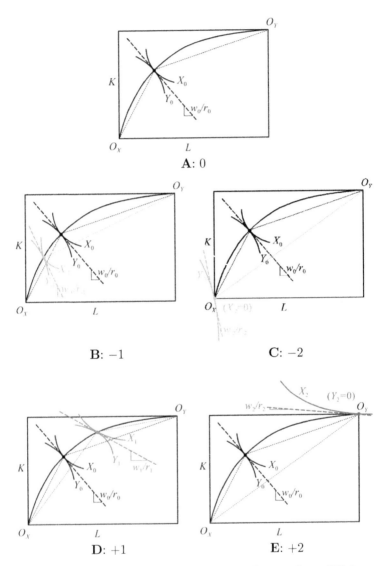

Fig. 1.2. Factor Proportions and Factor Prices along Efficiency Locus (A–E).

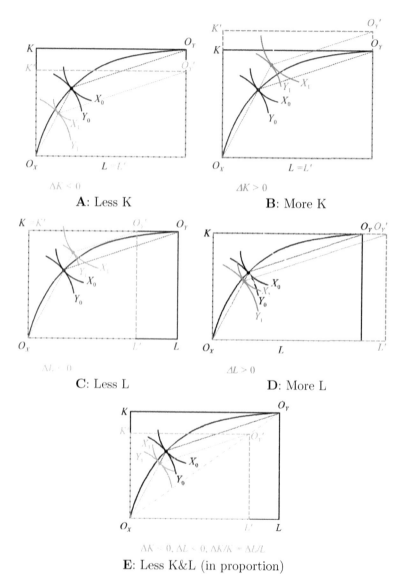

A: Less K

B: More K

C: Less L

D: More L

E: Less K&L (in proportion)

Fig. 1.3. Changes in Factor Endowments (A–E).

Key
K, L Quantities of factors capital and labor
r, w Rental price of capital and wage of labor
X, Y Quantities of goods X and Y

Explanation

The basic Edgeworth Production Box, shown above, has dimensions equal to the *factor endowments* (page 102) of a country, and it shows all of the ways that those endowments can be allocated across two industries for producing two goods, X and Y. The lower-left corner serves as the origin for measuring *allocations* (page 9) of factors to industry X, and the upper-right corner as the origin for allocations to industry Y. Thus every point in the box represents a particular allocation, with all of both factors allocated to the two industries in quantities given by the coordinates with respect to these two origins.

Production functions for each industry are represented by *isoquants* (page 153) drawn relative to these two origins, that for industry Y being rotated 180 degrees from the usual orientation. Thus the outputs of the two goods are represented by the two isoquants, one for each industry, passing through any particular point in the box.

An *efficient allocation* (page 82) is one for which these two isoquants are tangent, as shown at E_0 for X_0 and Y_0. The set of all such tangencies is the *efficiency locus* (page 82), the curve $O_X E_0 O_Y$. Under the usual assumption of *constant returns to scale* (page 47) in both industries, the efficiency locus cannot cross the upward-sloping diagonal of the box, and it must therefore lie either wholly above it, as shown, if industry X is *capital intensive* (page 32) compared to industry Y, or wholly below it in the opposite case.

The diagram can be used to illustrate the effects of factor reallocations along the efficiency locus on outputs and factor prices, where the latter appear via *isocost lines* (page 153) tangent to the isoquants. It can also be used to show the effects of changing factor endowments, under the assumption that prices of goods (and therefore of factors, due to *FPE* (page 112)) are held constant.

Factor Reallocation

If factors are reallocated from one industry to the other, as for example in response to a change in relative prices (which cannot easily be shown in this diagram), movement will be along the efficiency locus. If factors are moved into industry Y, then movement is down and to the left along this locus, to the point shown in Fig. 1.1 as E_{-1}. If factors are moved into industry X, then equilibrium moves up and to the right to point E_1.

Factor Proportions and Factor Prices along Efficiency Locus

At each point along the efficiency locus, factor proportions appear as the slopes of the rays from the two respective origins to the point. The ratio of the two factor prices at each point is given by the slope of the single straight line that is tangent to both isoquants at that point (single, because they are tangent to each other) as in Fig. 1.2A. Since factor proportions depend monotonically on relative factor prices, the two (different) ratios of factors employed in each industry must move in the same direction, as both factors are reallocated along the efficiency locus.

Thus, for a small reallocation into industry Y and out of industry X, numbered "−1" in Fig. 1.2B, the ratios of capital to labor employed rise in both, and this in turn requires that the relative wage of labor, w/r shown by the (absolute) slope of the tangent to the isoquants, rises as well. That is, both isoquants become steeper as we move down and to the left along the efficiency locus.

This process continues until the corner of the box is reached at O_X. At that point in Fig. 1.2C, all factors are employed in industry Y, whose factor proportions equal that of the country, and the factor prices are given by the slope of the Y-isoquant only. This is shown as the allocation numbered "-2".

Allocations "1" and "2" show the analogous movement of factors out of industry Y and into X. In both industries, this causes capital-labor ratios to fall and the relative wage of labor to fall as well.

Changes in Endowments

A change in factor endowments appears as a change in the dimensions of the box. This is most easily done holding one corner of the box fixed, O_X, and letting the opposite corner, O_Y, move to reflect the new factor endowments. Holding prices of goods and therefore factors constant (due to FPE), the ratios of capital to labor employed in each industry remain unchanged. Thus the new equilibrium allocation can be found by simply shifting the Y-industry factor-proportions ray along with O_Y, keeping it parallel to what it was before, and finding where it crosses the unchanged X-industry factor proportions ray.

The results, illustrated in Fig. 1.3 for "Less K," "More K," etc., are the *Rybczynski Theorem* (page 239) results that a rise in K or a fall in L cause more of both factors to be allocated to capital-intensive industry X, and thus the output of X to rise, while output of Y falls. A proportional change in both factor endowments, on the other hand, causes both outputs to rise or fall together, in the same proportion.

2. Integrated World Economy Diagram

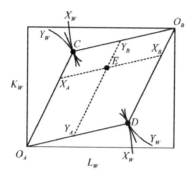

Fig. 2. Integrated World Economy Diagram.

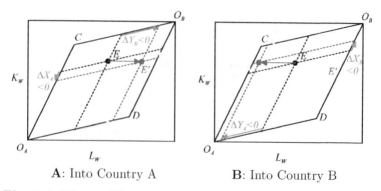

A: Into Country A   **B**: Into Country B

Fig. 2.1. Effects of Factor Reallocation Across Countries of Labor into A and B.

Key	
K, L	Factors capital and labor
X, Y	Goods X and Y
A, B, W	Countries A and B, and world W
O_A, O_B	Origins for graphing factors in countries A and B

Explanation

The diagram shows allocations of two factor endowments between two countries for given prices of the two goods that the countries are able to produce. The prices themselves do not appear in the diagram but enter instead through their corresponding (via *FPE* (page 112)) factor prices and the cost-minimizing ratios of factors that each industry would employ at those factor prices. The dimensions of the box are the combined factor endowments of the two countries, with each point inside the box representing a division of these endowments between them as measured from their respective origins O_A and O_B, much as in the *Edgeworth Production Box* (page 81). The industry factor ratios are the slopes of the rays $O_A C$ (and its parallel $D O_B$) for capital-intensive good X and $O_A D$ (and its parallel $C O_B$) for good Y. These rays form a parallelogram, within which lie all allocations of the two factors to the two countries consistent with their both producing both goods and thus having factor price equaliztion. (Outside this parallelogram it is simply not possible to fully employ both factors while still using them in these proportions.)

In most uses of the diagram, the prices of the goods are those that would prevail in equilibrium if the world contained only these two countries and if they were fully "integrated," in the sense that both goods and factors were able to move freely between them. These goods prices would then imply corresponding factor prices and factor proportions such that factors would be fully employed in the world economy, some producing good X and others good Y in the quantities demanded at those prices, X_W and Y_W. Thus the isoquants through points C and D in Fig. 2 represent these outputs, which may be represented with respect to either O_A or O_B, as shown.

The diagram can also be used to represent two countries that are not the whole world, or two regions within a country, facing arbitrary exogenous prices. In that case, X_W and Y_W become the outputs of only this part of the world if it alone is integrated and has FPE, and these outputs need not equal demand.

In either case, the diagram can be used to identify how factors are allocated to the two industries across the two countries, and thus how the two countries' outputs of X and Y depend on the country allocation of their combined factor endowments. For the particular allocation indicated at point E in Fig. 2, the dotted lines parallel to the sides of the parallelogram intersect the parallelogram at country A's allocation to industry X, X_A, etc.

Effects of Reallocating Factors Across Countries

If factors are reallocated from one of these two countries to the other, this does not change their combined outputs so long as the allocation remains inside the FPE parallelogram. The cases shown in Fig. 2.1 are for reallocation of labor from B to A, and from A to B. In both cases, the country receiving labor expands its employment of both factors in the labor-intensive industry, Y, and thus expands output there. And to keep both factors fully employed, it must reduce employment of both factors in the capital-intensive industry, X, and thus reduce its output of X. This is an example of the *Rybczynski Theorem* (page 239) in action. Reallocation of capital, not shown, would have analogous effects.

3. IS-LM-BP Diagram

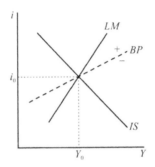

Fig. 3. Basic IS-LM-BP Diagram.

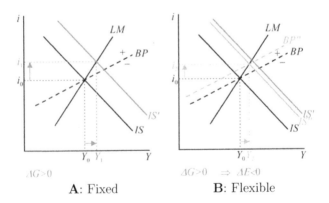

A: Fixed   **B**: Flexible

Fig. 3.1. Fiscal Stimulus (A and B).

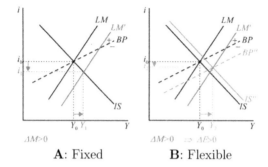

A: Fixed   **B**: Flexible

Fig. 3.2. Monetary Stimulus (A and B).

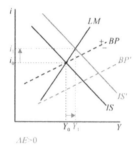

Fig. 3.3. Devaluation.

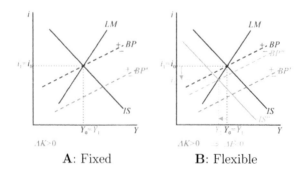

A: Fixed   **B**: Flexible

Fig. 3.4. Capital Inflow (A and B).

Key	
Y	National income and output
i	Interest rate (real = nominal since prices are constant)
IS	Goods market equilibrium (investment = savings)
LM	Money market equilibrium (demand for money, L, equals supply)
BP	Balance of payments (BOP) curve
E	Exchange rate (domestic currency price of foreign currency)
K	Exogenous capital inflow
G	Government spending
M	Money supply

Explanation

Equilibrium is at the intersection if IS and LM. With a pegged exchange rate this may lie off the BP curve, indicating a BOP in surplus (+) above or deficit (−) below. With a floating exchange rate, a secondary adjustment of the exchange rate, E, (with effects shown in light gray) must move the three curves so as to intersect in one place, in order to get equilibrium in the exchange market.

From the diagram, one can read the following effects of exogenous changes, for the case shown (which assumes relatively mobile capital and *sterilization* (page 257) of exchange market intervention — see notes below):

Fiscal expansion (Fig. 3.1)

An increase in government spending (or a tax cut) shifts the IS-curve to the right. With a fixed exchange rate this causes income and the interest rate both to rise. The rise in interest rate attracts a capital inflow that, with relatively mobile capital, is sufficient to create a BOP surplus. With a flexible exchange rate this is an excess demand for domestic currency, which therefore appreciates. The appreciation dampens the increase in both income and the interest rate.

Monetary expansion (Fig. 3.2)

An increase in the money supply shifts the *LM* curve to the right, raising income and lowering the interest rate. With a fixed exchange rate, both of these changes contribute to BOP deficit. With a flexible rate, this is an excess supply of domestic currency, which therefore depreciates. The depreciation further stimulates income, but dampens the fall in interest rate.

Devaluation (Fig. 3.3)

A devaluation of the otherwise fixed exchange rate stimulates demand for domestic goods shifting the *IS*-curve to the right, but also shifting the *BP* curve down and creating a BOP surplus. (This ignores the possibility of a *J-curve* (page 153) — see below.)

Capital Inflow (Fig. 3.4)

An exogenous capital inflow has no effect on *IS* or *LM* under a fixed exchange rate, since the central bank is sterilizing its effect on the interest rate. It merely causes a BOP surplus. With a flexible rate, however, this surplus causes an appreciation, which reduces demand and shifts the *IS*-curve to the left. Thus the capital inflow lowers income and the interest rate under a flexible exchange rate.

Notes

1. The relative slopes of the *LM* and *BP* curves are crucial to some of these results. The case shown assumes that capital is sufficiently mobile internationally that the BP curve is flatter than the *LM* curve. The extreme case of perfect capital mobility would have a horizontal *BP* curve.

2. In addition to the two cases shown, one could (and should) also look at the case of a fixed exchange rate with *non-sterilization* (page 194). In that case, whenever there is a BOP disequilibrium the money supply will be changing, rising with a surplus and falling with a deficit (which are in turn indicated by the + and − signs in the diagram). The *LM* curve therefore shifts until all three curves intersect at once.

3. Exchange rate devaluation (and depreciation) is shown as shifting the *IS* and *BP* curves both to the right. This requires that *import demand elasticities* (page 134) are large enough to satisfy the *Marshall-Lerner Condition* (page 173). Without this, as is perhaps likely in the short run, both would shift in the other direction. This is one possible cause of the *J-curve* (page 153), worsening the balance of trade in the short run, and also reducing aggregate demand.

4. An exogenous change in exports and/or imports due to any of a variety of causes ranging from changing trade policies to business cycle fluctuations abroad will have effects under fixed exchange rates similar to the devaluation shown above. Under a flexible exchange rate, however, matters are complicated by the need to know how an exchange rate change alters capital flows. Depending on the nature of expectations, among other things, anything — or nothing — is possible. In particular, it may be that, say, an exogenous increase in exports will be exactly offset, in its effects on the trade balance and aggregate demand, by an exchange rate appreciation.

5. The model here takes all foreign variables as given, under the assumption that this is a *small open economy* (page 248). If that is not the case, there will be *foreign repercussions* (page 110) from the foreign response to this country's changes in trade and capital flows, and results may change.

4. Lerner Diagram

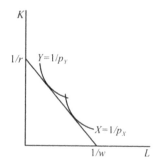

Fig. 4. Basic Lerner Diagram.

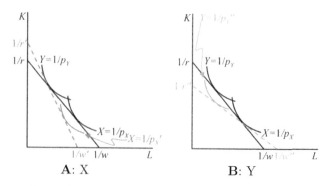

A: X   **B**: Y

Fig. 4.1. Price Changes — Increase in Price of X and Y (A and B).

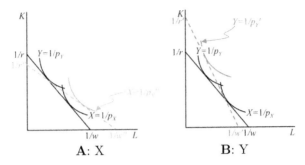

Fig. 4.2. Price Changes — Decrease in Price of X and Y (A and B).

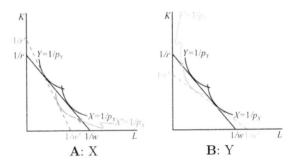

Fig. 4.3. Technological Change (Hicks Neutral) — Improvement in X and Y (A and B).

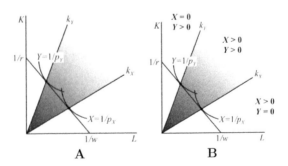

Fig. 4.4. Extensions: A, Diversification cone; and B, Patterns of Specialization.

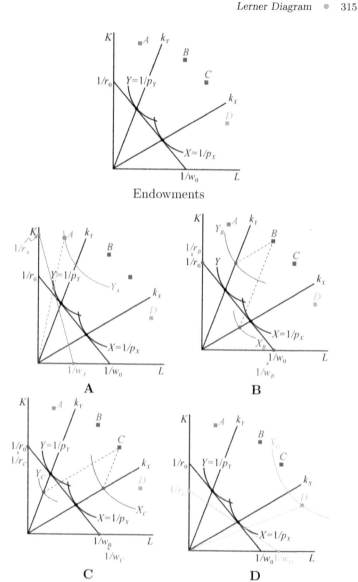

Fig. 4.5. Extensions — Factor Allocations and Factor Prices (Endowments, A–D).

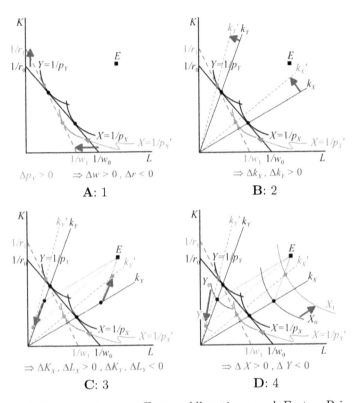

Fig. 4.6. Extensions — Factor Allocations and Factor Prices: Increase in Price of X (A–D).

Key	
K, L	Quantities of factors capital and labor
r, w	Rental price of capital and wage of labor
X, Y	Quantities of goods X and Y
p_X, p_Y	Prices of goods X and Y
K_X, K_Y	Capital employed in production of goods X and Y
L_X, L_Y	Labor employed in production of goods X and Y
k_X, k_Y	Capital-labor ratio employed in diversified production of goods X and Y

Explanation

The basic Lerner Diagram, shown above, uses *unit-value isoquants* (page 285) and *unit isocost lines* (page 284) to determine the *factor prices* (page 103) that are consistent with positive production of two goods under perfect competition. The unit-value isoquants incorporate both *nominal* (page 191) prices and *technology* (page 268), both of which are taken as given for the diagram. The unit isocost line is then determined within the diagram as the straight line tangent to both of the unit-value isoquants — the "*common tangent* (page 42)". The factor prices represented by (the reciprocals of) the intercepts of this isocost line permit both industries to just break even and therefore permit both to produce without a positive profit. If only one such common tangent exists, as it appears above, then these factor prices are the unique ones consistent with positive production at the goods prices for which the unit-value isoquants were drawn.

The diagram can be used as a powerful tool for deriving many of the results of the *Heckscher-Ohlin Model* (page 126). It is especially useful for finding the effects of a change in the prices of goods on factor prices, but with the extensions shown it can also determine other things.

Price Changes (Figs. 4.1–4.2)

A price change appears in the diagram as a shift of a unit-value isoquant. An increase in the price of good X, for example, means that a smaller quantity of good X is worth one dollar. With *linearly homogeneous* (page 164) technologies, the new unit-value isoquant is just a shrunken version of the old, contracted inward toward the origin by the fraction of the price increase.

As shown, an increase in the price of X, then, shifts the X-isoquant inward, causing the common tangent to rotate clockwise. From the intercepts, the wage rises and the rental falls. A fall in price of X has the opposite effects, while a change in the price of Y is analogous.

Technological Change (Fig. 4.3)

A technological improvement for producing a good causes the isoquant for the same quantity to be shifted inwards. The shift need not be proportional, but the figure above assumes *Hicks-neutral* (page 127) progress, for which it is. Thus the picture looks exactly the same as that for an increase in the price of the good. The effects are correspondingly the same, except that one must be careful in distinguishing changes in quantities from changes in values for a good with a changed technology.

Extensions

The Lerner Diagram provides a convenient starting point for further analysis of the Heckscher-Ohlin Model. The figure can be used to determine, essentially in the following order,

- industry factor ratios (techniques) corresponding to diversification,
- the diversification cone,
- patterns of specialization,

and with addition of a point representing factor endowments

- factor employment in each industry, and
- industry outputs.

The effects on all of these variables can therefore be derived, for any initial pattern of specialization, due to changes in anything exogenous to the diagram: prices, technology, and factor endowments.

The Diversification Cone (Fig. 4.4.A)

If factor prices are those given by the common tangent, as they must be for both goods to be produced, then the cost-minimizing techniques of production in the two industries are at the two points of tangency. Therefore, the factor ratios at these points of tangency, and the rays with these slopes labeled k_X and k_Y above, represent these techniques. The diversification cone is the set of all factor endowments lying on or between these rays.

Patterns of Specialization (Fig. 4.4.B)

The reason for calling it the diversification cone, aside from its shape, is that only for factor endowments lying inside the cone — between the rays k_X and k_Y — will a country produce both goods. Otherwise it would not be able to employ both factors fully, since it would be using either a higher or lower ratio of factors in both industries than it has in its endowment. Outside the cone, therefore, the country completely specializes, producing only the most labor-intensive good, X, below the cone and only the most capital intensive good, Y, above it.

Factor Allocations and Factor Prices (Fig. 4.5.)

Outside the cone, the factor allocations are simple. The entire endowment is employed in one industry. In order for firms to do that willingly, they must face factor prices that induce them to hire factors in the same proportions as the endowment. Therefore, factor prices outside the cone are **not** given by the common tangent, but rather by the slope of the operating industry's isoquant at the factor ratio of the country's endowment.

Inside the cone, factor prices **are** given by the common tangent, and the industries employ factors in the ratios k_X and k_Y. With two factors and two goods, there is only one way that factors can be fully employed given this constraint. It can be found by constructing lines parallel to the k_X and k_Y rays from the point representing the country's factor endowment to where each intersects the other industry's ray. The point of intersection is the amount of factors allocated to that industry.

Effects of a Price Change (Fig. 4.6)

All of this can be combined to determine the effects of changes in variables that are exogenous to the diagram, such as prices. The case shown is an increase in the price of good X. The price increase pulls the unit-value isoquant for X in toward the origin. This causes the common tangent to rotate clockwise, becoming steeper and representing a higher relative price of labor compared to capital. In nominal terms, the wage rises and rental falls. These changes cause both industries to substitute toward using less labor and more capital, moving up and to the left along their isoquants to higher ratios of capital to labor. This increase in the capital-labor ratios of diversification means that the diversification cone rotates counterclockwise. Some factor endowments that previously would have involved specialization in the more capital-intensive industry now will accommodate both industries, while other factor endowments that were inside the cone but closer to its bottom edge are now below it, switching from producing both goods to producing only X. For endowments that remain within the cone, factors must be reallocated in order to keep them fully employed at the new higher capital labor ratios. The more labor-intensive industry, even though it now employs a higher ratio of capital to labor, also must expand, employing a larger amount of both factors. The capital-intensive industry Y, on the other hand, employs less of both factors and contracts. Thus, for a country within the cone, the output of X rises and the output of Y falls.

Notes

1. The Lerner Diagram works only for *linearly homogeneous* (page 164) technologies. With that assumption, every isoquant for an industry is exactly like every other, just scaled inward or outward, and a single isoquant — such as the unit-value isoquant — completely describes the technology. Without linear homogeneity or something equivalent to it, the Lerner Diagram would make no sense and could not be used.

2. Only Hicks-neutral technological change is illustrated above. However, one of the counter-intuitive messages of the Lerner Diagram is that this neutrality is not very important for the effects of technological change on factor prices. An improvement in the technology for producing X, for example, will pull its unit-value isoquant inward no matter how it may be biased in favor of labor or capital, and as long as the other isoquant does not change, the common tangent must get steeper. Thus if both goods are produced so that the country is (and remains) inside the diversification cone, technological progress in the

labor-intensive industry causes a rise in the relative wage regardless of any factor bias in the progress itself.

3. The isoquants above do not display a *factor intensity reversal* (page 102). If they did, then there could be two common tangents, not one, and with multiple reversals there could be even more. For each common tangent there is a corresponding diversification cone.

5. Offer Curve Diagram

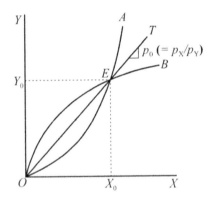

Fig. 5. Basic Offer Curve Diagram.

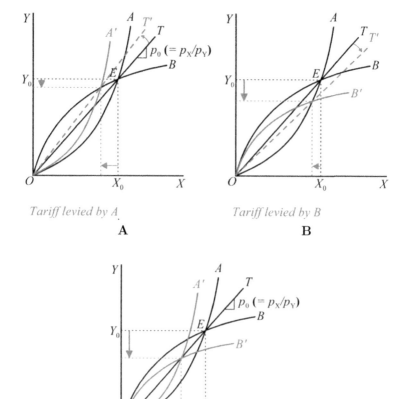

Tariff levied by A

A

Tariff levied by B

B

Tariffs levied by A and B

A&B

Fig. 5.1. Tariff (A, B, A&B).

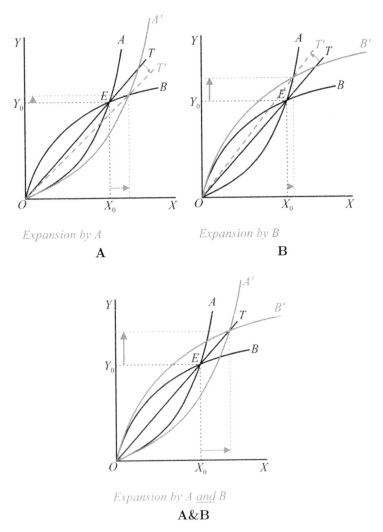

Fig. 5.2. Expansion (A, B, A&B).

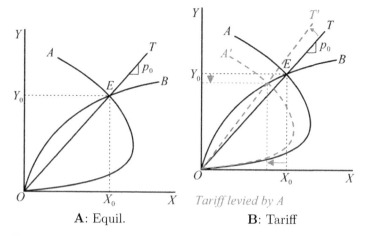

Fig. 5.3. Variants: Inelastic Demand by Country A (A and B).

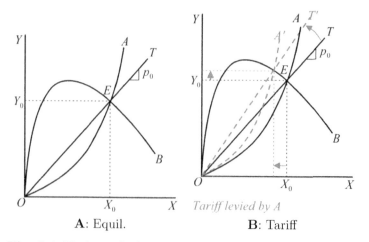

Fig. 5.4. Variants: Inelastic Demand by Country B (A and B).

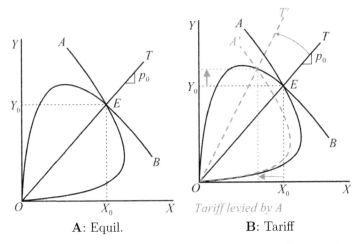

A: Equil.   **B**: Tariff

Fig. 5.5. Variants: Inelastic Demand by Both (A and B).

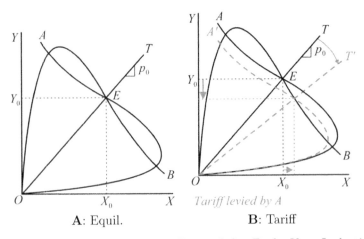

A: Equil.   **B**: Tariff

Fig. 5.6. Variants: Inelastic Demand by Both *Very* Inelastic (A and B).

Key

X, Y	Quantities of goods X and Y
OA, OB	Initial offer curves of countries A and B
OA', OB'	Offer curves of countries A and B after shock
OT, OT'	Price lines for the initial and the new equilibria.
E	The initial equilibrium
X_0	The quantity of X exported by A and imported by B at E.
Y_0	The quantity of Y exported by B and imported by A at E.

Explanation

The offer curve OA records the quantities of good X that country A supplies to the world market for export **and** the quantities of good Y that it demands from the world market as imports, for all prices. The prices are only implicit in the diagram, represented as rays from the origin the slopes of which are the prices of good X relative to good Y. This is possible since balanced trade (which is assumed throughout), requires that $p_Y Y = p_X X$, and therefore that $Y/X = p_X/p_Y$. Thus the offer curve can be read as giving the quantity of good X that country A is willing to export in exchange for various quantities of imported good Y, or equivalently as the amounts of both X and Y that it is willing to trade at various prices along rays from O.

Offer curve OB is similarly defined for country B, except that the directions of trade for it are reversed. This is why it is something of mirror image of OA. That is, it records quantities of good Y that B will export in exchange for various quantities of imports of good X. In equilibrium, of course, country B must import what A exports and vice versa, which is why equilibrium is found where the two curves intersect, at E.

By representing both good X and good Y in a single diagram in this way, the intersection of the two offer curves depicts equilibrium in both markets simultaneously, something that is possible (indeed necessary) because of *Walras' law* (page 290).

Offer curves need not be upward sloping throughout. If they are, as drawn in Fig. 5, that says that the country is willing to spend more, in exports, for additional quantities of imports as their price falls (and the relative price of exports therefore rises). If this is true, it means that the demand for imports is *elastic* (page 83), and therefore such offer curves are often themselves called "elastic." If demand for imports instead becomes *inelastic* (page 140) at low import prices — which is possible but not theoretically necessary — then the offer curve bends back on itself as shown in the variants in Figs. 5.3–5.6. This, as the pictures show, can lead to different sorts of responses of prices and quantities of trade to various shocks.

Tariff (Fig. 5.1)

The effects of a tariff on a country's offer curve depend on how the tariff revenue is spent. If, as is customary to assume, it is *redistributed* (page 231), then the tariff in a *non-distorted* (page 193) economy unambiguously reduces the desired quantities traded at any given world price. Thus the offer curve shifts in toward the origin along every ray. Beyond this, one cannot say much about the size of the shift, which depends on both preferences and the constraints of technology and factor endowments. Nonetheless, this is often enough to determine qualitatively the effects on equilibrium prices and quantities, at least on the world market.

As shown in the panels of Fig. 5.1 with both offer curves elastic a tariff by either country (or both) reduces the quantities of both goods traded. The effect on the world price (*terms of trade* (page 269)) depends (not necessarily simply) on the sizes of the two tariffs, each country's terms of trade tending to *improve* (page 136) most the larger is its own tariff and the smaller is the other country's. This, of course, is the reason for the likelihood of *retaliation* (page 236) when a country seeks to use an *optimal tariff* (page 200).

Expansion (Fig. 5.2)

Economic expansion, due either to factor accumulation or technological progress, tends to cause a country to trade more at any given prices, and thus shifts its offer curve out away from the origin. This is not inevitable, however, as illustrated elsewhere with the *trade and transformation curve diagram* (page 343), which shows that if expansion is sufficiently biased in favor of the import-competing good, desired trade may decrease. The figures above, however, all assume that economic expansion in a country causes it to trade more, for given prices.

The outward shift of a country's offer curve that results is therefore just the opposite of the inward shift due to a tariff, although the exact shape of the change could well be different. Not much more therefore needs to be said about this case.

Variants (Figs. 5.3–5.6)

Implications of a tariff (and of expansion, for that matter) can be somewhat different when import demands are inelastic than when they are elastic, as the variants shown above illustrate. For a country that levies a tariff, having its own import demand be inelastic does not matter a great deal, except perhaps to the sizes of the changes that result. But having the foreign offer curve be inelastic matters a lot.

When country A levies a tariff against a world whose demand for its export is inelastic, then the effect is actually to *increase* its quantity of imports, not reduce it. The reason is that by reducing its demand for imports at the initial price it causes the price of its imports to fall and of its exports to rise. But the inelastic foreign demand means that the other country increases its expenditure on imports when their price rises, and their expenditure *is* their exports. So the price of their exports must fall by enough to induce the tariff-levying country to buy more of them. Get that?

Things seem to get even stranger if both countries have inelastic import demands, especially in the extreme case shown in Fig. 5.6. Here, almost everything seems to go nuts, as country A's tariff seems to cause it to push *up* the price of its imports and down the price of its exports, therefore causing it to export more and import less. This appearance is deceiving, however, for all of this weirdness started from an equilibrium that, on inspection, would have been unstable. In the unlikely event that the world started from the unstable equilibrium at E in Fig. 5.6, the tariff would actually have caused the system to move to the stable equilibrium northwest of it, with results much more like the other cases.

Notes

1. Offer curves need not be nearly as smooth and well behaved as shown above. In the *Ricardian Model* (page 237), for example, they include straight lines from the origin and kinks. And in general, especially once a tariff is imposed, they need not even be concave to the origin.
2. The offer curves shown above are drawn only in one quadrant of the diagrams. However, in fact they extend beyond the origin into the negative quadrant, where the directions of trade are reversed. If preferences are well behaved, they will not intersect in that negative quadrant, but if consumers are heterogeneous, they may.
3. The slope of an offer curve at the origin is the country's autarky price. In fact, country A's offer curve lies wholly above a price line through the origin with slope equal to its autarky relative price, and country B's lies wholly below such a line for it. This in turn illustrates that a trade equilibrium must be at prices that lie between the two countries' autarky prices.
4. Offer curves work only with two goods and two countries, not more. To use them in more complicated worlds, it is necessary to aggregate. That is not too hard, especially for countries under ideal conditions (no distortions). Studying country A, for example, we can interpret country B as the entire rest of the world.

6. Specific-Factors Model

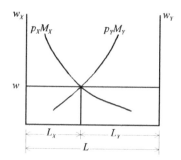

Fig. 6. Specific-Factors Model.

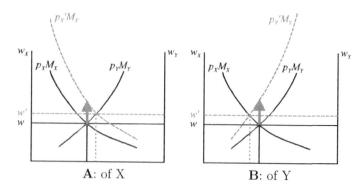

Fig. 6.1. Increase in Price (A and B).

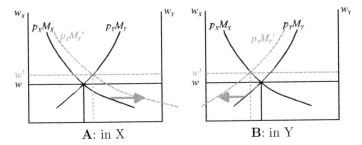

Fig. 6.2. Increase in Endowment of Specific Factor (A and B).

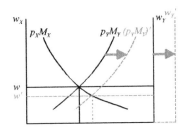

Fig. 6.3. Increase in Endowment of Labor.

Key	
w_X, w_Y	Wages of labor in industries, X, Y (both equal to w in equilibrium)
p_X, p_Y	Prices of X, Y
M_X, M_Y	Marginal product of labor in industry X, Y
L_X, L_Y	Labor employed in industry X, Y (sum to labor endowment L in equilibrium)

Explanation

The economy has two sectors and three factors. Each sector has a specific factor that is confined to it, and each also employs labor, which is perfectly mobile between them. Figure 6 depicts the labor market, the fixed supply of labor (the labor endowment) being its width, and the two sectors' demands for labor drawn as functions of the wage from opposite corners. Demand for labor in each sector is given by a curve the height of which is the value of labor's marginal product in the sector: pM. Equilibrium is at the intersection of these two curves, determining both the common wage and the allocation of labor between the sectors.

Effects of Changing Prices

A rise in the price of either good shifts its sector's labor demand curve proportionally upward. This causes its intersection with the unchanged labor demand curve of the other sector to move up along that curve, increasing both the equilibrium common wage and employment in the sector where the price has risen.

Implicit in this is that output rises in the sector with the higher price and falls in the other sector. Also, since the wage rises by less than the upward shift of the curve (the heavy arrow in Fig. 6.1, showing the size of the price increase), it follows that the nominal wage of labor rises relative to the unchanged price but falls relative to the increased price, implying that the effect on the real wage is, from this information, ambiguous.

Also implicit in the figure are the effects on real returns to specific factors, which respond to changes in labor employment by rising in the expanding sector and falling in the contracting sector.

Effects of Changing Endowments of Specific Factors

An increase in the endowment of a specific factor in a sector makes labor in that sector more productive. Assuming *constant returns to scale* (page 47), the marginal product of labor depends only on the ratio of factors, and therefore the marginal product curve shifts horizontally by the percentage change in the specific factor, as shown in Fig. 6.2. Like the price increases above, this raises the equilibrium employment in the sector with more of the specific factor, and raises the equilibrium nominal wage in both.

Output rises in the expanding sector, due now to the increases in both factors, while output in the other sector contracts. Since prices in this case are fixed, the rise in nominal wage is also an increase in real terms.

The real return to the non-expanded specific factor goes up, since it depends on its ratio to employed labor. The real return to the expanded specific factor goes down, analogously, since employment of labor in that sector expands by less than the increase in the specific factor (shown again by the heavy arrow in Fig. 6.2).

Effects of Changing Endowment of Labor

An increase in endowment of labor expands the horizontal dimension of the figure. Holding its left side fixed in Fig. 6.3, the right side moves to the right by the amount of the increased endowment, and since the Y-sector labor demand is drawn relative to the vertical axis on the right, it shifts horizontally by the same absolute amount. The result is a fall in the equilibrium wage and a rise in employment of labor (and thus both output and returns to specific factors) in both sectors.

7. Tariff in Partial Equilibrium

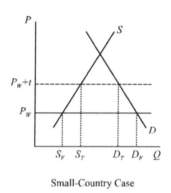

Small-Country Case

Fig. 7. Tariff in Partial Equilibrium.

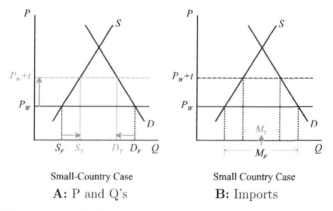

Small-Country Case
A: P and Q's

Small Country Case
B: Imports

Fig. 7.1. Small Country Case, Effects of Tariff: A and B.

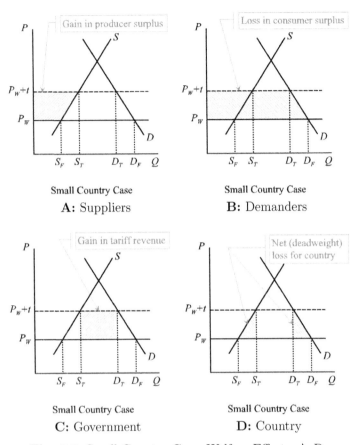

Fig. 7.2. Small Country Case, Welfare Effects: A–D.

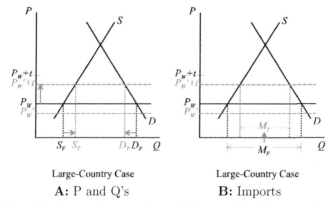

Fig. 7.3. Large Country Case, Effects of Tariff: A and B.

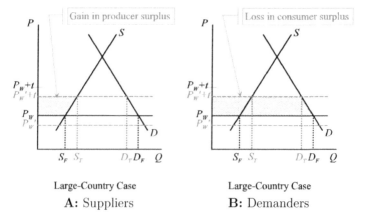

Fig. 7.4. Large Country Case, Welfare Effects: A–D.

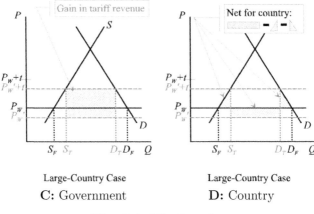

Large-Country Case
C: Government

Large-Country Case
D: Country

Fig. 7.4. (*Continued*).

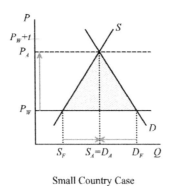

Small Country Case

Fig. 7.5. Prohibitive Tariff, Effects on: P, Q's and welfare.

Key	
P, Q	Price and quantity of good
S, D	Domestic supply and demand in importing country
F, T	Equilibrium values under free trade and tariff
t	*Specific tariff* (page 253)
P_W	Price of good on world market

Explanation

The diagram shows upward-sloping supply and downward-sloping demand for a good inside a country. The world price, P_W, is assumed to be below the country's autarky price, so that it has excess demand at the world price and will import the good if it is free to do so. If that were not the case, a tariff on imports would have no effect. Thus, with free trade, the country supplies and demands the good in the amounts S_F and D_F respectively, as determined by the supply and demand curves in Fig. 7.

A tariff raises the domestic price above the world price by the amount of the tariff, so long as the good continues to be imported. The effects on the domestic market depend on whether the tariff induces any change in the world price. In the small-country case of Figs. 7.1 and 7.2, the country's imports are too small to matter for the world market and the world price remains unchanged. If the importing country is large, however, its reduced demand for imports causes the world price to fall by an amount that cannot be determined with this diagram alone. The large-country case shown in Figs. 7.3 and 7.4 simply assumes an arbitrary fall in the world price. Finally, if the tariff is larger than the gap between the country's autarky price and the world price, then it is "prohibitive," reducing imports of the good to zero in Fig. 7.5.

Small-Country Case

In the small-country case, the world price remains unchanged, and therefore the domestic price must rise by the full amount of the tariff. This rise in price causes domestic supply to rise and domestic demand to fall, along the respective supply and demand curves in Fig. 7.1. Since the quantity of imports is the difference between demand and supply, imports are reduced by both of these changes.

Effects on welfare within the country can be measured by various areas in Fig. 7.2. The rise in price benefits suppliers, as measured by the increase in *producer surplus* (page 219), which is the area to the left of the supply curve between the old and new prices. The same price increase hurts demanders, as measured by the decrease in *consumer surplus* (page 48), which is the analogous area to the left of the demand curve. In addition to these effects on the market participants, the tariff-levying government also benefits in the form of increased government revenue from the tariff, which is simply the rectangle representing the tariff itself multiplied by the new level of imports. This tariff revenue acrues directly to the government, but presumably indirectly to the domestic population as taxpayers.

The net of these three changes is necessarily a loss in the small country case, since the gains to suppliers and government are both subsumed within the larger area of loss to demanders. The net loss appears as two triangles, with height equal to the size of the tariff and width equal to the amounts by which supply and demand have changed. Together these triangles measure the *deadweight loss* (page 61) from the tariff, and they exist only to the extent that the tariff has induced changes in the behavior of the market participants.

Large-Country Case

The small-country analysis also implies that a country of any size will demand less from the world market, as a result of a tariff, for any given world price. This reduced demand from the world market, if the country is large enough to matter at all, causes the world price to fall. The size of this fall depends on properties of the world market that do not appear here, although it is normally smaller than the tariff itself.

The fall in world price implies that the domestic price rises by less than the tariff. Qualitatively, the rising domestic price has the same effects on domestic suppliers and demanders as in the small-country case, but quantitatively both the gain to suppliers and the loss to demanders are reduced, since the price increase is smaller. The tariff revenue, on the other hand, is *not* reduced by the fall in world price. On the contrary, with a specific tariff the tariff revenue is larger here, since the size of the tariff itself is the same and the quantity of imports (which has fallen less) is larger. In Fig. 7.4C, the rectangle of tariff revenue is no longer fully subsumed within the area of lost consumer surplus, but instead extends below it.

The net welfare effect of the tariff on a large tariff-levying country can therefore be positive. This is the case, in Fig. 7.4D, if the portion of tariff revenue shown by the upward-sloping-cross-hatched rectangle below P_W is larger than the sum of the two downward-sloping-cross-hatched triangles of dead weight loss. If so, this is a case of an *optimal tariff* (page 200) that has successfully altered the importing country's *terms of trade* (page 269) in its favor. Indeed, the benefit depends entirely on being able to push down the world price, which the country pays for its imports, and thus occurs at the expense of foreign exporters. (The effect on welfare abroad is does not appear in this figure.)

Prohibitive Tariff

If a tariff is set high enough, it will choke off all trade in the good. For this to happen in the small country, the tariff need only be as large as the difference between its *autarky price* (page 15) (i.e., the price P_A at which domestic supply equals domestic demand) and the world price. For it to happen in a large country, the same must be true, except that the relevant world price is the one that will prevail after the country's imports are zero. In either case, however, the result, shown in Fig. 7.5, is that the country moves to its autarky equilibrium with the autarky price P_A, and this is the case even if the tariff is made still larger. That is, once the tariff is large enough to eliminate trade, further increases in the tariff have no effect on anything.

The welfare effect of a prohibitive tariff is analogous to a non-prohibitive tariff, in that suppliers gain and demanders lose. However, there is no tariff revenue, since imports are zero, and as a result the deadweight loss from the tariff is maximized.

Notes

1. The analysis here uses a *partial equilibrium* (page 205) model, thus focusing only on the market for a single good and ignoring any interactions with other markets. This is justified if the market in question is too small to matter for all other markets, in which case unfortunately it may be too small too matter for anything. Fortunately, the partial equilibrium model also provides a good approximation to what would be found with a more complete general equilibrium model even for a market that does matter for others, as long as the feedbacks through those markets on itself are small. In practice, whether justified or not, the partial equilibrium model is very commonly used.

2. What **is** critically important in use of this analysis is that this tariff be the only one being changed, or one of only a few. If tariffs are being changed on most products that a country trades, as for example during implementation of a *trade round* (page 277), then results are likely to differ substantially from what one would get from just adding up the effects of multiple partial equilibrium analyses.

8. Trade and Transformation Curve Diagram

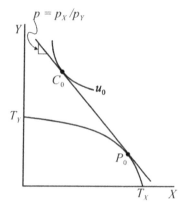

Fig. 8. Basic Trade and Transformation Curve Diagram.

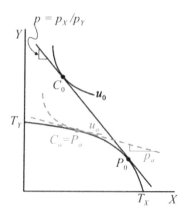

Fig. 8.1. Autarky.

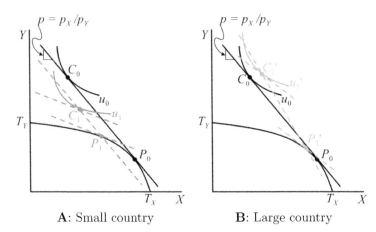

A: Small country   **B**: Large country

Fig. 8.2. Tariff (A and B).

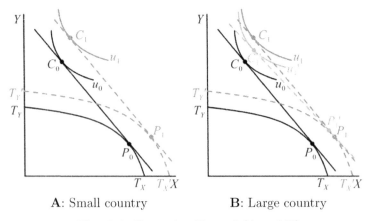

A: Small country   **B**: Large country

Fig. 8.3. Expansion Neutral (A and B).

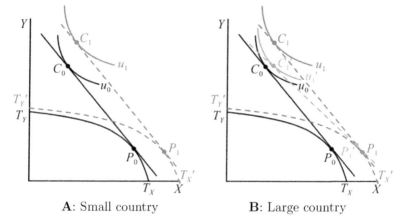

A: Small country   **B**: Large country

Fig. 8.4. Expansion — Export Biased (A and B).

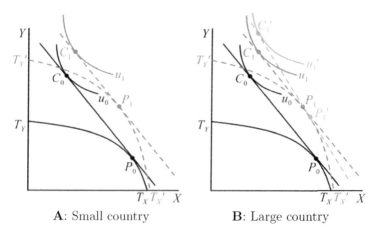

A: Small country   **B**: Large country

Fig. 8.5. Expansion — Import biased (A and B).

Key	
X, Y	Outputs of goods X and Y
T_X, T_Y	Maximum output of goods X and Y
$T_X T_Y$	Transformation curve
p_j	Price of good j, $j = X,Y$
p	Relative price of good X
P_i	Production point in equilibrium i
C_i	Consumption point in equilibrium i
u_i	Utility (community welfare) in equilibrium i

Equilibria:

0	Free trade (initial position)
a	Autarky
1	New position with tariff or expansion

Explanation

The trade and transformation curve diagram combines information about *technology* (page 268) and *endowments* (page 86) represented by a *transformation curve* (page 279) with information about prices represented by *price lines* (page 216) to determine levels of production, consumption, and therefore trade. By using *community indifference curves* (page 42) the diagram also provides an easy representation of effects on a country's *welfare* (page 291).

The basic diagram shown above starts with the transformation curve, $T_X T_Y$, the position and shape of which depend on the technologies for producing the two goods, X and Y. It is usually drawn *concave* (page 45) to the origin, as shown, representing either *diminishing returns* (page 68) due to *specific factors* (page 252) in the two industries or differences in their relative *factor intensities* (page 102) in the *Heckscher-Ohlin Model* (page 126). The curve is linear in the *Ricardian Model* (page 237), and kinked-linear with *Leontief technologies* (page 161). The position and shape also depend on factor endowments, the curve extending further in the direction of the good for which the country has relatively the most specific or intensive factors.

Prices are added to the diagram via a downward-sloping *price line* (page 216), along which the combined value of goods is constant. A competitive economy maximizes the value of output at the prices facing producers, so if these are domestic prices, production is determined by a tangency between the transformation curve and the price line, as at P_0 above. The value of a country's output is also its income, so this price line is also the budget line of consumers in the aggregate. Representing their preferences by a family of community indifference curves, the consumption point is found as a tangency with this price line, as at C_0 above. The level of aggregate welfare is the utility reached by this indifference curve, u_0 above.

Finally, the quantities traded are found by comparing production and consumption. This can be done by adding the *trade triangle* (page 277) to the diagram. Its horizontal side shows the trade of good X (in this case an export, since production is to the right of consumption), and its vertical side shows trade in good Y (import, here).

The diagram can be used for a wide variety of theoretical exercises, including the following:

Comparison of free trade and autarky (Fig. 8.1)

In *autarky* (page 15), the country must produce what it consumes. Therefore the best that it can do is to consume on the highest indifference curve that it can reach. This is also what a competitive economy will actually do, since the same price line that induces production at P_a induces consumption there as well. The figure shows immediately that the level of welfare is lower in autarky than with free trade, and also that a country will export the good whose relative price in autarky is lower than the price that will prevail with trade. Trade causes the output of the export good to rise and that of the import good to fall.

Effects of a tariff (Fig. 8.2)

A *tariff* (page 264) causes the domestic price of the imported good to be higher than the world price, and thus the domestic relative price of the exported good, X in this case, to be lower. If the country is *small* (page 248), so that the world price remains unchanged with the tariff, then the tariff faces producers with a flatter price line, to which they respond by producing less of good X and more good Y, at a tangency of the transformation curve with this flatter price line. The budget line of the country as a whole is still given by world prices, however, now passing through this new producdtion point, P_1. To have *balanced trade* (page 19), consumption must be on this line, at a point of tangency between an indifference curve and another domestic price line parallel to that facing producers. The effects of the tariff in the small country include a drop in welfare compared to free trade, and a reduction in the quantities traded. The large-country case differs, in that the world price of the exported good rises when less of it is supplied to the world market, and this steepens the price line, both world and domestic, as shown. The main difference from the small country case is that the large country's welfare may rise, as shown.

Expansion (Figs. 8.3–8.5)

Production possibilities can expand due either to an advance in technology or to an accumulation of factors. In either case, the transformation curve shifts outward, but it can do this in various ways depending on the cause of the expansion. The diagrams above show three cases, neutral and biased toward goods X and Y respectively. For a small country, trade expands in the first two of these cases, but it declines in the third. For a large country, these changes imply that the world price of X falls and rises respectively. When it falls, as it does most with export-biased expansion, this undermines the benefits of the expansion and may conceivably lower welfare altogether, although it does not in the case shown.

Notes

1. The diagrams are drawn assuming *homothetic preferences* (page 129). That is why the consumption points move radially outward in the small-country cases of expansion. Without that, effects of trade could

be somewhat different, depending on which good has the higher income elasticity.

2. The diagrams all assume *balanced trade* (page 19). Without that, there must be a *capital inflow* (page 32) or outflow, which will enable the country to consume either more or less than its income from production. This can be handled by shifting price lines out and in respectively.

3. The tariff analysis assumes that the tariff revenue is *redistributed* (page 231) to consumers. That is why the price line they face is further out than the one faced by producers, since consumer income includes these transfers.

Part III
Lists of Terms in International Economics by Subject

Lists of Terms in
International Economics
by Subject

1. Arguments for Protection (page 12)

Balance of payments (page 17)
Cultural (page 56)
Domestic distortions (page 74)
Employment (page 85)
Environmental protection (page 87)
Externalities (page 100)
Fairness (page 104)
Foreign investment (page 110)
Income redistribution (page 137)
Infant industry (page 140)
Labor standards (page 157)
Monopoly (page 180)
National defense (page 185)
Non-economic objectives (page 193)
Optimal tariff (page 200)
Patriotism (page 206)
Pauper labor (page 206)
Revenue (page 237)
Second-best (page 243)
Self-sufficiency (page 244)
Strategic industry (page 258)
Strategic trade policy (page 258)
Sunset industry (page 260)
Terms of trade (page 269)

2. International Commodity Agreements and Organizations

Association of Natural Rubber Producing Countries (page 14)
International Cocoa Organization (page 146)
International Coffee Organization (page 146)
International Cotton Advisory Committee (page 146)
International Grains Council (page 147)
International Jute Organization (page 148)
International Lead and Zinc Study Group (page 148)
International Olive Oil Council (page 149)
International Rubber Study Group (page 149)
International Sugar Organization (page 149)
International Tropical Timber Organization (page 150)
Organization of Petroleum Exporting Countries (page 202)

3. Effects

Laursen-Metzler effect (page 158) of terms of trade on expenditure
Magnification effect (page 168) of exogenous prices and endowments in the *Heckscher-Ohlin model* (page 126)
Terms of trade effect (page 269) of a tariff

4. Empirical Findings (page 85)

Leontief paradox (page 160)
Mystery of the missing trade (page 184)

5. Fragmentation (page 112): Terms and Types

Delocalization (page 65)
Disintegration (page 71)
Internationalization (page 150)
Intramediate trade (page 151)
Intra-product specialization (page 151)
Kaleidoscope comparative advantage (page 154)
Multistage production (page 183)

Outsourcing (page 202)
Slicing up the value chain (page 247)
Splintering (page 254)
Subcontracting (page 259)
Vertical specialization (page 289)

6. GATT Articles*

1	Article I	General *Most Favored Nation* (page 181) Treatment
2	Article II	Schedules of *Concessions* (page 46)
3	Article III	*National Treatment* (page 186) on Internal Taxation and Regulation
4	Article IV	Special Provisions relating to Cinematograph Films
5	Article V	Freedom of Transit
6	Article VI	*Anti-dumping* (page 4) and *Countervailing Duties* (page 52) [Superseded by later agreements]
7	Article VII	*Valuation for Customs Purposes* (page 60) [Superseded by later agreement]
8	Article VIII	Fees and Formalities connected with Importation and Exportation
9	Article IX	Marks of Origin
10	Article X	Publication and Administration of Trade Regulations
11	Article XI	General Elimination of *Quantitative Restrictions* (page 224)
12	Article XII	Restrictions to Safeguard the *Balance of Payments* (page 17)
13	Article XIII	Non-discriminatory Administration of *Quantitative Restrictions* (page 224)
14	Article XIV	Exceptions to the rule of Non-discrimination
15	Article XV	Exchange Arrangements
16	Article XVI	*Subsidies* (page 260)
17	Article XVII	*State Trading Enterprises* (page 256)

18   Article XVIII   Governmental Assistance to Economic
                                    Development [Includes exception for *infant
                                    industries* (page 140)]
19   Article XIX   Emergency Action on Imports of Particular
                                    Products [*Safeguards* (page 240)]
20   Article XX   General Exceptions [*Non-economic
                                    objectives* (page 193) (health, safety)]
21   Article XXI   Security Exceptions [*National defense*
                                    (page 185)]
22   Article XXII   Consultation
23   Article XXIII   Nullification of Impairment [*Dispute
                                    settlement* (page 71)]
24   Article XXIV   Territorial Application, Frontier Traffic,
                                    Customs Unions (page 60) and *Free-trade
                                    Areas* (page 113)
25   Article XXV   Joint Action by the Contracting Parties
26   Article XXVI   Acceptance, Entry into Force, and
                                    Registration
27   Article XXVII   Withholding or Withdrawal of Concessions
28   Article XXVIII   Modification of Schedules; Tariff
                                    Negotiations
29   Article XXIX   The Relation of this Agreement
                                    to the *Havana Charter* (page 125)
30   Article XXX   Amendments
31   Article XXXI   Withdrawal
32   Article XXXII   Contracting Parties
33   Article XXXIII   *Accession* (page 4)

*These titles are taken from the Text of the General Agreement on Tariffs and Trade, dated 1986 but referred to in the Final Act of the Uruguay Round Negotiations as GATT 1947.

7. Indexes (page 139)

Balassa   index   (page   19)   of   *revealed   comparative   advantage*
    (page 236)
Consumer price index (page 47)

Grubel-Lloyd index (page 123) of *intra-industry trade* (page 151)
Implicit price deflator (page 133)
Trade intensity index (page 275)
Trade restrictiveness index (page 277)

8. Memberships

European Union Members

Member	Joined	Member	Joined
Austria	1995	Italy	1958
Belgium	1958	Latvia	2004
Cyprus	2004	Lithuania	2004
Czech Republic	2004	Luxembourg	1958
Denmark	1973	Malta	2004
Estonia	2004	Netherlands	1958
Finland	1995	Poland	2004
France	1958	Portugal	1986
Germany	1958	Slovakia	2004
(East Germany)	1990	Slovenia	2004
Greece	1981	Spain	1986
Hungary	2004	Sweden	1995
Ireland	1973	United Kingdom	1973

Euro Zone Members

Members			
Austria	France	Ireland	Netherlands
Belgium	Germany	Italy	Portugal
Finland	Greece	Luxembourg	Spain

Group of Ten (page 123) Members

Belgium	Germany	Netherlands	United Kingdom
Canada	Italy	Sweden	United States
France	Japan	Switzerland	

(Yes, there are eleven members of the Group of Ten. The
"Ten" refers to the *IMF* (page 132) members, to which
Switzerland was added.)

Organization of American States (page 202) Members

Antigua and Barbuda	Guyana
Argentina	Haiti
The Bahamas	Honduras
Barbados	Jamaica
Belize	Mexico
Bolivia	Nicaragua
Brazil	Panama
Canada	Paraguay
Chile	Peru
Colombia	Saint Kitts and Nevis
Costa Rica	Saint Lucia
Cuba*	Saint Vincent and the Grenadines
Dominica	Suriname
Dominican Republic	Trinidad and Tobago
Ecuador	United States of America
El Salvador	Uruguay
Grenada	Venezuela
Guatemala	

*Cuba is a member but its government has been excluded from participating since 1962.

OECD Members as of January 2006

Member	DAC?*	Joined OECD
Australia**	yes	1971
Austria**	yes	1961
Belgium**	yes	1961
Canada**	yes	1961
Czech Republic	no	1995
Denmark**	yes	1961
Finland	yes	1969
France**	yes	1961
Germany**	yes	1961 (East Germany added 1990)
Greece**	yes	1961

Member	DAC?*	Joined OECD
Hungary	no	1996
Iceland**	no	1961
Ireland**	yes	1961
Italy**	yes	1961
Japan	yes	1964
Korea	no	1996
Luxembourg**	yes	1961
Mexico	no	1994
Netherlands**	yes	1961
New Zealand	yes	1973
Norway**	yes	1961
Poland	no	1996
Portugal**	yes	1961
Slovak Republic	no	2000
Spain**	yes	1961
Sweden**	yes	1961
Switzerland**	yes	1961
Turkey**	no	1961
United Kingdom**	yes	1961
United States**	yes	1961

*Member of Development Assistance Committee
**Original member when OECD replaced *OEEC*
(page 196).

OPEC Members as of January 2006

Member	Joined	Withdrew
Algeria	1969	
Ecuador	1973	1993
Gabon	1975	1995
Indonesia	1962	
Iran	1960	
Iraq	1960	
Kuwait	1960	
Libya	1962	
Nigeria	1971	

Member	Joined	Withdrew
Qatar	1961	
Saudi Arabia	1960	
United Arab Emirates	1967	
Venezuela	1960	

Warsaw Pact Members

Members (1955)

Albania	People's Republic of Albania
Bulgaria	People's Republic of Bulgaria
Czechoslovakia	Czechoslovak Republic
East Germany	German Democratic Republic
Hungary	Hungarian People's Republic
Poland	Polish People's Republic
Rumania	Rumanian People's Republic
Soviet Union	Union of Soviet Socialist Republics

9. Models (page 178)

Heckscher-Ohlin model (page 126)
IS-LM model (page 152)
IS-LM-BP model (page 152)
Mundell-Fleming model (page 183)
Ricardian model (page 237)
Ricardo-Viner model (page 238)
Specific-Factors model (page 253)
2x2x2 model (page 281)

10. Non-tariff Barriers (page 194)

Advance deposit requirements (page 6)
Anti-dumping (page 10)
Border tax adjustments (page 25)
Countertrade (page 52)
Countervailing duties (page 52)
Customs procedures (page 59)

Domestic content requirements (page 74)
Embargos (page 84)
Exchange controls (page 93)
Government procurement practices (page 120)
Import licensing (page 134)
Preferential trading arrangements (page 214)
Prohibitions (page 221)
Quotas (page 226)
Rules of origin (page 239)
Special entry procedures (page 252)
Standards (page 255)
State trading (page 256)
Subsidies (page 260)
Tariff quotas (page 265)
Technical barriers (page 267)
Variable levies (page 288)
Voluntary export restraints (page 289)
Voluntary restraint agreements (page 290)

11. Other Non-tariff Measures (page 194)

Export limitations (page 98)
Export requirements (page 99)
Export subsidies (page 99)
Voluntary import expansions (page 289)

12. Paradoxes (page 204)

Leontief paradox (page 160)
Lerner paradox (page 161)
Metzler paradox (page 175)

13. Preferential Trading Arrangements (page 214)

African Economic Community (page 7)
Andean community (page 10)

Andean Pact (page 10)
ASEAN Free Trade Area (page 12)
Australia-New Zealand Closer Economic Relations Trade Agreement (page 15)
CAFTA (page 29)
Canada-US Auto Pact (page 29)
Canada-US Free Trade Agreement (page 29)
Caribbean Basin Initiative (page 34)
Central American Common Market (page 35)
Central European Free Trade Agreement (page 36)
Common Market of Eastern and Southern Africa (page 41)
Cotonou agreement (page 52)
European Free Trade Association (page 91)
European Union (page 357)
Generalized system of preferences (page 118)
Gulf Cooperation Council (page 123)
Israel-US Free Trade Agreement (page 153)
LAFTA (page 157)
LAIA (page 158)
Lomé Convention (page 166)
MERCOSUR (page 175)
NAFTA (page 184)

14. Techniques of Analysis (page 268)

Hat algebra (page 125)
Meade geometry (page 174)

15. Theoretical Propositions (page 270)

Factor price equalization theorem (page 103)
Gains from trade theorem (page 116)
Heckscher-Ohlin theorem (page 126)
Kemp-Wan theorem (page 155)
Lerner Symmetry theorem (page 161)
Rybczynski theorem (page 239)
Stolper-Samuelson theorem (page 258)

16. Trade Disputes (page 274)

Banana war (page 19)
Beef hormone (page 21)
Chicken war (page 37)
Foreign Sales Corporation (page 110)
Shrimp-turtle (page 246)
Softwood lumber (page 250)
Tuna-dolphin (page 281)

17. Trade Rounds (page 277)

Rounds of Multilateral Negotiation under
the GATT and WTO

1	1947	Geneva Round
2	1949	Annecy Round
3	1950–51	Torquay Round
4	1955–56	Geneva Round
5	1960–61	*Dillon Round* (page 68)
6	1963–67	*Kennedy Round* (page 155)
7	1973–79	*Tokyo Round* (page 271)
8	1986–94	*Uruguay Round* (page 286)
9	2002–	*Doha Round* (page 73)

18. United Nations Organizations (page 285)

(For a complete list of **all** U.N. organizations, see the U.N.'s *alphabetic index*. The following are just the ones most relevant to international economics.)

International Development Association (page 146)
International Centre for Settlement of Investment Disputes (page 145)
International Bank for Reconstruction and Development (page 145)
International Finance Corporation (page 147)
International Labor Organization (page 148)

International Monetary Fund (page 148)
Multilateral Investment Guarantee Agency (page 183)
United Nations Conference on Trade and Development (page 285)
World Bank (page 293)
World Intellectual Property Organization (page 293)
World Trade Organization (page 293)

19. United States Government Units
   (dealing with international economic matters)

Customs Service (page 60)
Court of International Trade (page 53)
International Trade Administration (page 150) (ITA)
International Trade Commission (page 150) (ITC)
United States Trade Representative (page 286) (USTR)

Part IV
Origins of Certain Key Terms in International Economics

Origins of Certain
Key Terms in
International Economics

CES function

Arrow et al. (1961, pp. 225–226) (page 371) described their empirical motivation to "derive a mathematical function having the properties of (i) homogeneity, (ii) constant elasticity between capital and labor, and (iii) the possibility of different elasticities for different industries." They named it the *CES function* (page 36) and estimated it across industries and countries.

Comparative advantage

Ruffin (undated) credits the concept of *comparative advantage* (page 42) and the *law of comparative advantage* (page 159) to *Ricardo (1951–1973)* (page 380), in a discovery that Ruffin dates to early October 1816. The law was developed in Ricardo's celebrated chapter on foreign trade, while the term "comparative advantage" seems to have first appeared in a later chapter (Ricardo (1951–1973), Vol I, p. 263). In crediting Ricardo, Ruffin disagrees with *Chipman (1965)* (page 373) who credits *Torrens (1815)* (page 382). From what I see in this debate, Torrens deserves credit for first recognizing the possibility that a country will import a good in which it has an *absolute advantage* (page 3), even though he did not work out the full conditions needed for this to happen, as Ricardo did.

Continuum of goods

The first to model trade with a *continuum of goods* (page 49) were *Dornbusch, Fischer, and Samuelson (1977)* (page 374), who also use that term in their title. They cite an unpublished paper by Charles Wilson, also dated 1977, that further explores their model, but in the published version of that paper, *Wilson*

(1980) (page 383), he credits them with having suggested this modification of traditional trade theory.

Currency area

Mundell (1961, p. 657) (page 379) spoke of "...defining a *currency area* (page 57) as a domain within which exchange rates are fixed ...". Perhaps because the exchange rates among separate national currencies are seldom if ever truly fixed, the term has come to mean a group of countries that share a common currency. Mundell also coined the term "optimum currency area" which is now more commonly expressed as *optimal currency area* (page 200).

Diversification cone

Dixit and Norman (1980, p. 52) (page 374) attribute this to *Lerner (1952)* (page 378) and *McKenzie (1955)* (page 378). I see nothing in Lerner to justify this. McKenzie, however, makes considerable use of the concept in the form of a set of factor endowments within which *factor price equalization* (page 103) occurs, though he does not give it a name. Since he projects factor requirements and factor endowments onto a *simplex* (page 240), his set appears as a triangle, though a cone is implicit. I do not yet know who may have preceded Dixit and Norman in using this term.

DUP activity

Bhagwati (1982) (page 372) introduced this acronym for *directly unproductive profit-seeking activity* (page 69). After listing a variety of activities that fit this description, including *rent seeking* (page 233), *revenue seeking* (page 237), and others, he said (p. 990), "Thus, these are aptly christened DUP activities."

Edgeworth-Bowley box

The origins of this are examined by *Tarascio (1972)* (page 382). The *Edgeworth-Bowley box* (page 81) diagram got its name when *Bowley (1924)* (page 373) drew a box around a rotated version of an indifference curve diagram of *Edgeworth (1881)* (page 374). However, Bowley did not claim originality, and *Pareto (1906)* (page 379) had actually been the first to draw and use the actual box diagram.

Fragmentation

Used to mean a splitting up of production processes, the term *fragmentation* (page 112) was first introduced by *Jones and Kierzkowski (1990)* (page 376), who start their analysis by noting (p. 31) that increasing returns and specialization encourage a growing firm to "switch to a production process with *fragmented* production blocks connected by service links .... Such fragmentation spills over to international markets." (Italics in original.) Many other terms have been used with the same, or related, meanings, as listed in this Glossary (please see pp. 354–355), but "fragmentation" seems to have caught on most widely.

Immiserizing growth

The term *"immiserizing growth"* (page 132) was used by *Bhagwati (1958)* (page 372) and it seems unlikely that anyone used it before him, since he seems to have coined the word "immiserizing." As for the concept, Bhagwati credits *Johnson (1953* (page 376), *1955* (page 376)) with identifying a form of immiserizing growth and also with working out the conditions for Bhagwati's form of it in an unpublished note. Long before both of them, *Edgeworth (1894, pp. 39–40)* (page 374) had shown, though only by example, that increased production of exports could so reduce their relative price that the country loses or, as Edgeworth put it, is "damnified by the improvement." He in turn credits *Mill (1821)* (page 378) with noting the possible worsening of the terms of trade, though Mill apparently incorrectly equated this worsening with a necessary decline in welfare. (I have not read Mill and am taking Edgeworth's word for this.)

Law of comparative advantage

See *comparative advantage* (page 367).

Lerner diagram

The *Lerner diagram* (page 369) was first drawn by Lerner in an unpublished seminar paper in 1933. He used *unit-value isoquants* (page 285) together with *unit isocost lines* (page 284) to show the relationship between goods prices and factor prices in the *HO model* (page 126). That paper was reproduced, "as it was originally written" according to the journal editor, as *Lerner*

(1952) (page 378). I don't know who first called it the Lerner diagram, although *Findlay and Grubert (1959)* (page 375) made extensive use of the diagram, attributing it to Lerner.

Some (including myself, until I learned better) have called it the *Lerner-Pearce diagram* (page 161), giving credit also to *Pearce (1952)* (page 380). In fact, although Pearce in this article was debating Lerner regarding the likelihood of factor price equalization, he used *unit isoquants* (page 284), not unit-value isoquants, for the purpose. Since these do not align in equilibrium with a single unit isocost line, they cannot be used in the same way, and they do not achieve the essential simplicity of Lerner's construction.

Rent seeking

Rent seeking (page 233) was introduced to the trade literature by *Krueger (1974)* (page 377), who defined it generally but applied it to *quantitative restrictions* (page 224) on trade. She noted (p. 291) that government restrictions on economic activity "give rise to rents ..., and people often compete for the rents." She called this competition rent seeking, a term that she apparently coined and that has caught on hugely.

Bibliography

Alexander, Sidney. 1952. "The Effects of Devaluation on a Trade Balance," *IMF Staff Papers*, (April), pp. 359–373. See *absorption approach* (page 3).

Anderson, James E. and J. Peter Neary. 1996. "A New Approach to Evaluating Trade Policy," *Review of Economic Studies* 63, (January), pp. 107–125. See *trade restrictiveness index* (page 277).

Antweiler, Werner and Daniel Trefler. 2002. "Increasing Returns and All That: A View from Trade," *American Economic Review* 92, (March), pp. 93–119. See *intramediate trade* (page 151).

Armington, Paul S. 1969. "A Theory of Demand for Products Distinguished by Place of Production," *IMF Staff Papers* 16, (March), pp. 159–178. See *Armington assumption* (page 12).

Arndt, Sven W. 1997. "Globalization and the Open Economy," *North American Journal of Economics and Finance* 8, pp. 71–79. See *intra-product specialization* (page 151).

Arrow, K.J., H.B. Chenery, B.S. Minhas, and R.M. Solow. 1961. "Capital-Labor Substitution and Economic Efficiency," *Review of Economics and Statistics* 53, (August), pp. 225–251. See *CES function* (page 36), *homohypallagic* (page 129), and *SMAC function* (page 248).

Balassa, Bela. 1964. "The Purchasing Power Parity Doctrine: A Reappraisal," *Journal of Political Economy* 72, pp. 584–596. See *Balassa-Samuelson effect* (page 19).

Balassa, Bela. 1965. "Trade Liberalization and 'Revealed' Comparative Advantage," *Manchester School* 33, pp. 99–123. See *revealed comparative advantage* (page 236).

Baldwin, Robert E. 1948. "Equilibrium in International Trade: A Diagrammatic Analysis," *Quarterly Journal of Economics* 67, (November), pp. 748–762. See *Baldwin envelope* (page 19).

Baldwin, Robert E. 1969. "The Case Against Infant Industry Protection," *Journal of Political Economy* 77, (May–June), pp. 295–305. See *infant industry protection* (page 140).

Bentham, Jeremy. 1789. *An Introduction to the Principles of Morals and Legislation*, London: Hafner, 1948, p. 326. See *international* (page 145).

Bergson, Abram. 1938. "A Reformulation of Certain Aspects of Welfare Economics," *Quarterly Journal of Economics* 52, (February), pp. 310–334. See *Bergsonian social welfare function* (page 22).

Bergsten, C. Fred. 1975. *Toward a New International Economic Order* Lexington, MA: Lexington Books. See *bicycle theory* (page 22).

Bergsten, C. Fred. 1997. "Open Regionalism," *The World Economy* 20, (August), pp. 545–565. See *open regionalism* (page 199).

Bhagwati, Jagdish. 1958. "Immiserizing Growth: A Geometrical Note," *Review of Economic Studies* 25, (June), pp. 201–205. See *immiserizing growth* (page 132).

Bhagwati, Jagdish. 1982. "Directly Unproductive Profit-Seeking (DUP) Activities," *Journal of Political Economy* 90, (October), pp. 988–1002. See *DUP activities* (page 76).

Bhagwati, Jagdish. 1984. "Splintering and Disembodiment of Services and Developing Nations," *The World Economy* 7, (June), pp. 133–143. See *splintering* (page 254).

Bhagwati, Jagdish. 1985. "Protectionism: Old Wine in New Bottles," *Journal of Policy Modeling* 7, pp. 23–34. See *quid pro quo FDI* (page 225).

Bhagwati, Jagdish. 1987. "Quid Pro Quo DFI and VIEs: Political-Economy-Theoretic Analyses," *International Economic Journal* 1, pp. 1–14. See *VIE* (page 289).

Bhagwati, Jagdish. 1988. *Protectionism* Cambridge, MA: MIT Press. See *bicycle theory* (page page 22).

Bhagwati, Jagdish. 1991. *The World Trading System at Risk*, Princeton, NJ: Princeton University Press. See *stumbling block* (page 259).

Bhagwati, Jagdish and Vivek H. Dehejia. 1994. "Freer Trade and Wages of the Unskilled — Is Marx Striking Again?" in Jagdish Bhagwati and Marvin Kosters, eds., *Trade and Wages: Leveling Wages Down?*, Washington D.C.: American Enterprise Institute, pp. 36–75. See *kaleidoscope comparative advantage* (page 154).

Bhagwati, Jagdish and Arvind Panagariya, eds. 1996. *The Economics of Preferential Trade Agreements*, College Park: Center for International Economics, University of Maryland. See *preferential trading arrangement* (page 214).

Bhagwati, Jagdish and T.N. Srinivasan. 1980. "Revenue Seeking: A Generalization of the Theory of Tariffs," *Journal of Political Economy* 88, (December), pp. 1069–1087. See *revenue seeking* (page 237).

Bowley, Arthur. 1924. *The Mathematical Groundwork of Economics*. See *Edgeworth-Bowley box* (page 81).

Brander, James A. and Paul Krugman. 1983. "A 'Reciprocal Dumping' Model of International Trade," *Journal of International Economics* 15, (November), pp. 313–321. See *reciprocal dumping* (page 230).

Brander, James A. and Barbara J. Spencer. 1981. "Tariffs and the Extraction of Foreign Monopoliy Rents under Potential Entry," *Canadian Journal of Economics* 14, (August), pp. 371–389. See *strategic trade policy* (page 258).

Brander, James A. and Barbara J. Spencer. 1984. "Tariff Protection and Imperfect Competition," in Henryk Kierzkowski, ed., *Monopolistic Competition and International Trade*, Oxford Univ. Press. See *strategic trade policy argument for a tariff* (page 258).

Bruno, Michael. 1963. *Interdependence, Resource Use and Structural Change in Israel*, Jerusalem: Bank of Israel. See *domestic resource cost* (page 75).

Bruno, Michael. 1972. "Domestic Resource Costs and Effective Protection: Clarification and Synthesis," *Journal of Political Economy* 80, (January–February), pp. 16–33. See *domestic resource cost* (page 75).

Chipman, John S. 1965. "A Survey of the Theory of International Trade: Part I, The Classical Theory," *Econometrica* 33, pp. 477–519. See *comparative advantage* (page 42).

Christensen, Laurits R., Dale W. Jorgenson, and Lawrence J. Lau. 1973. "Transcendental Logarithmic Production Frontiers," *Review of Economics and Statistics* 55, (February), pp. 28–45. See *translog function* (page 279).

Coase, Ronald. 1960. "The Problem of Social Cost," *Journal of Law and Economics* 3, (October), pp. 1–44. See *Coase theorem* (page 39).

Corden, W. Max. 1966. "The Structure of a Tariff System and the Effective Protective Rate," *Journal of Political Economy* 74, (June), pp. 221–237. See *effective rate of protection* (page 82).

Corden, W. Max. 1974. *Trade Policy and Economic Welfare* Oxford: Clarendon Press. See *conservative social welfare function* (page 46).

Cournot, A. 1897. *Researches into the Mathematical Principles of the Theory of Wealth*, New York. See *Cournot's law* (page 53).

Deardorff, Alan V. 1979. "One-Way Arbitrage and Its Implications for the Foreign Exchange Market," *Journal of Political Economy* 87, (April), pp. 351–364. See *one-way arbitrage* (page 198).

Deardorff, Alan V. 1982. "The General Validity of the Heckscher-Ohlin Theorem," *American Economic Review* 72, (September), pp. 683–694. See *comvariance* (page 53).

Dixit, Avinash K. and Gene M. Grossman. 1982. "Trade and Protection with Multistage Production," *Review of Economic Studies* 59, pp. 583–594. See *multistage production* (page 183).

Dixit, Avinash K and Victor Norman. 1980. *Theory of International Trade* London: Cambridge University Press. See *integrated world economy* (page 142).

Dixit, Avinash K. and Joseph E. Stiglitz. 1977. "Monopolistic Competition and Optimum Product Diversity," *American Economic Review* 67, (June), pp. 297–308. See *Dixit-Stiglitz function* (page 73).

Dornbusch, Rudiger. 1976. "Expectations and Exchange Rate Dynamics," *Journal of Political Economy* 84, (December), pp. 1161–1186. See *exchange rate overshooting* (page 95).

Dornbusch, Rudiger, Stanley Fischer, and Paul A. Samuelson. 1977. "Comparative Advantage, Trade, and Payments in a Ricardian Model with a Continuum of Goods," *American Economic Review* 67, (December), pp. 823–839. See *DFS model* (page 68), *continuum-of-goods model* (page 49).

Dornbusch, Rudiger, Stanley Fischer, and Paul A. Samuelson. 1980. "Heckscher? Ohlin Trade Theory with a Continuum of Goods," *Quarterly Journal of Economics* 95, (September), pp. 203–224. See *DFS model* (page 68), *continuum-of-goods model* (page 49).

Dunning, J.H. 1979. "Explaining Changing Patterns of International Production: In Defence of an Eclectic Theory," *Oxford Bulletin of Economics and Statistics* 41. See *OLI paradigm* (page 197).

Edgeworth, Francis. Y. 1881. *Mathematical Psychics.* See *Edgeworth-Bowley box* (page 81).

Edgeworth, Francis. Y. 1894. "The Theory of International Values," *Economic Journal* 4, (March), pp. 35–50. See *immiserizing growth* (page 132).

Ethier, Wilfred. 1974. "Some of the Theorem of International Trade with Many Goods and Factors," *Journal of Economic Perspectives* 4, pp. 199–206. See *core propositions* (page 50).

Feenstra, Robert C. 1998. "Integration of Trade and Disintegration of Production in the Global Economy," *Journal of Economic Perspectives* 12, (Fall), pp. 31–50. See *disintegration* (page 71).

Findlay, Ronald and Harry Grubert. 1959. "Factor Intensities, Technological Progress and the Terms of Trade," *Oxford Economic Papers*, pp. 111–121. See *Lerner diagram* (page 369).

Fisher, Irving. 1930. *The Theory of Interest*, New York: Macmillan. See *Fisher effect* (page 107).

Fleming, J.M. 1962. "Domestic Financial Policies under Fixed and under Floating Exchange Rates," *IMF Staff Papers* 9, pp. 369–379. See *Mundell-Fleming model* (page 183).

Frankel, Jeffrey. 1997. *Regional Trading Blocs in the World Economic System* Washington, DC: Institute for International Economics. See *trade intensity index* (page 275), *natural trading partner* (page 186), *supernatural trading bloc* (page 261).

Friedman, Milton. 1953 . "The Case for Flexible Exchange Rates," *Essays in Positive Economics*, Chicago: University of Chicago Press. See *stabilizing specualtion* (page 255).

Friedman, Milton. 1969. "The Optimum Quantity of Money," *The Optimum Quantity of Money and Other Essays*, Chicago: Aldine Publishing Company. See *Friedman rule* (page 114).

Grossman, Gene M. and Elhanan Helpman. 1999. "The Internationalization of Economic Activity," National Science Foundation grant, July. See *internationalization* (page 150).

Grossman, Gene M. and Alan Krueger. 1993. "Environmental Impacts of a North American Free Trade Agreement," in Peter M. Garber, ed., *The Mexico-U.S. Free Trade Agreement*, Cambridge, MA: MIT Press, pp. 13–56. See *environmental Kuznets curve* (page 87).

Grubel, Herbert G. and Peter J. Lloyd. 1975. *Intra-Industry Trade: The Theory and Measurement of International Trade in Differentiated Products*, New York: Wiley. See *Grubel-Lloyd index* (page 123), *intra-industry trade* (page 151).

Haberler, Gottfried von. 1937. *The Theory of International Trade with Its Applications to Commercial Policy*, New York: Macmillan. See *specific factor* (page 252).

Harberger, Arnold C. 1950. "Currency Depreciation, Income, and the Balance of Trade," *Journal of Political Economy* 58, pp. 47–60. See *Harberger-Laursen-Metzler effect* (page 124).

Heckscher, Eli. 1919. "The Effect of Foreign Trade on the Distribution of Income," *Ekonomisk Tidskrift*, pp. 497–512. See *Hecksher-Ohlin model* (page 126).

Hicks, John R. 1940. "The Valuation of the Social Income," *Economica*, (May). See *Kaldor-Hicks criterion* (page 154).

Hummels, David, Dana Rapoport, and Kei-Mu Yi. 1998. "Vertical Specialization and the Changing Nature of World Trade," *FRBNY Economic Policy Review*, (June), pp. 79–99. See *vertical specialization* (page 289).

Johnson, Harry G. 1953. "Equilibrium Growth in an Expanding Economy," *Canadian Journal of Economics and Political Science* 19. See *immiserizing growth* (page 132).

Johnson, Harry G. 1954. "Optimum Tariffs and Retaliation," *Review of Economic Studies* 21, pp. 142–153. See *optimal tariff argument* (page 200), *tariffs and retaliation* (page 266).

Johnson, Harry G. 1955. "Economic Expansion and International Trade," *Manchester School* 23, pp. 95–112. See *immiserizing growth* (page 132).

Jones, Ronald W. 1965. "The Structure of Simple General Equilibrium Models," *Journal of Political Economy* 73, (December), pp. 557–572. See *hat algebra* (page 125), *magnification effect* (page 168).

Jones, Ronald W. 1971. "A Three-Factor Model in Theory, Trade, and History," in Bhagwati, *et al.*, eds., *Trade, Balance of Payments, and Growth: Essays in Honor of C. P. Kindleberger*, Amsterdam: North-Holland. See *Ricardo-Viner model* (page 238).

Jones, Ronald W. 1977. "'Two-ness' in Trade Theory: Costs and Benefits," *Special Papers in International Economics* No. 12, International Finance Section, Princeton University, (April). See *two-ness* (page 282).

Jones, Ronald W. and Henryk Kierzkowski. 1986. "Neighborhood Production Structures, with an Application to the Theory of International Trade," *Oxford Economic Papers* 38, pp. 59–76. See *neighborhood production structure* (page 187).

Jones, Ronald W. and Henryk Kierzkowski. 1990. "The Role of Services in Production and International Trade: A Theoretical Framework," in Ronald W. Jones and Anne O. Krueger, eds., *The Political Economy of International Trade: Essays in Honor of Robert E. Baldwin*, Cambridge, MA: Blackwell, pp. 31–48. See *fragmentation* (page 112).

Jones, R.W. and J. Scheinkman. 1977. "The Relevance of the Two-Sector Production Model in Trade Theory," *Journal of Political Economy* 85, (October), pp. 909–936. See *two-ness* (page 282).

Kaldor, Nicholas. 1939. "Welfare Propositions of Economics and Interpersonal Comparisons of Utility," *Economic Journal* 49, (September), pp. 549–552. See *Kaldor-Hicks criterion* (page 154).

Katrak, Homi. 1977. "Multinational Monopolies and Commercial Policy," *Oxford Economic Papers* 29, (July), pp. 283–291. See *strategic trade policy argument for a tariff* (page 258).

Kemp, Murray C. and Henry Wan, Jr. 1976. "An Elementary Proposition Concerning the Formation of Customs Unions," *Journal of International Economics* 6, (February), pp. 95–97. See *Kemp-Wan theorem* (page 155).

Keynes, John Maynard. 1936. *The General Theory of Employment, Interest, and Money* London: MacMillan. See *Keynesian* (page 155) and *liquidity trap* (page 164).

Krueger, Anne O. 1974. "The Political Economy of the Rent Seeking Society," *American Economic Review* 64, (June), pp. 291–303. See *rent seeking* (page 233).

Krugman, Paul R. 1979a. "Increasing Returns, Monopolistic Competition, and International Trade," *Journal of International Economics* 9, (November), pp. 469–479. See *new trade theory* (page 190).

Krugman, Paul R. 1979b. "A Model of Balance-of-Payments Crises," *Journal of Money, Credit and Banking* 11(3), pp. 311–325. See *canonical model of currency crises* (page 30).

Krugman, Paul R. 1987. "Pricing to Market When the Exchange Rate Changes," in Sven W. Arndt and J. David Richardson, *Real-Financial Linkages Among Open Economics* Cambridge, MA: MIT Press, pp. 49–70. See *pricing to market* (page 217).

Krugman, Paul R. 1991a. *Geography and Trade* Cambridge, MA: MIT Press. See *new economic geography* (page 190).

Krugman, Paul R. 1991b. "The Move Toward Free Trade Zones," in *Policy Implications of Trade and Currency Zones*, symposium sponsored by The Federal Reserve Bank of Kansas City, Jackson Hole, Wyoming, August 22–24. See *GATT-Think* (page 117).

Krugman, Paul R. 1996. "Does Third World Growth Hurt First World Prosperity?" *Harvard Business Review* 72, pp. 113–121. See *slicing up the value chain* (page 247).

Kuznets, Simon. 1955. "Economic Growth and Income Inequality," *American Economic Review* 65, (March), pp. 1–28. See *Kuznets curve* (page 155).

Laursen, Svend and Lloyd A. Metzler. 1950. "Flexible Exchange Rates and the Theory of Employment," *Review of Economics and Statistics* 32, (November), pp. 281–299. See *Harberger-Laursen-Metzler effect* (page 124).

Leamer, Edward E. 1996. "The Effects of Trade in Services, Technology Transfer and Delocalisation on Local and Global Income Inequality," *Asia-Pacific Economic Review* 2, (April), pp. 44–60. See *delocalization* (page 65).

Leibenstein, Harvey. 1966. "Allocative Efficiency vs. 'X-Efficiency'," *American Economic Review* 56, (June), pp. 392–415. See *X-efficiency* (page 294).

Leontief, Wassily. 1933. "The Use of Indifference Curves in the Analysis of Foreign Trade," *Quarterly Journal of Economics* 57, (May), pp. 493–503. See *community indifference curve* (page 42).

Leontief, Wassily. 1954. "Domestic Production and Foreign Trade: The American Capital Position Reexamined," *Economia Internatiozionale* 7, (February), pp. 3–32. See *input-output table* (page 141), *Leontief paradox* (page 160).

Lerner, Abba P. 1936. "The Symmetry between Import and Export Taxes," *Economica* 3, (August), pp. 306–313. See *Lerner symmetry theorem* (page 161).

Lerner, Abba P. 1952. "Factor Prices and International Trade," *Economica* n.s. 19, (February). See *Lerner diagram* (page 369).

Linder, Staffan Burenstam. 1961. *An Essay on Trade and Transformation*, New York: Wiley and Sons. See *Linder hypothesis* (page 163).

Lipsey, R.G. and Kelvin Lancaster. 1956. "The General Theory of Second Best," *Review of Economic Studies* 24, pp. 11–32. See *second best* (page 242).

Mayer, Wolfgang. 1974. "Short-Run and Long-Run Equilibrium for a Small Open Economy," *Journal of Political Economy* 82, (September–October), pp. 955–967. See *Ricardo-Viner model* (page 238).

McKenzie, Lionel W. 1955. "Equality of Factor Prices in World Trade," *Econometrica* 23, (July), pp. 239–257. See *diversification cone* (page 72).

Meade, James Edward. 1952. *A Geometry of International Trade*, London: Allen and Unwin. See *Meade geometry* (page 174), *trade indifference curve* (page 275).

Metzler, Lloyd. 1949. "International Demand and Domestic Prices," *Journal of Political Economy* 57, (August), pp. 345–351. See *Metzler paradox* (page 175).

Mill, James. 1821. *Elements of Political Economy*. See *immiserizing growth* (page 132).

Mill, John Stuart. 1848. *Principles of Political Economy and Some of Their Applications to Social Philosophy*. See *vent for surplus* (page 288).

Minhas, Bagicha S. 1962. "The Homohypallagic Production Function, Factor-Intensity Reversals, and the Heckscher-Ohlin Theorem," *Journal of Political Economy* 70, (April), pp. 138–156. See *homohypallagic* (page 129).

Mundell, Robert A. 1960. "The Pure Theory of International Trade," *American Economic Review* 50, (March), pp. 67–110. See *Cournot's law* (page 53).

Mundell, Robert A. 1961. "A Theory of Optimum Currency Areas," *American Economic Review* 51, (September), pp. 657–665. See *currency area* (page 57), *optimal currency area* (page 200).

Mundell, Robert A. 1962. "The Appropriate Use of Monetary and Fiscal Policy under Fixed Exchange Rates," *IMF Staff Papers* 9, (March), pp. 70–79. See *assigment problem* (page 13), *Mundell-Fleming model* (page 183).

Mundell, Robert A. 1963. "Capital Mobility and Stabilization Policy under Fixed and Flexible Exchange Rates," *Canadian Journal of Economics and Political Science* 9, (November), pp. 475–485. See *Mundell-Fleming model* (page 183).

Mussa, Michael. 1974. "Tariffs and the Distribution of Income: The Importance of Factor Specificity, Substitutability, and Intensity in the Short and Long Run," *Journal of Political Economy* 82, (November–December), pp. 1191–1204. See *Ricardo-Viner model* (page 238).

Myint, Hla. 1958. "The 'Classical Theory' of International Trade and the Underdeveloped Countries," *Economic Journal* 68, (June), pp. 317–337. See *vent for surplus* (page 288).

Neary, Peter. 1978. "Short-Run Capital Specificity and the Pure Theory of International Trade," *Economic Journal* 88, (September), pp. 488–510. See *Ricardo-Viner model* (page 238).

Ohlin, Bertil. 1933. *Interregional and International Trade*, Cambridge, MA: Harvard University Press. See *Heckscher-Ohlin model* (page 126), *Ohlin definition* (page 197), *price definition* (page 215).

Ohyama, Michihiro. 1972. "Trade and Welfare in General Equilibrium," *Keio Economic Studies* 9, pp. 37–73. See *revealed preference* (page 236).

Pareto, Vilfredo. 1906. *Manual of Political Economy*. See *Edgeworth-Bowley box* (page 81).

Pearce, Ivor F. 1952. "The Factor Price Equalization Myth," *Review of Economic Studies* 19(2), pp. 111–120. See *Lerner-Pearce diagram* (page 369).

Porter, Michael E. 1990. *The Competitive Advantage of Nations*, New York: Free Press. See *Porter's diamond* (page 211).

Pöyhönen, Pentti. 1963. "A Tentative Model for the Volume of Trade Between Countries," *Weltwirtschaftliches Archiv* 90(1), pp. 93–99. See *gravity model* (page 121).

Prebisch, Raúl. 1950. "The Economic Development of Latin America and its Principal Problems". See *Prebisch-Singer hypothesis* (page 212).

Preston, Samuel H. 1975. "The Changing Relation between Mortality and Level of Economic Development," *Population Studies* 29, pp. 231–248. See *Preston curve* (page 214).

Ricardo, David. 1951–1973. *The Works and Correspondence of David Ricardo*, edited by Piero Sraffa and M. Dobbs, Vols. I-XI, Cambridge: Cambridge University Press. See *comparative advantage* (page 42).

Robinson, Joan. 1932. *The Economics of Imperfect Competition*, London: Macmillan. See *monopsony* (page 180).

Ruffin, Roy J. Undated. "David Ricardo's Discovery of Comparative Advantage." See *comparative advantage* (page 42).

Rybczynski, T.M. 1955. "Factor Endowments and Relative Commodity Prices," *Economica* 22, pp. 336–341. See *Rybczynski theorem* (page 239).

Samuelson, Paul A. 1939. "The Gains from International Trade," *Canadian Journal of Economics and Political Science* 5, pp. 195–205. See *gains from trade theorem* (page 116), *revealed preference* (page 236).

Samuelson, Paul A. 1948. "International Trade and the Equalisation of Factor Prices," *Economic Journal* 58, (June), pp. 163–184. See *factor price equalization* (page 103), *Heckscher-Ohlin model* (page 126).

Samuelson, Paul A. 1949. "International Factor-Price Equalisation Once Again," *Economic Journal* 59, (June), pp. 181–197. See *factor price equalization* (page 103), *Heckscher-Ohlin model* (page 126).

Samuelson, Paul A. 1953. "Prices of Factors and Goods in General Equilibrium," *Review of Economic Studies* 21, (October), pp. 1–20. See *Heckscher-Ohlin model* (page 126), *reciprocity conditions* (page 230).

Samuelson, Paul A. 1954. "The Transfer Problem and Transport Costs, II: Analysis of Effects of Trade Impediments," *Economic Journal* 64, (June), pp. 264–289. See *iceberg transport cost* (page 131).

Samuelson, Paul A. 1962. "The Gains from International Trade Once Again," *Economic Journal* 72, (December), pp. 820–829. See *gains from trade theorem* (page 116), *utility possibility frontier* (page 287).

Samuelson, Paul A. 1964. "Theoretical Notes on Trade Problems," *Review of Economics and Statistics* 23, pp. 145–154. See *Balassa-Samuelson effect* (page 19).

Samuelson, Paul A. 1971. "Ohlin Was Right," *Swedish Journal of Economic* 73, pp. 365–384. See *Ricardo-Viner model* (page 238).

Samuelson, Paul A. 1981. "Bergsonian Welfare Economics," in S. Rosefielde, ed., *Economic Welfare and the Economics of Soviet Socialism: Essays in Honor of Abram Bergson*, Cambridge, MA: Harvard University Press, pp. 223–266. See *Bergsonian social welfare function* (page 22).

Sanyal, Kalyan K. and Ronald W. Jones. 1982. "The Theory of Trade in Middle Products," *American Economic Review* 72, (March), pp. 16.31. See *middle product* (page 176).

Scitovszky, Tibor de. 1942. "A Reconsideration of the Theory of Tariffs," *Review of Economic Studies* 9, (Summer), pp. 89–110. See *Scitovszky indifference curve* (page 242).

Singer, H.W. 1950. "U.S. Foreign Investment in Underdeveloped Areas: The Distribution of Gains Between Investing and Borrowing Countries," *American Economic Review, Papers and Proceedings* 40, (May), pp. 473–485. See *Prebisch-Singer hypothesis* (page 212).

Smith, Adam. 1776. *An Inquiry into the Nature and Causes of the Wealth of Nations.* See *division of labor* (page 73), *vent for surplus* (page 288).

Solow, Robert M. 1956. "A Contribution to the Theory of Economic Growth," *Quarterly Journal of Economics* 70, pp. 65–94. See *neoclassical growth model* (page 188).

Solow, Robert M. 1957. "Technical Change and the Aggregate Production Function," *Review of Economics and Statistics* 39, (August), pp. 312–320. See *Solow residual* (page 250).

Stolper, Wolfgang and Paul A. Samuelson. 1941. "Protection and Real Wages," *Review of Economic Studies* 9, (November), pp. 58–73. See *Stolper-Samuelson theorem* (page 258).

Suganami, H. 1978. "A Note on the Origin of the World 'International'," *British Journal of International Studies* 4(3), October, 1978, pp. 226–232. See *international* (page 145).

Swan, Trevor W. 1955. "Long-Run Problems of the Balance of Payments," written but unpublished in 1955, later published in Arndt and Corden, eds., *The Australian Economy* 1963. See *Swan diagram* (page 262).

Swan, Trevor W. 1956. "Economic Growth and Capital Accumulation," *Economic Record* 32, pp. 334–361. See *neoclassical growth model* (page 188).

Tarascio, Vincent J. 1972. "A Correction: On the Geneology of the So-Called Edgeworth-Bowley Diagram," *Western Economic Journal*, (June), pp. 193–197. See *Edgeworth-Bowley box* (page 81).

Tinbergen, Jan. 1962. *Shaping the World Economy: Suggestions for an International Economic Policy*, New York: Twentieth Century Fund. See *gravity model* (page 121).

Tobin, James. 1978. "A Proposal for International Monetary Reform," *Eastern Economic Journal* 4, pp. 153–159. See *Tobin tax* (page 271).

Torrens, Robert. 1815. *Essay on the External Corn Trade*, London: J. Hatchard. See *comparative advantage* (page 42).

Travis, William Penfield. 1964. *The Theory of Trade and Protection*, Cambridge, MA: Harvard University Press. See *integrated world economy* (page 142).

Trefler, Daniel. 1995. "The Case of the Missing Trade and Other Mysteries," *American Economic Review* 85, (December), pp. 1029–1046. See *mystery of the missing trade* (page 178), *home bias* (page 128).

Vanek, Jaroslav. 1968. "The Factor Proportions Theory: The n-Factor Case," *Kyklos* 4, (October), pp. 749–756. See *Heckscher-Ohlin-Vanek theorem* (page 126).

Vernon, Raymond. 1966. "International Investment and International Trade in the Product Cycle," *Quarterly Journal of Economics* 80, (May), pp. 1900–1207. See *product cycle* (page 220).

Vernon, Raymond. 1971. *Sovereignty at Bay: The Multinational Spread of US Enterprises*, New York: Basic Books. See *OBM* (page 196).

Viner, Jacob. 1950. *The Customs Union Issue*, New York: Carnegie Endowment for International Peace. See *trade creation* (page 273), *trade diversion* (page 274).

Williams, John H. 1929. "The Theory of International Trade Reconsidered," *Economic Journal* 39, (June), pp. 195–209. See *vent for surplus* (page 288).

Williamson, John H. 1990. "What Washington Means by Policy Reform," in John Williamson, ed., *Latin American Adjustment: How Much Has Happened?* Washington, D.C.: Institute for International Economics. See *Washington Consensus* (page 291).

Wilson, Charles. 1980. "On the General Structure of Ricardian Models with a Continuum of Goods: Applications to Growth, Tariff Theory, and Technical Change," *Econometrica* 48, (November), pp. 1675–1702. See *continuum of goods* (page 367).

Wonnacott, P. and M. Lutz. 1989. "Is There a Case for Free Trade Areas," in J. Schott, ed., *Free Trade Areas and U.S. Trade Policy* Washington, D.C.: Institute for International Economics. See *natural trading partners* (page 186).